EXCELLENCE IN LIFE

EXCELLENCE IN LIFE

O P Shukal

GYAN PUBLISHING HOUSE
NEW DELHI-110002

Excellence in Life

ISBN: 81-212-0963-3

Published in 2008 in India by
Gyan Publishing House
5, Ansari Road, Darya Ganj,
New Delhi-110002
Phones : 23282060, 23261060
Fax : 011-23285914
E-mail: books@gyanbooks.com
Website: www.gyanbooks.com

Lasser Type Setting by: Rudra Computer Graphics, Delhi
Printed at : Singhal Print Media, Delhi

Dedicated To

To my mother - Bhagwati Devi Shukal and my father - Bua Dutt Shukal,
who inspired me to write the book, to share my experiences.

Content

Preface

We live in 21st century, where information is readily available on internet websites and in books, but we have to learn to utilize the knowledge in the right direction; at the right time. Civilization has reached a critical phase of development, where science has made inroads into every aspect of human activity. No one has time to go through the details, as such, the book has been written based on three principles:

1. Principle of brevity - British Prime Minister Sir Winston Churchill; when assumed office during Second World War; saw that his office was flooded with hundreds of files of urgent nature; all awaiting prime minister's decision; he propounded the principle of brevity. Churchill ordered that one-page reports be prepared on all the pending files; files be resubmitted along with one-page reports for decision; one-page reports helped in quickly grasping the subject matter; all the pending files were disposed off in record time. For this achievement, he was declared as the most successful Wartime Prime Minister of United Kingdom.

2. Principle of specifics - avoids the use of words, like: good / bad; fast / slow; low / high; more / less, as these are comparative words and meaning differs from person to person. As such, things have been specified in clear terms. Language used has been simple; length of sentence is controlled, where it could be read / spoken without loosing

one's breadth; action performed is directly expressed in active voice; passive voice sentences are avoided. Each chapter is divided into serial numbered topics; topics have been further divided into subtopics; serial numbered topics help for quick reference and location in the text.

3 Principle of sharing - is based upon the thinking that knowledge grows, when shared with others. Aim of the book is, that: Author has vision; Book has information; Readers have resources; Let's join hands to enrich human life.

About the author

Om Prakash Shukal was born at Narsingh Garh, near Bhopal in Madhya Pradesh; has done double graduation in marine engineering with steam and motor subjects (Diesel) subjects; again has done degree course in mechanical engineering with boiler subjects. He served in the Indian Navy for 14 years and was awarded War Service Medal in Indo-Pak war of 1965.

He joined department of Atomic Energy in 1966, as Scientific Officer Engineer (Mech) and opted for further higher studies to pass 18 written papers of Nuclear Engineering to operate and maintain Atomic Power Stations. He served in the Department of Atomic Energy for 29 years at different senior positions; retired on superannuation in 1994 from Government of India Service; researched internet websites and hundreds of books on religion, creation, life, intelligence, astrology, language, interviews, management and wisdom for 10 years to develop this book to share knowledge and experience with the readers.

Acknowledgements

In my book 'Excellence in Life', I have tried to analyse the intricacies of human life. I think that it will help humanity to measure its footsteps into future.

In bringing this book to completion, I have been helped and inspired by many people.

Firstly, I wish to thank my wife Prem Lata, for providing inspiration and support in writing the book.

I am also very much thankful to my daughter Purnima and sons Arun and Tarun for their comments and suggestions.

I also had the opportunity to study scriptures, astrological and management books etc. Their contents have become a part of my knowledge, many thanks to those writers as well.

I am also thankful to various Internet websites whose contents provided as a back up data for compiling the book.

Further, to say I am very much thankful to the readers, who have chosen this book to study. I hope that the information, as contained in the book, will help readers to achieve 'Excellence in Life'.

Introduction

0.1. Excellence in life - means advancement in career and leading a life of contentment; this requires efficient performance of duties towards family, society and country. Some achieve excellence early in life, while others late, as it depends upon their efforts, aspiration and willpower. Excellence in life is a never ending process, as this requires right knowledge in the right areas of human activity. This demands working at a higher level of efficiency, which means one has to become jack-of-all-trades and have mastery in his professional area. One is born with certain in-born instincts, which make him suitable for a particular profession, this profession is to be adopted in life; this leads to advancement in career.

One has to aim high in career; has to adopt a practical approach; has to learn to solve his problems, as they arise in life. This requires life-time-plan of studies; one has to learn to live in the present; has to treat his past as an experience; has to live with hope to do better in future. This requires positive thinking, formation of habit to rely on self, rather on others. In this direction, choosing good friends may help, as they can push up or pull down, boost or break, encourage or discourage, as all this depends upon friends.

0.2. Human life - is most precious, as even angels' dream to enjoy it on Earth. Treat the present life as an opportunity, which if lost; can never be regained. Utilize the present moment as the best moment of life; acquire right knowledge in the right direction; remembering that human life is unique in itself. Fix excellence as goal in life; put efforts to achieve excellence; God helps in this noble cause.

0.3. Basic aspects of human life - are four

1. Religious aspect has three paths: 1. Devotional, 2. Knowledge, 3. Deeds and finally these paths lead to realization of one's religion's limits.
2. Spiritual aspect embraces three stages: 1. Cleaning, 2. Meditation, 3. Studies of spiritual books and these stages finally lead to enlightenment. Both these aspects create a feeling of contentment in life.
3. Scientific aspect involves study of: 1. Creation, 2. Life, 3. Intelligence and these studies finally lead to reality.
4. Materialistic aspect involves study of: 1. Astrology, 2. Language, 3. Interview, 4. Management, 5. Wisdom and studies finally lead to higher earings. Both these aspects lead to advancement in career. Contentment in life and advancement in career achieve excellence in life. This is illustrated on the back cover of this book.

0.4. Achievers of excellence in life

1. Galileo Galilee (1564 - 1642 AD) - studied different subjects; developed mastery over cosmos; performed experiments; observed every phenomenon; discussed his findings, but never got tired out of his failures, instead derived strength from them. He was not bothered about his criticism, but continued with his experiments with more vigour, till final conclusions could be drawn; based on conclusions, he established scientific laws.

He supported Copernican theory that planets orbit the Sun; Church declared Copernicanism as false and erroneous in 1616; commanded Galileo not to defend or hold this doctrine. Galileo was undaunted by the Church ruling; published his observations, which brought forth the wrath of Pope; Galileo was sentenced to house imprisonment for life. Galileo was right, but suffered due to innocence of others.

2. Albert Einstein (1879 - 1955 AD) - the American scientist was born on 14.03.1879 at Ulm in South Germany; father was an electrician; Einstein got interested in electro-magnetism at the tender age of four years; Uncle Jacob taught him mathematics. Einstein was not a brilliant student at school; did graduation at the age of 22 years; father expired in 1902; he became a school

teacher; later became a patent-inspector. In 1905, he got world fame, when he propounded six theories:

1. Theory of relativity
2. Theory of photoelectric effect.
3. Theory of browning motions.
4. Mass and energy equation.
5. Unified field theory on electromagnetism.
6. Gravitational phenomenon in 1920.

In 1909 - Einstein became an associated professor in Zurich University; later served as faculty in Prague and Berlin Universities. In 1921 - Einstein was awarded Noble Prize for his research in photo-electric effects. In 1952 - Einstein was requested to become president of Israel, but he declined the offer in favor of scientific research.

One day, a student asked from Einstein, what is the velocity of light? Einstein replied, "I don't know, my son". Student, Oh! You are noble prize winner; you don't know the velocity of light? Einstein said, "I know where to look for it, but my son, you don't and this is the difference between you and me". Once Einstein said, "The best minds reach a particular frontier, beyond which they can't think; beyond that frontier of science God exists". Einstein before his death donated his brain for scientific research; expired on 18.04.1955 at the ripe age of 76 years.

3. Stephen Hawkins (1945 - alive) - born on 08.01.1945 at Oxford, England, UK; at the age of 21 years, suffered an attack of ALS (An incurable disease) in which motor neurons suffer an irreversible damage; lost control over his speech and even could not stand on his own feet, leave alone walking. He uses wheel chair; is completely dependent on others; his indomitable spirit prevails; he uses speech-synthesizers. He is professor of science at the renowned Oxford University; has written many books on cosmology; has traveled widely in the world. He visited India on a wheelchair; lectured at many places; his each speech was applauded.

1

Aspects

Modern scientific view is that human life has four basic aspects: 1. Religious aspect, 2. Spiritual aspect, 3. Scientific aspect, 4. Materialistic aspect and as described below:

1. Religious aspect - is with us since ages, but it depends upon the support of finances as provided by the materialistic aspect of life. Religious aspect is only one wing of a bird, which cannot fly on a single wing. Religious aspect maintains that God created the universe and mankind. Further it belives that God is an External-being and one can seek him through worship.

Religious aspect begins in the childhood, when a child accompanies his parents to a place of worship. He embarks on an outward journey, seeks his God in places of worship, undertakes fasts to purify himself, and studies his religious scriptures to understand religion's philosophy.

2. Spiritual aspect - developed during the last 3,000 years and depends to a lesser extent on the finances as obtained from materialistic aspect. Spiritual aspect maintains that God is an Internal-being and one has to seek him within through meditation.

Spiritual aspect begins where the boundaries of religious aspect loose their identity. One starts to seek satisfaction through spiritual things, like meditation, where the real truth lies. One abandons his outward journey, embarks on an inward journey to seek and realize God within.

3. Scientific aspect - is of recent origin. The aspect has developed as science advanced, but it still requires further development to understand the intricacies involved in religious

practices. Scientific studies indicate that religious prayers produce vibrations, which affect human mind. This creates a feeling of oneness with the divine. Research work is still going on to determine the truth.

Science has become very important in modern day life. It is better to understand its wider implications and meaning. Word science comes from Latin scientia, which means knowledge attained through verifiable means and is based on evidence, as available in nature.

Hypothesis is based on an assumption rather than on fact, which has been neither well supported nor yet ruled out by experimentation.

Theory is a logically self-consistent framework, which describes the behaviour of certain natural phenomena and is open to falsification, if new evidence surfaces.

Law is a scientific generalization based on a large number of observations, that is taken as fully verified. This has caused a revolution in the religious-concepts, as held so far. Few centuries ago, what ever is written in the scriptures, was taken for granted to be true. As science advanced, it gave convincing evidence and proved that the information as contained in the religious scriptures was based on the knowledge as available then in the olden days, as such; scriptural knowledge is due for revision.

Science has advanced beyond comprehension of a common man and new branches have come up, which are:

1. Atheism - is the belief that there is no God.
2. Theology - is the study of religions and religious beliefs.
3. Ontology - is the study of existence of human life.
4. Epistemology - is the study of source, nature and limitations of knowledge, as held by the various religions, but it neither interferes into the religious beliefs nor propogates new ideas for adoption, just gives the right information.

4. Materialistic aspect - is with us since civilization. This aspect maintains that one has to earn his livelihood through right means. As civilizations advanced, requirements increased to have comfortable shelter, enjoy tasty food, which provides nutrients as well, travel at faster speeds to save time, have adequate lighting at night hours to work longer, communicate quickly with others,

have clean water supply and drainage system, have good clothing, which provides protection against inclement weather and all this requires money, which has to be earned. This aspect is concerned with ones career.

RELIGIOUS ASPECT

1.1. Religion

Mohandas Karam Chand Gandhi - the father of the Indian nation said, that religion is not alien to us, it is always within us, with some consciously, with others unconsciously, but it is always there.

Every religion has a distinct style of worship, has a particular prayer to offer to its Godhead. Name of Godhead and place of worship depends upon the religion one follows, but what ever religion one follows, does not matter in human life, as all the religions are equally good for their followers. There is no need to change one's religion in favour of another or force anybody else to adopt any particular religion in preference to any other religion. Every culture has developed its own religion, its own myth, its own philosophy and even have researched to find after-life.

Every religion gives an identity to its follower and provides them with moorings to follow a particular path, but it is a scientific fact that human race is one throughout the world. Mankind may differ in colour, structure, appearance or speak a different language, bur it does not matter in human life.

Main task of a religion is to bring awareness into the minds of the followers that they are inherently divine. It is the social customs and environment, which has created the divide between different religions, however every religious philosophy, has exalted many and have given them enlightenment.

Religion is like a cocoon, which man weaves around him to lie inert and passive until science tears it open with a revelation to allow mankind freedom of expression above religious thinking. It is easier to bore a tunnel through a mountain than to break open the religious cocoon, which man has built around him. In the past, millions in India have abandoned their homes, have dwelt in solitude, have practiced every form of austerity, have penanced, have prayed day and night and still the goal of enlightenment have eluded them, while some have achieved enlightenment with much less efforts.

Religious activity patterns in the dirt on the floor of Chauvet Caves in France, which remained undisturbed during the past 25,000 years, indicate dancing showing that some form of religious activity had taken place, but no written record exists, so it is impossible to ascertain what people believed in or what their religious practices were?

History of religions reveals that most of the religions have come up during the past few centuries, while mankind has existed from the past 3.6 million (36 lakh) years. It has been observed that after the death of the founders of religions, it was their disciples, who have advocated their philosophies and the religious scriptures were written much later. Places of worship have come up still much later, but the process of building new places of worship is still going on in all parts of the world in all religions.

Few generations ago, religious scriptures were commonly accepted as true and reliable, but advancement in science has lead that religious beliefs are subject to review in the context of scientific evidence. This has lead that teaching of Bible in classrooms in America has been abandoned and a scientific committee now advises Pope.

In much of Eastern Europe, Russia and China the impact of communist ideology has reduced the importance of religion. Secularism has increased, while in Western Europe, affluence and freedom of expression exist, the tolerance for other religions have increased. In Netherlands 50 % of the population claim to have no religion, but the quest for religious insight is still strong. In 1983, Martin Palmer - founded ICOREC (International Consultancy on Religion, Education and Culture), which is lauded very much these days.

Two examples of so called miracles

On 21.09.1995 and again on 21.08.2006 - thousands of Hindu devotees flocked to temples in North India to see the Deities taking milk, which was disappearing from the spoons of devotees, scientists stated that this was not due to slurping by the idols, rather it was caused by surface tension- a force that pulls the liquid towards the statue and capillary action, through which the milk was leaching into the statues through tiny pores on the surface of the stone and is similar to the phenomenon by which water reaches the top of a tree through roots.

On 18.08.2006 - on Friday seawater turned sweet in Mumbai's Mahim Creek, attracted thousand of Muslim devotees, scientists advised not to take the seawater, as it was highly polluted and this happened due to heavy rains on a vast area, which dropped the level of salt, but crowds kept on filling their mouths and bottles, until police intervened.

However, it is presumed that the founders of religions did have some kind of contact with what they considered a divine being, who was reachable by following certain religious doctrine of human life.

1.2. Three streams of religions

Scholars, who keep track of world's religions, have identified 9,900 distinctive religions and this figure may increase or decrease with time, but for the purpose of study, these religions can be categorized into three streams: 1. Prophetic, 2. Philosophical and 3. Hybrid, as given below:

1. Prophetic stream of religions - are also called Abrahamic religions and are founded by Prophets like: Judaism, Christianity, Islam etc. These religions have prophetic traditions, as one of their distinctive prophets was sent to recall the people to their proper role in God's plan. These religions have few scriptures to study, as such, are easy to follow and understand.

2. Philosophical stream of religions - developed much before Christ. These religions are based on philosophy, like: Hinduism, Buddhism, Jainism etc. These religions require studies of many scriptures, as such, are difficult to understand. These religions have a common root in the Vedic culture and are influenced by the belief that all existence is cyclical in nature; universe arises, exists, declines and fades to be replaced by a new universe. This view is presently supported by scientific evidence.

3. Hybrid stream of religions - are mixtures of prophetic and philosophical religions. These religions are based on faith and

developed with time into separate religious streams, like: Taoism in China, Shinto in Japan, Sikhism in Punjab in India and Bahai's in Iran and Israel. These religions are simple to follow, as few scriptures are to be studied to comprehend them.

Six major religions of the world:

In course of time, the major religions split into denominations, but the number of followers increased and the following data is given, which is subject to change with time, but gives an over all idea of the magnitude involved:

1. Christians	= 200.0 crore,	Roman Catholic	=	130.0 crore
		Orthodox ———	=	24.0 crore
		Protestants ——	=	23.5 crore
		Pentecostal ——	=	11.5 crore
		African Sects —	=	11.0 crore
		Total		200.0 crore 33 % of world's population
2. Muslims —	= 130.0 crore,	Sunni ————	=	94.0 crore
		Shiite ————	=	12.0 crore
		Others ———	=	24.0 crore
		Total		130.0 crore 21 % of world's population

3. Hindus ——	= 90.0 crore	14 % of world's population
4. Buddhists -	= 36.0 crore	6 % of world's population
5. Chinese —	= 22.0 crore	4 % of world's population
6. Sikhs ——	= 2.0 crore	0.3 % of world's population
7. Others ——	= 126.0 crore	20.8 % of world's population
Total ———	= 606.0 crore	World's present population

Four major religions in India:

1.	Hindus ———	= 82 crore	80 % of population
2.	Muslims ——	= 12 crore	12 % of population
3.	Christians ——	= 3 crore	3 % of population
4.	Sikhs ————	= 2 crore	2 % of population

Others ————	=	3 crore	3 % of population
Total ————	=	102 crore	

1.3. Origin of seven religions

1. Zoroastrianism - is the oldest religion of the Western world, which was prevalent in ancient Persia (Iran) and had reincarnation idea of Hindu Religion. Zoroastrianism has incarnation of Vrithragna (Indra) and idea of Prophethood (Messiahhood) came from the Western religions of Judaism, Christianity and Islam. The founder of the religion was Zoroastra and followers are called Parsees. They believe that Fire is God and consider it so sacred, that they do not burn their dead bodies in it, but keep the dead bodies at a place for vultures to eat. The religion has its origin in Persia (Iran) and Parsees of India still follow this religion. It seems that many ideas in Jewish and Christian mythology came from this religion, like: angels, heaven, hell etc.

2. Christianity - has the largest number of followers in the world. It began as a movement within Judaism and the founder was Jesus Christ (4 BC - 29 AD, age 33 years). Jesus Christ was born on 25th December in 4 BC at Bathleham in Israel, his father was Yusuf - who was carpenter and mother was Virgin Mary. Jesus Christ was Jew in the Roman province of Palestine (Israel). Mary and Joseph lived in Nazareth in Galilee. As per New Testament, they travelled to Bethlehem, near Jerusalem in response to a Roman census.

Christ's popularity as Messiah had alarmed the Romans and Jewish authorities. When Jesus moved to Jerusalem, his disciple Judas betrayed him and Roman governor Pontius Pilate sentenced Jesus to be crucified (The Roman method of execution for serious criminals). Jesus was made to carry his own cross on his back and was crucified on Friday in 29 AD. Church of Holy Sepulchre in Jerusalem (Israel) encompasses the rock of Golgotha, where Jesus Christ was crucified.

St. Peter and St. Paul made Christianity the world religion. Mark and Luke in 185 AD propagated four gospels of Christianity and declared the gospels to be authoritative, though they had never met Jesus. It suited them to delete the gospel of Thomas, who was close to Jesus. (Celts people were living at Jerusalem in Israel in those days. They used to worship Nature as God and considered 31st October to be the last day of the year. Their New Year started on 1st November)

The three cosmic functions of: 1. Generator, 2. Operator and 3. Destroyer gave birth to the word GOD in Christianity in English language. Christ was the Son of God. As time passed, Christianity split into two denominations: 1. Catholics and 2. Protestants. The sacred places are: 1 Mount Arafat in Turkey - where Noah's ark landed, 2. Mount Sinai presently under Israeli occupation - where God revealed Ten Commandments to Moses and 3. Mount Olympus in Greece - is believed to be the home of God.

Bible - is a holy book about God and His relationship with human beings. The scripture contains a long history of God's revelations of Himself to man, from Adam to Moses down to the Apostles - the twelve disciples chosen by Christ to preach the Gospel - the first four books of the New Testament. Bible is world's most selling book, as year after year millions of copies are sold. Bible has been printed in 2,000 languages, but many find the book hard to understand. Bible is divided into: Old Testament (Originally written in Hebrew) and New Testament (Originally written in Greek in 380 AD) and is the revelation of St. John

The major festivals are: 1. New Year Day (1st January) - celebrated throughout the world with rejoicing and feasting, 2. Good Friday - the day of crucification of Jesus Christ, 3. Easter - the day of resurrection of Christ, 4. Christmas (25th December) - birthday of Jesus Christ, which is traditionally celebrated with exchange of greetings and gifts.

3. Islam - has the second largest number of followers in the world. Prophet Mohammed Sahib (570 AD - 632 AD, age 62 years) was the founder of the religion. He was born on 25th May 570 AD at Mecca in Saudi Arabia, his mother was Bibi Amina and father was Hazrat Abdullah - who was a businessman. Mohammed Sahib at the age of 25 years married a rich widow, named Khadija.

Prophet Hazarat Ebrahim at Mecca in Saudi Arabia built Kaba. It is obligatory in Islam to perform Haj in one's life at this place. During Haj, person wears Ihram (Two plain unstitched lengths of cloth). Muslims perform the ceremonial journey between two hillocks, called Safa and Marwa. They pledge to devote to the call of Allah (God), as the great Ismail and his mother did. During the journey, persons throw pebbles at the pillars of Jamarat to confirm that they will chase Satan away, as Prophet did.

Prophet Mohammed Sahib had four Khalifas, who helped him in spreading Islam. Twelve years after death of Prophet Mohammed Sahib, Zaid Ibn Thabit wrote Quran and the Islamic laws were framed over the next several hundred years with extensive elaborations from Hadith tradition. Later Mullahs introduced Veil (Burkha) system in the religion.

Islam has five major beliefs

1. There is no god, but Allah (God) and Mohammad Sahib is his prophet.
2. Prayer (Salah) - is to be performed five times: 1. after dawn and before sunrise (Fajr), 2. sun's descent and late afternoon (Zuhr), 3. sun halfway through descent and befóre sunset (Asr), 4. between sunset and the red glow fades (Maghrib) and 5. between dusk and midnight (Isha). Islamic calendar is lunar, is not adjusted to keep pace with the Solar year and is counted from Prophet Mohammad's move to Madina in 622 AD.
3. Fasting (Sawn) - in the 9th month of Ramadan fasting is held, where an adult refrains from eating, drinking, smoking and conjugal relations from dawn to dusk.
4. Welfare tax (Zakat) - community has a right on the surplus wealth of an individual and is 2.5 % of the annual income, which is distributed amongst the needy.
5. Pilgrimage (Hajj) - Muslims are expected to perform holy pilgrimage to Makkah during the month Dhu-L-Hijja atleast once in a lifetime.

Mosque is a holy place for the Muslim community to meet and pray. Prophet Mohammad Sahib built the first Mosque in Madina and as time passed, Islam split into two denominations: 1. Sunnis and 2. Shias. Islam originated in Saudi Arabia and the major festivals are:

1. Muharram - is the 1st month of the year and 10th Muharram is martyrdom of Ali, when young men subject themselves to physical testing.

2. Ramadan - is the 9th month of fasting and Muslims refrain from eating, drinking, smoking and conjugal relations from dawn to Sunset.
3. Eid-Ul-Fitr - end of fasting month, heralded by sight of new Moon and Eid Mubarak is celebrated.
4. Dhu-L-Hijja - pilgrimages to Makkah and 10th day Prophet Ibrahim's offer to sacrifice his son Ishmael, when God desired and a lamb was sacrificed instead of Ishmael.
5. Maulid-Al-Nabi - Birthday of Prophet Mohammad Sahib.

4. Jainism

1st Tirthankar was Rishabha. 23rd Tirthankar was Parshva, who lived in 900 BC and advocated adoption of Jain philosophy. Last 24th Tirthankar was Lord Vardhamana Mahavira (598 BC - 526 BC, age 72 years) - he was born on 27.03.598 BC, at the age of 30 years, wandered naked, lived on little food, received alms, spent most of his time in silence, frequently stood still like a statue and after 12 years of suffering, achieved Omniscience (Kevala). He at the age of 72 years attained liberation (Moksha).

Jainism's main theme is non-injury (Ahinsa), monks and nuns wear a small mask over their mouth to stop any insect going into their mouth. They strain water, before taking. Each Tirthankar has a symbol and Mahavira has lion. Jainism believes that the universe follows an eternal pattern of rise and fall. In each age, there are 24 Tirthankaras (Bridge makers), who help men and women cross the gap between life and death. Jain means the follower of Jinas (Spiritual- victors).

As time passed, Jainism split into two denominations: 1. Digambara and 2. Shvetambara:

1. Digambara (Sky clad) - believe that complete nudity is necessary to signify detachment from material life. They believe that women are incapable of achieving enlightenment and they must wait to be reborn as men. Most of the Digambaras live in North India.
2. Shvetambara (White clad) - held that white robes are equally acceptable and they mostly live in South India.

The five principles of Jainism are: 1. Complete avoidance of harm to any living-being (Ahinsa), 2. Truthfulness is avoidance of saying anything harmful to others (Satya), 3. Non-stealing is avoidance of greed and exploitation (Asatya), 4. Chastity(Brahma-charya) monks and nuns are celibate and faithfulness is important, 5. Detachment (Aparigraha) consider material pleasures as illusions and avoidance of accumulation of wealth.

The religion has its origin in India. Mount Abu in Rajasthan is famous for Dilwara Temples and major festivals are: 1. Jinendra Rath Yatra, 2. Mahavira Jayanti (Birth of Lord Mahavira), 3. Shree Shantinath Janam, 4. Shree Parshvanath Jayanti and holy symbol is Upright-hand, which signifies responsibility of every individual to act with wisdom.

Jain scriptures - Bhadrabhanu Swami was the last man, who knew all the Jain scriptures by heart. Jains were concerned that the knowledge of Holy Scriptures might be lost, so in 360 BC a conference of monks was arranged at Patliputra (Patna) in Bihar. In the conference, the contents of the sacred texts were arranged into scriptures: 1. Anga - 11 texts, 2. Upangas - 12 texts, 3. Pakinnakas - 10 texts, 4. Chedas - 6 texts, 5. Mulasutra - 4 texts, 6. Sutras - 2 texts and 7. Kalpasutra - contains biographies of the 24 Tirthankaras.

Jain philosophy is based on non-existence of God as creator and sustainer. Jainisn believes that the goal of life is liberation (Kevala). Universe is neither created nor sustained by a super power; it is beginning less, endless and operates in accordance with natural laws. They believe that reality exists in soul (Jive) and in without soul (Ajiva). Jains contention is that bad deeds (Karmas) make the soul heavy and good deeds make it light.

5. Buddhism

Siddhartha Gautam Buddha (567 BC - 487 BC, age 80 years) - was the black divine person, who had flat face, thick lips, curly hair of Negro origin, who established Buddhism, which spread through out Asia. Buddha means enlightened one. Buddha while meditating under a Bodhi tree at Bodhgaya attained enlightenment. He learnt the four noble truths: 1. Truth of suffering (Dukha) is the central fact of life, 2. Truth of origin of suffering (Samudaya) is the reason for suffering; 3. Truth of cessation of suffering (Nirodha) is a way to end the suffering, 4. Truth of path is to end the suffering

(Marga). Truth of path is eight fold: 1. Right views, 2. Right thoughts, 3. Right speech, 4. Right action, 5. Right livelihood, 6. Right effort, 7. Right mindfulness and 8. Right contemplation.

Buddha gave his first sermon to a small group of disciples at Sarnath. After 200 years of Buddha's death, King Ashoka gave the religion international dimensions and it spread beyond India. Different cultures as existed over there, influenced the religion and four different forms of Buddhism developed, which are:

1. Theravada Buddhism - is the teachings of the elders, is popular in Myanmar (Burma), Malaysia, Ceylon, Thailand and Vietnam. Scriptures were written in Pali language on palam-leafs in Sri Lanka. Palam-leaf collection is called Tripitaka (Three baskets) as the manuscripts were kept in three wooden baskets: 1. Sutha basket - contained discourses of Buddha, 2. Vinaya basket - contained rules and 3. Abhidhamma basket - contained knowledge.
2. Mahayana Buddhism - is the great vehicle, which is popular in Tibet, West China and Mongolia. Scriptures were written in Sanskrit language during 1st century AD.
3. Eastern Budhism - is popular in East China, Korea and Japan.
4. Indian Buddhism - is popular in Indonesia, Borneo and Celebes.

Religion has its origin in India. Major festival is Buddha Jayanti - celebrated on full Moon day as birth and liberation (Mahaparinirvana) of Buddha. Buddhists usually begin an act of devotion before a shrine by reciting: "I take refuse in the Buddha". Pilgrimage centers are: 1. Lumbini - Buddha's birth place, 2. Bodhgaya - Buddha's enlightenment, 3. Sarnath - Buddha delivered his first sermon and 4. Kushinagar - here Buddha died.

Buddhism's philosophy rejects the ritualistic aspects of Vedas, caste system, believe in deeds (Karma), transmigration of soul from one birth to another, life's goal is end of change (Nivana) and there is no creator, no God, as such, no union with God. Dharmapada is a sacred book, which contains 42 verses. Dharmapada represents Buddha's teachings and views. Buddhisms believes that a man should enlighten himself from the life of evil, passion, lust, hatred and anger. Salvation comes from knowledge and pure thoughts, while desire and attachments are the cause of suffering.

6. Sikhism

Sikh means follower or disciple and the worship place is called Gurdwara (The door of the Guru), which is normally attached with Langar (Free kitchen). Nanak Dev Ji was the founder of the religion. He was the first Guru and his successor Gurus spread the movement in Punjab and in other parts of India.

Sikh Gurus

1st Guru Nanak Dev Ji (1469 – 1539 AD, age 70 years) - was born on 14th April 1469 (Traditional birth celebration is held in mid Lunar month of Karthak, which falls in November) at Talwandi (Nankana Sahib) near Lahore in Punjab in Pakistan. His mother was Mata Tripta and father was Kalyan Rai Bedi - known as Mehta Kalu, who was a land officer.

Guru Nanak Dev Ji wrote many hymns and founded the town of Kartarpur in Punjab. He was born to a Hindu family and worked for a local Muslim Governor. He discussed religion with both Hindus and Muslims.

One day, Nanak Dev Ji's clothes were found on the river bank and he was feared drowned, but after three days, he returned. He did not talk for a day, but next day, he said that there is neither Hindu nor Muslim, so whose path shall I follow? He said that I shall follow God's path and God is neither Hindu nor Muslim. He said that external rituals are irrelevant and God cannot be defined by any religion. Nanak Ji traveled to Sri Lanka in the south, to Makkah in Saudi Arabia in the west, to Afghanistan in the north and established a community at Kartarpur.

2nd Guru Angad (1504 – 1552 and Guru from 1539 AD) - one day, Nanak Dev Ji chose a successor named Lehna and renamed him as Angad - meaning part of him. Angad Ji developed Gurmukhi script in which Guru Granth Sahib was originally written.

3rd Guru Amardas (1479 – 1574 and Guru from 1552) - he organized Sikh community and introduced the custom of calling the members on Baisakhi and Devali. He developed the custom of Langar (Free community meal).

4th Guru Ram Das (1534 – 1581 and Guru from 1574) - he was son-in-law of Guru Amar Das ji. He founded the city of Amritsar and dug the bathing pool (Sarovar). He made Amritsar a pilgrimage center. His hundreds of compositions are included in Guru Granth Sahib including the Lavan - the wedding hymn.

5th Guru Arjan (1563 – 1606 and Guru from 1581) - he was son of Guru Ram Das Ji. He completed building of Golden Temple at Amritsar. He collected the hymns of his predecessors into Adi Granth and installed this in Golden Temple. Arjan Ji was tortured and killed by the Mughal Emperor Jahangir. He became the first martyr.

6th Guru Hargobind (1595 – 1644 and Guru from 1606) - he was son of Guru Arjan and was imprisoned for a short while, but soon developed good relations with Jahangir. He built Gurdwaras and repaired others.

7th Guru Har Rai (1630 – 1661 and Guru from 1644) - he was grand son of Guru Hargobind. He had good knowledge about medicines, opened hospitals, where treatment was free.

8th Guru Har Krishan (1656 – 1664 and Guru from 1661) - younger son of Guru Har Rai. He became Guru at the age of 5 years. Emperor Aurangzeb viewed him with suspicion, the young Guru was summoned to Delhi, kept under house arrest, where he contracted smallpox and died at the age of 8 years.

9th Guru Tegh Bahadur (1621 – 1675 and Guru from 1664) - he was second son of Guru Hargobind and his name was Tyag Mal, but before he became Guru, he was given the name Degh Bahadur. After he became Guru and looking to his resistance to Emperor Aurangzeb's attempt to impose Islam, he earned the name Tegh Bahadur. He was executed after refusing to embrace Islam.

10th Guru Gobind Singh (1666 – 1708 and Guru from 1675) - he was son of Guru Tegh Bahadur and his original name was Govind Rai, but took the name Singh, when he founded Khalsa. He sanctioned use of military force in defence of justice, but was killed by an assassin. He wrote many hymns, which were collected after his death into Dasam Granth and Mugal Emperor immured his two sons alive in a wall at Sirhind in Punjab.

Guru Gobind Singh declared that the collection of hymns, known as Adi Granth is the Guru for all time to come and in 19th century, the writing was standardized, so each copy has exactly the same number of pages. Guru Granth Sahib is treated as one would treat the highly honoured human Guru. Guru Granth Sahib has its own separate room, where at night five beloved Sikhs (Panj Pyaras) carry him for rest. Excerpts from Guru Granth Sahib are available in the form of Gutkha.

Guru Gobind Singh gave all Sikhs the name Singh (Lion) for men and Kaur (Princess) for women, to abolish all traces of caste system. Five K's of the religion are: 1. Kesh- uncut hair, 2. Kanga- comb to keep the hair tidy, 3. Kara- a steel bangle symbolizing one God, 4. Kirpan- a dagger reminder of readiness to fight against oppression and 5. Kacchera- short trouser / breeches signifying readiness to ride into battle and all Sikhs carry them. Sikhism believes in one God, who is timeless, without form, cannot be found by human efforts, but reveals Himself to those, who seek Him through prayer and unselfish life-style.

Sikhism teaches equality, service and protection of the week against injustice. Four Gurudwaras associated with Guru Gobind Singh are marked with special sanctity and are: 1. Patna Sahib in Bihar (His birth place), 2. Anandpur Sahib in Punjab (Ceremony of Baptism), 3. Akal Takht in Golden Temple at Amritsar in Punjab, from where edicts are issued and 4. Nanded Sahib in Maharashtra, where he died.

In 1604 AD, Bhai Gurudas Ji wrote Granth Sahib in Gurumukhi under the direction of Guru Arjan Dev Ji. Bhai Manik Singh under the guidance of Guru Gobind Singh Ji re-edited Garanth Sahib at Damdama Sahib. Guru Gobind Singh seeing his end near declared that after his death Shree Guru Granth Sahib will be the living Guru for the Sikh community. Guru Granth Sahib was instituted as Guru for all time in 1708 AD.

Shree Guru Granth Sahib has the sayings of Guru Nanak Dev Ji, Guru Anangad Dev Ji, Guru Amardas Ji, Guru Ramdas Ji, Guru Arjundev Ji and words of Kabir, Farid, Namdev, Ravidas, Surdas, Jaidev and Dhanna. Guru Granth Sahib has 2026 Shabad, 305 Asatpadiya, 145 Chand and was installed in Har Mandir Sahib at Amritsar in 1604 AD. Recitation of Shree Guru Granth Sahib is called Sahaj Pat, when time factor is ignored and continuous recitation is called Akhand Pat, which gets completed in 48 hours.

Religion has its origin in India and major festivals are: 1.Baisakhi (13th April) - is based on Solar Calendar to commemorate founding of Khalsa, 2. Martyrdom of Guru Arjan Dev, 3. Divali (Four day festival and ends on 2nd day of Kartik month, 4. Guru Nanak's birthday (Full Moonday of Kartik month), 5. Hola Mohalla (Full Moonday of Phalgun month) - contests of athletics, horsemanship and martial art.

Khanda is the insignia of the Sikh religion, which represents the universal creative power, in the center is double-edged sword - symbol of primal and almighty power of the creator, circle (Chakra) - symbolizes one God with no beginning or end and symbol of infinity, two swords - on the outside symbolize spiritual (Piri) and temporal (Miri) balance in universe. This shows Sikh's readiness to defend truth and justice.

Sikhism's philosophy is that attachment to material objects is the primary cause of rebirth, which takes place on the basis of past actions (Karmas), liberation (Mukti) from the cycle of birth and death can be achieved by being conscious towards the divine teacher (Gurmukh). Philosophy does not believe in incarnation of God in human form, disapproves asceticism and self mortification as path to enlightenment. Sikhs do recitation of hymn (Japa), sing devotional prayer (Kirtan) and sing the names (Nam-simran).

Sikhism teaches that God is the creator of the universe, its existence and continued survival depends on his Will (His Hukum). God is both with attributes (Saguna) and without attributes (Nirguna) and is called truth (Sat). True God (Sat Guru) is timeless-being (Akal Purkh), is creator (Kartar) and praise to God (Wahi-Guru).

7. Bahaism

Bahaism is a recent religion and originated in 19th century in Iran. Religion is based on the belief that Mirza Husayn Ali in (1817 – 1892 AD) - was the prophet sent by God and is known as glory of God (Bahaullah). Siyyid Ali Mohammad - a young Shia Muslim in 1844 AD, announced that he is a gate (Bab) through whom God communicates with humanity. He was executed in 1850 AD and the disciples were persecuted.

Bahaullah appointed his son Abdul Baha as the authority and during his time, Bahai faith became international with headquarters at Haifa in Israel. He taught that God has provided successive revelations to mankind through series of prophets to bring humanity to maturity and he was the last Prophet. The central theme of his teaching was the unity of all people. He said that Earth is one country and mankind it's citizens.

Religion is based on principles of economic justice, equal rights for men and women, education for all, break-down of barriers of race, class and creed. Bahai's holy symbol is interlocked triangles, which signify interdependence of all people.

There are about 50, 00,000 Bahai's worldwide in 175 countries. The holy places are: 1. Spiritual center in Haifa, 2. Tomb of Baaullah, 3. Shrine of Bab and are situated in Israel. Holy scripture is Bahaullah's Kitab-I-Aqdas - a book of laws, which he wrote in Arabic and Persian.

Bahai calendar has 19 months, each month has 19 days, making 361 days, and remaining 4 days are for celebrations, giving gifts and for hospitality. Bahai's believe that God has revealed himself through different prophets, like: 1. Krishna, 2. Moses, 3. Buddha, 4. Christ and 5. Mohammad. They gave revelations, which were appropriate for their times. Bahai's believe that they are capable of forming one world, rather than diverse nations of different races and religions. They place emphasis on social life to create one world, under one government with one religion of Bahai faith.

1.4. Hindu Religion

. India had an indigenous black-population, which found its way into the Indian subcontinent about 50,000 years ago from Ethiopia. They were from two origins of population: 1. East side of Red Sea and 2. West side of Red Sea. They had established an empire, known as Indus (Sindhu) Valley Civilization and ruled over a vast area stretching from Egypt to East India. The great Indian Rishi Manu, who divided Hindu society into four castes, belonged to Egypt and this happened in an era beyond the reach of history.

Godfrey Higgins - the British archaeologist,. author and historian said that in 1,500 BC, Indus Valley Civilization Empire was invaded by a tribe from North of India, igniting a series of wars upon the Indian subcontinent, which lasted 1,000 years. Rig Veda - the most ancient scripture describes this confrontation.

Hindu Religion is world's oldest living religion (Dharma) and is about 8,500 years old. The roots of the religion lie in the Indus (Sindhu) Valley Civilization, which had 300 settlements as early as 5,000 BC. Religion is very complex in nature, is very wide, is very deep, is very vast and is philosophical in nature, as such; the religion has been dealt in more detail. Indus Valley Civilization suffered heavy losses due to recurring floods in the Indus River, which forced the Hindus to migrate to other parts of India. This migration took place from 1,800 BC to 1,700 BC.

Aryans - were fire worshippers, they settled along the banks of River Saraswati around 1,500 BC and their religious practices got merged Into the Hindu practices. The combined religious practices were carried to other parts of India. Dr Sarvepalli Radhakrishnan, the former president of India said that Hinduism is more a way of life than a set of beliefs.

Sanatana Dharma - was the original name of the Hindu Religion. World Hindu came from Hind - the Old Persian name for India and Hinduism meant the religion of the people of India. India's original name was Bharat - the land of King Bharata, who was son of Shakuntala and Dushyanta. Hindu religion is a conglomeration of many faiths, beliefs, cults, doctrines and has no central authority or hierarchy. Hindus mostly live in India and Nepal. Hindu Religion regards all forms of worship as merely different paths to reach the God (Parbrahman). Hinduism is like a great river into which over the period of past 3,000 years, many streams have flowed in. The streams are the beliefs and practices of the numerous ethnic groups and their cultures that exist in the Indian subcontinent.

Europeans - came to India around 1650 AD to draw the geographical map of the country. They changed the name of the religion from Sanatana Dharma to Hinduism, as the followers of the religion were living on the Eastern side of Hindukush Mountain (Afghanistan / Pakistan border) and called the followers Hindus. They changed the name of the country from Bharat Varsh to India, as the country was situated on the Eastern side of the River Indus (Flowing through Pakistan) and Hind Maha Sagar to Indian Ocean.

Caste system - Hindu religion in the beginning, had no caste system, but as work culture grew complex, Rishi Manu divided the Hindu society into four castes (Jati), depending upon the occupational profession, the people followed. Four castes are:

1. Brahmins - performed priestly work in temples and organized religious functions.
2. Kshatriyas - performed soldierly work and protected the people from aggression.
3. Vaishyas - did business and supplied goods to the society.
4. Shudras - performed physical work and helped people in their household work.

As time passed, caste system became hereditary in nature and caste prejudices grew. There are approximately 3,000 castes in the Hindu society and each caste forms a distinct unit in itself in respect of social gatherings and usually marry within their own caste to maintain traditions.

Hindu festivals - are based on Lunar Calendar of 12 months and one extra month is added every five years to keep pace with the seasons in India. Each month is divided into a bright fortnight (Moon waxing) and a dark fortnight (Moon waning). Month ends with full Moon day (Purnima). Festivals are:

1. Makar Sankranti (14th January fixed as per Solar year) - is the transit of Sun into the 10th Makar Rashi is celebrated with rejoicing.
2. Shiva Ratri (New Moon night of every month) - is the night of Lord Shiva and Mahashivaratri (13th / 14th dark half of Magh month) - is the great night of Lord Shiva.
3. Sarasvati Puja (5th day of bright half of Magh month) or Basant Panchmi - Sarasvati is the goddess of arts and learning and people wear yellow clothes, as symbol of royalty and warmth of the spring season.
4. Holi (Full Moon Day of Phalgun month) - is the grain harvest festival of India. Festival is the most boisterous spring festival, celebrated with bonfires, jokes, fun, dancing, colored water and powder is thrown on people.
5. Ram Naomi (9th day of bright half of Chaitra month) - birthday of Lord Rama.

6. Rath Yatra (16th day of Asadha month) - huge image of Lord Vishnu (Jaggannath) is placed on a wooden chariot and pulled through the streets.
7. Raksha Bandhan (Full Moon day of Sravana month) - sisters tie Rakhi on the right hand of brothers to secure protection.
8. Janma Ashtmi (8th day of Bhadra month) - birthday of Lord Krishna.
9. Ganesh Chaturthi (4th day of bright half of Bhadrapad month) - idols of Lord Ganesha are installed; on 13th day the idols are taken out in procession and immersed in water.
10. Navaratri (10 Days of bright half of Aswin month) - Durga the concert of Shiva has many forms, like: as Kali - destroys, as Parvati - faithful wife of Lord Shiva, as Durga - destroyer of evil demons.
11. Dussehra (A day after Navaratri) - effigy of Ravana is set on fire.
12. Diwali (13th day of dark half of Aswin month) - is the most widely celebrated festival, traders close their accounts, Lakshmi - the goddess of wealth is worshiped. This is the brightest festival, where every house gets illuminated with lamps and candles, so that Lakshmi can come in. The festival also marks the return of Lord Rama from his exile. Festival heralds the beginning of New Hindu Year.
13. Kumbha Mela - is held every twelve years in rotation in India at four places: 1. Allahabad - confluence of three rivers Ganga, Jamuna and the legendry Sarasvati, 2. Hardwar - Ganges river, 3. Ujjain - Shipra river and 4. Nasik -Godavari river. People in millions bathe in these holy rivers.

Eight theories on the existence of God

Hinduism defines God (Eishwara) through theories and no theory supersedes any other. Each theory holds equally good and no theory has been proved to be right or wrong. All the eight theories evolved from time to time, as religion progressed through the ages. Theories are:

1. Adhyatmic (Spiritual) theory - states that the existence of God is merely an experience, not a reality, however through spiritual practices like meditation, God can be realized internally (In the

heart) in reality, who has consciousness, as such, spiritual perception of God is true and else is false.

2. Ardhnarishvara (Half male and half female) theory - God is perceived as having a body consisting of half portion as male and the other half as female. This is the form of Shiva and he does not marry, as he is complete in himself.

3. Assumption theory - is based upon the following assumptions:

1. God existed - before the visible universe came into being and He will continue to live even, if the universe comes to an end.
2. God has no power - but all power comes from Him.
3. God has no knowledge - but all knowledge flows from Him.
4. God has no strength - but all strength is derived from Him.
5. God has no wealth - but all wealth comes from Him.
6. God has no form - but any form can be assigned to Him.
7. God has no language - but prayer can be offered in any language to Him.
8. God has no religion - but all religions put claim on Him.
9. God has no gender - but any gender can be assigned to Him.
10. God has no name - but any name can be assigned to Him.

4. Aum theory - is an Upanishad theory, which states that the sound wave 'Aum' pervades in the universe. 'Aum' is known as Brahm Nad i.e. Godly sound, which was produced, when a point explosion, called Bindu Vishphot took place. 'Aum' sound wave was produced before anything else appeared in the universe, as such, the word 'Aum' is used before every prayer and hymn (Mantra) of Hindu Religion. This is phenomenon in science is also known as Big Bang theory.

5. Brahman theory - is a Vedantic theory, where Brahman simultaneously exists as Parbrahman - as omniscient consciousness. Brahman is a Sanskrit language word, where 'Brh' means to grow and manifest. Brahman is male (Purusha) and is the prime soul, who administers every aspect of the universe. The theory was popular from 2,000 BC to 500 BC. and religious stories (Gathas) became very popular during Mughal period, which re-established Hinduism with greater force and avoided the forcible conversion to Islam.

6. Nirankar theory - God has no form, as such, cannot be perceived through the five human senses (1. Eyes, 2. Ears, 3. Nose, 4. Tongue and 5. Touch), but He has consciousness and controls every thing and knows what is happening in the universe.

7. Sakar theory - states that God assumes a form, when sins increase beyond a limit. He chooses his own birth date, time and place and after taking birth restores righteousness (Dharma) in society. God's birth is known as incarnation (Avatar) and the manifested form is called Bhagwan, which is a Sanskrit word, where: 1. 'Bha' - means Earth (Bhumi), 2. 'Ga' - means sky (Gagan), 3. 'V' - means air (Vayu), 4. 'A' - means fire (Agni) and 5. 'N' - means water (Nir).

8. Samarth Guru theory - states that God is complete (Purn) in Himself, while remaining complete, He makes others also complete and even then He remains complete by Himself, as such, Samarth Guru is real God.

Two scientific theories on the existence of God

1. Abstract Entity theory - states that Entity has consciousness, which existed before the universe came into being and after having created the universe, Entity remains present everywhere in it. Entity administers all the basic functions of everything else. Abstract Entity theory is based on Four Fundamental Forces:

1. Gravitational Force - is the weakest force, but it acts over very long distances, is felt by every particle according to its mas, is always attractive in nature, force makes the Earth rotate on its axis and makes it to revolve around the Sun.

2. Electromagnetic Force - is the flow of electrons from negative to positive side, the flow gives rise to electrical current, which produces magnetism, but the force interacts at very low energy levels.

3. Weak Nuclear Force - is responsible for radioactivity, which holds the protons and neutrons together in the nucleus of an atom. The force has a curious property called confinement, which binds the nuclear particles together in an atom.

4. Strong Nuclear Force - holds the quarks, the constituent parts of protons and neutrons together. The force is attractive

between unlike particles and repulsive between like particles. Electromagnetic attraction between negatively charged electrons and positively charged protons in an atom, cause the electrons to orbit around the protons in an atom.

All the particles of the Four Fundamental Forces exist in nature only in different states and at high energy levels; they all behave in a similar manner. Scientist Albert Einstein said that as science advances, all the Four Fundamental Forces would be united, some explanation would be found for it in future and Abstract Entity would be renamed as God.

2. Super Intelligent Mind theory - DNA is not merely a molecule with a pattern, but is a Code, which has language and has information storage mechanism. All codes are created by a conscious mind, therefore DNA is a proof of the existence of a Super Intelligent Mind, but research is this direction is of very recent origin and much more is yet to come.

Hindu Deities - fall into three categories and are worshiped in three different modes:

1. Asuric Deities - are demonic in nature and are worshiped in fierce mode (Tamoguna). If one is successful in his worship, he acquires power to control and destroy others.
2. Devta and Devi Deities - are of divine in nature and are worshiped in gentle mode (Rajoguna). If one is successful in his worship, he acquires material wealth and achieves prosperity in life.
3. Mukti Deities - are liberation granting and are worshiped in truth mode (Sattoguna). If one is successful in his worship, he attains liberation and escapes the cycle of birth and death. His soul merges with the Supreme-being.

Twelve Devtas (Divine males):

1. Agni Devta (Fire) - in Rig-veda largest number of hymns are devoted to Fire Devta and his consort is Swaha.
2. Indira Devta - his favourite weapon is thunderbolt and rain is at his command and his consort is Indrani.
3. Vishwa Karma Devta - is the divine architect of universe and is son of Lord Brahma.

4. Yam Devta - is the deity of death and is embodiment of the rule of law and imparts justice according to one's deeds.
5. Narad Devta - is shown as a wandering seer going from place to place and is reputed to have invented Veena, the musical instrument.
6. Dhanvantri Devta - is the physician.
7. Hanuman Devta - has the most strength.
8. Vayu Devta - the controller of winds and atmosphere.
9. Balaram Devta - looks after agriculture.
10. Mitra Devta - fosters friendship.
11. Ganesha Devta - is the elder son of Lord Shiva and is knowledgeable (Vinayaka). He is remover of obstacles (Vighneshvara) and is worshiped in the beginning of every event to get his blessings. His vehicle is mouse.
12. Kartikeya Devta - is the younger son of Lord Shiva and is known by different names, as Subramaniam, Skanda, Guha, Shadannana and Sanmukha (Six face). His vehicle is peacock.

Three Devis (Divine females):

1. Ambika Devi - she lures devils to death.
2. Amman Devi - she keeps summer epidemics away.
3. Aranyani Devi - she protects the wild animals and forests.

Five Matas (Divine mothers):

1. Kali - portrays destructive energy.
2. Lakshmi - provides wealth and prosperity.
3. Saraswati - helps in studies and gives knowledge.
4. Shakti family - consists of 1. Durga, 2. Parwati and 3. Amba.
5. Santoshi - she is for the betterment of housewives.

Four dual (Female - male) forms:

1. Radha - Krishna
2. Sita - Rama
3. Uma - Mahesh
4. Lakshmi - Narayana

Hindus believe in trinity of Godheads (Lords):

1. Lord Brahma - the creator is depicted seated on a lotus - the symbol of glorious existence. He has four heads, four hands, in one hand - holds sacrificial tool (Sruva), in second hand - holds books of knowledge (Vedas), in third hand holds water pot

(Kamandalu) and in fourth hand - holds rosary (Mala). His vehicle is swan (Hansa), concert is Saraswati and does not contain opposites within himself. He belonged to Shudra Caste.

He introduced divine (Eish) system in the religion and the head of the system is named Eishwara (God), the land where the system prevailed is called Asia, which continues even today. Mythologically it is believed that Lord Brahma had one head, but acquired three more, when he created woman from his own body, fell in love with her, but she hid herself from him, so to see her from every side, Lord Brahma grew three more heads, one on his left side, another on his right side and the third on his back side.

2. Lord Vishnu - is the preserver. He has four hands, in one hand - holds conch shell (Sankha) to produce divine sound 'Aum', in second hand - holds disk the wheel of time (Chakra), in third hand - holds lotus (Padma) for glorious existence and in fourth hand - holds mace (Gada) indicating power. His vehicle is eagle (Garuda), he rests on a bed of coiled serpent named Sheshanag and his concert is Lakshmi - the Devi of wealth.

He contains good and evil. He has opposites within himself and maintains order in society. When evil gets an upper hand; he incarnates (Avatar) and assumes certain special powers (Kalas), which help him to restore righteousness (Dharma). He takes birth on a pre-determined date, time and place. We humans take birth as per our previous traits (Sanskars). Wherever Vishnu is worshipped, sacred basil plant (Tulasi) is kept, as the plant is considered sacred and leaves are used in worship. His other names are Venkateshwara and Satya Narayana.

3. Lord Mahesh (Shiva) - is portrayed in a meditating posture in a happy mood with matted hair adorned which crescent (Moon), has a coiled serpent around his neck, has trident (Trishul) in one hand and body smeared with ashes. His vehicle is bull (Nandi) - the symbol of strength. He is destroyer and maintains balance in nature. He as Lord of dance (Nataraja) is shown with left foot raised - the symbol of liberation, his downward pointing left hand - the symbol where a worshiper finds refuge, his third vertical eye - destroys the evil, his whirling hair - hold the Ganges, his halo - is the symbol of cosmos, his statue surrounded by a circle of flame - is the symbol of end of life in flames (Destruction), his dance - the

symbol of eternal movement of universe and life. When the cycle of dance ends - it gives rise to new life, when he beats his small drum (Damru) - he summons a new creation. This religious phenomenon has impressed the Western world much, as it tallies with the present scientific observations.

Twelve abodes (Jyotirlingas) of Lord Shiva:

1. Bhimshankar - on Brahmpur Mountain in Kamrup district in Assam.
2. Ghushmeshwar - on the bank of River Banas at Shiwar village in Sawai Madhopur district in Rajasthan.
3. Kedarnath - on the bank of River Mandakini in Uttarakhand.
4. Mahakaleshwar - on the bank of River Kshipra at Ujjain in Madhya Pradesh.
5. Mallikarjun - on the bank of River Krishna in Tamilnadu.
6. Nageshwar - in Dwarukwan forest near Dwarka in Gujarat.
7. Onkareshwar - on the bank of River Narbada in Khargon district in Madhya Pradesh.
8. Rameshwaram - in Ramnad district in Tamilnadu.
9. Somnath - in Kathiawar in Saurashtra in Gujarat.
10. Triyambkeshwar - on the bank of River Godavari at Nasik in Maharashtra.
11. Vaidnath - at Devghar in Bihar.
12. Vishvanath - on the bank of River Ganges at Banaras in Bihar.

Seven eternal-beings (Chiranjeevis)

1. Ashwathama - son of Guru Dronacharya learnt the art of invoking the ultimate weapon of destruction (Brahmastra) and during Mahabharata War, entered the camp of Panadavas, killed the male members and lastly he was over powered by the Pandavas. He was granted the boon of eternal-being (Chiranjeevi), but was condemned to live forever with a wound, which will never heal.

2. Bali - was the famous alms giving king, who surrendered all what he had to the Brahmin Vaman (Lord Vishnu's incarnation), but Vaman had to humble himself, when Bali knew who was Vaman, as such, Bali was granted the boon of eternal-being.

3. Hanuman - the symbol of service, courage, devotion, energy and righteousness. Sita the wife of Lord Rama bestowed upon him the boon of eternal-being and blessed him to remain ever youthful and energetic. Hanuman expressed his wish to listen to the stories of Lord Rama (Ram Katha), as such, whenever, wherever Rama Katha is recited, Hanuman is invariably present in some form or other. Rishi Vashishta and Vishvamitra were his compatriots.

4. Kirpacharya - was the great teacher, who upheld the great traditions of morality and impartiality as a teacher, as such, was granted the boon of eternal-being.

5. Parshuram - the master of weapons (Astras), scriptures (Shastras), martial arts and divinity. He led a simple life, when ever he was wrong, he never hesitated to accept his mistake, and he stood for strength. He achieved excellence in life and was granted the boon of eternal-being.

6. Vibhishana - the brother of king Ravana of Lanka, surrendered to lord Rama with full faith and preached what he believed, as such, he was granted the boon of eternal-being for righteousness and fearlessness.

7. Vyas - the great scholar, writer of Vedas, Mahabharata and Srimad Bhagavatam, was granted the boon of eternal-being for being the ultimate visionary of mankind.

Hindu time counting (Kalganna) system

Hindus see time as a circle. When this concept was realized by the American scientist Einstein, he elaborated and said that time is a curve and space is a curve as well, which eventually make a circle. Hindu time counting system is as follows:

1 Truti = 1 / 33,750 second - is smallest unit of time.

1 Kalpa = 1,000 Chaturyug = 14 Manvanter = 432, 00, 00,000 year (432 crore year) - is the longest unit of time and is the life span of Lord Brahma. This is the present age of Earth.

1 Chaturyug = 43, 20,000 years and from one Chaturyug to the next Chaturyug, there is Sandhi-Kal (Combining time period), which is not counted in the previous Chaturyug or in the next Chaturyug. 1 Chaturyug (Four yugs) = [Satyug 17,28,000 years (4 x Kaliyug) + Tretayug 12,96,000 years (3 x Kaliyug) + Dwaperyug

8,64,000 years (2 x Kaliyug) + Kaliyug 4,32,000 years (1 x Kaliyug)] = 43,20,000 years and 71 Chaturyug = 1 Manvanter and 1,000 Chaturyug = 14 Manvanter

Currently, 27 Chaturyug (Mahayug) have passed and 28th Chaturyug's Satyug, Tretayug, Dwaperyug have passed and Kaliyug's 5,108th year is passing (2006 AD)

1. Lord Brahma's life - Hindu time counting system states that Lord Brahma lives in cycles of Kalpa and the cycles keep on repeating, in the following manner: Lord Brahma's life = 1 Kalpa = 1,000 Chaturyug = 14 Manvanter = 432 crore-year = 100 Brahma-year = life of Earth and human race appear and disappear in a cyclic manner, presently we are in 51st year of Brahma-year, 15,500 core-year have passed since the present Brahma was born and will live for another 49 Brahma-year. After present Brahma's death, another 100 Brahma-year will pass, until he is re-born as Brahma again and he will re-create a new universe, which will follow another cycle, however the present creation of universe is as follows:

1	Sandhi Kal	=	17,28,000 years (Joining period)
6	Manvanter	=	184,03,20,000 year (30,67,20,000 x 6)
7	Sandhi Kal	=	1,20,96,000 year (17,28,000 x 7 = 1,20,96,000)
27	Chaturyug	=	11,66,40,000 year (43,20,000 x 27)
1	Satyug	=	17,28,000 year
1	Tratayug	=	12,96,000 year
1	Dwaperyug	=	8,64,000 year
	Current Kaliyug	=	5,108 year

Total = 197, 29, 49,108 year (Current year of Sarashti Calendar). It is a mystery as to how these figures were got calculated thousands of years ago. The figure 197.2949 crore-year roughly coincides with the period, when Earth's outer crust got formed and life sprang on Earth.

2. Resolution (Sankalpa) - when a Hindu performs a worship, he says that in the 7th Vaivasvat Manvanter, in the 28th Chaturyuga, in the Shavetvarah Kalpa, in Kaliyuga's 5,107th year (3,045 + 2062 Vikram Samvat), I resolve to perform this worship and when these figures are added together, it works out 197, 29, 49,107 year - the current year of Sarashti Calendar. This is a wonder of Hindu Religion's time counting system.

3. Eras (Yugs) - Hindu religion believes that a new civilization begins after a grand deluge (Pralaya), which comes after 2, 16,000 years, where most of life on Earth gets destroyed and after a transition period, new civilization begins. The present civilization started in this manner and has passed through three Eras (Yug): Satyug, Tratayug, Dwaperyug and the current civilization is passing through Kaliyug. Kaliyug began at midnight of 17 / 18 February, 3102 BC, but there is difference of opinion on the number of years contained in each Era. Mythology gives these figures in multiples of Kaliyug years and these figure runs in millions of years, which are not tenable as per current scientific view, as such, logical figures have been worked out, which are in multiples of Satyug years. The table gives the details:

Yuga	*Mythological*	*Logical*	*Gregorian period*
1. Satyyug	17,28,000 yrs (4 x Kaliyug)	4,800 yrs (1 x Satyug)	10302 BC – 9102 BC
2. Tratayug	12,96,000 yrs (3 x Kaliyug)	3,600 yrs (2 x Satyug)	9102 BC – 6702 BC
3. Dwaperyug	8,64,000 yrs (2 x Kaliyug)	2,400 yrs (3 x Satyug)	6702 BC – 3102 BC
4. Kaliyug	4,32,000 yrs (1 x Kaliyug)	1,200 yrs (4 x Satyug)	3102 BC – 1698 AD
Total	43,20,000 years	12,000 years	

Figure 43, 20,000 years roughly coincides with the advent of human life on Earth and the sequence of Eras is in the descending order. Descending phase from Satyug to Kaliyug is associated with deterioration of righteousness (Dharma), which manifests as decrease in the span of human life and moral standards. On completion of descending phase, ascending phase begins from Kaliyug (1,200 year) back to Satyug and this cycle keeps on repeating.

In 700 BC, King Yudhister noticed the appearance of Kaliyug, handed over his throne to his grand son and retired to the Himalayas to die. As per Sri Yukteswar the ascending phase from Kaliyug began in September 499 AD and from September 1699

AD, we are living in the ascending phase of Dwaperyug. Evidence suggests that this may be happening, as the average life span of man is increasing, while another view is that we are currently living in the ascending phase of Kaliyug.

Four Yugs (Eras)

1. Satyuga (Golden) - majority of people experience spirituality, there is no dance (Natya) performance, because it is a period free from unhappiness and misery. People communicate directly through thought process, temples are not necessary because people feel the omni-presence of God and wars are rare, but they do occur.

2. Tratayuga (Silver) - majority of people harness mental power, men assume political power and inventions dissolve the illusion of time and distance. People communicate directly through thought process, temples are not necessary, because people feel the omni-presence of God and wars are rare, but they do occur.

3. Dwaperyuga (Bronze) - majority of people experience spiritual energies, science flourishes, inventions are abundant that dissolve the illusion of time and distance. Mostly power remains in the hands of women, temples, wars and writings are hallmark of the Yuga. End of Yuga was associated with the demise of Lord Krishna.

4. Kaliyuga (Iron) - majority of people remain aware of the physical aspect of human existence, material wealth and mostly the power remains in the hands of men. People's relationship with the spiritual life is governed by superstitions, temples, wars and writings are hallmark of the Yuga.

It is said that from Satyug Era to Kaliyug Era, there is a gradual decline of righteousness (Dharma), wisdom, knowledge, intellectual capacity, life span, emotional and physical strength and it has been calculated that the Kaliyuga Era began on 18.02.6810 BC at 02:20 hours in the Ashlesha constellation (Nakshtra) on Sunday, 13th Tithi of dark fortnight (Krishna Paksha) of Bhadrapad month of Vikram Samvat, when all the seven planets were in one sign (Rashi) and calendar depict that current Kaliyug's 5108th (3102 BC + 2006 AD) have passed, but it seems that this figure is not tenable as per present scientific calculations and it is presumed that the Kaliyug Era had ended in 1698 AD and we are passing through an ascending phase of the Kaliyug Era, where better human sense prevails and world peace will be restored by 2015 AD.

Lord Vishnu's nine incarnations (Avtars)

Hindus believe that when sins (Papams) increase beyond a limit; Lord Vishnu incarnates to restore peace and order in the society; for this he assumes special powers (Kalas).

YUG	AVTAR	KALAS
1. Satyug	1st Kachch (Tortoise) and 2nd Machch (Fish)	01
	3rd Varah (Bore) and 4th Vaman (Pigmy Brahmin)	02
	5th Narasingh (Head of lion and body of man) and 6th Parshuram (Brahmin warrior)	03
2. Tratayug	7th Bhagwan Rama (King of Ayodhiya) (7323 BC – 7281 BC, age of 42 years)	12
3. Dwaperyug	8th Bhagwan Krishna (King of Dwarka) (5659 BC – 5534 BC, age 125 years)	16
4. Kaliyug	9th Lord Buddha (567 BC – 487 BC, age 80 years) and established Buddhism	24
	10th Nishkalank (Birth in future)	24
	11th Not named (Birth in distant future)	64

Details of incarnations (Avatars)

1st Tortoise incarnation (Kachch Avatar) - took the newly created Earth on his back to render stability to the trembling Earth. It is mythologically believed that this support still exists, but science does not support this hypothesis.

2nd Fish incarnation (Matsya Avatar) - after a grand deluge (Prayalaya), the four Vedas remained drowned in the water, so fish incarnation descended into the water and brought the Vedas up. He instructed Lord Brahma to create the world.

3rd Bore incarnation (Varaha Avatar) - in the periodically repeated grand deluge (Prayalaya), Earth sank in the deep water; Bore incarnation descended into the water and brought the Earth up with tusks. This type of grand deluge is also held in other religions.

4th Dwarf Brahmin incarnation (Vaman Avatar) - King Bali through his devotion and penance defeated Indra Devta. He extended his rule over the three worlds. When Bali was making a religious offering, Dwarf Brahmin approached Bali and asked for land, which he could measure in three steps. Dwarf Brahmin (Vaman) measured heaven in first step, Earth in second step and stopped short for the third step, so Bali went to the subterranean region called Patal-lok. It is said that King Bali's capital was at Mahabalipuram; near Chennai in Tamilnadu, but does it suggest that South India was the so called Patal-lok?

5th Head of lion and body of man incarnation (Narasingh Avatar) - Lord Brahma had given the boon to the King Hiranya Kashyap that no man or animal born in the natural process would kill him, that he would neither die in the day nor in the night, that he would neither die on Earth nor in the heaven either by fire, water or any weapon. Lord Vishnu took birth with head of lion and body of man, who was neither man nor animal, took birth out of a split pillar, put Hiranya Kashyap on his thighs, and tore his body with his claws in twilight, which was neither day nor night.

6th Brahmin warrior incarnation (Parasuram Avatar) - at the close of Era Satyug, Kshatriya kings ruled the Earth. Their ministers very corrupt, goddess Earth (Prithvi) prayed to Lord Vishnu and he took birth as a Brahmin warrior (Parasuram) through a descent from sage Bhrigu. He defeated the Kshatriya Kings 21 times.

7th Lord Rama incarnation (7323 BC – 7281 BC, age 42 years) - he was Surya Vanshi Kshtriya Ruler of Ayodhya. He is depicted as holding a bow and an arrow indicating readiness to destroy evil. He is commonly pictured in a family style with wife Sita, brother Lakshman and devotee Hanuman sitting near Rama's feet. He was born at Ayodhya in Uttar Pradesh on 9th Tithi of Shukal Paksha in Chaitra Month of Vikram Samvat at 12 Noon in Tratayuga on 04.12.7323 BC (Calculated date).

Lord Rama at the age of 38 years' killed Ravana - the Brahmin Ruler of Lanka to rescue his wife Sita from his captivity. Lanka was so prosperous in those days that it glittered like gold. Lord Rama at the age of 42 years drowned himself (Jal Samadhi) in the River Saryu in 7281 BC (Calculated date). Ramayana describes his deeds.

8th Lord Krishna incarnation (5659 BC – 5534 BC, age 125 years) - he was Yadava Ruler of Dwarka. He is depicted as playing flute (Murali), who spreads the melody of love. He is generally shown with his childhood devotee Radha and the pair symbolizes eternal love between people and God.

He is the most commonly worshipped Lord. He delivered the message of Gita to Arjuna during Mahabharata War at the battlefield at Kurushetra in Haryana in India. He was born on 8th Tithi of dark fortnight (Krishna Paksha) of Bhadra month of Vikram Samvat at midnight at Mathura in Uttar Pradesh on 27.07.5659 BC (Calculated date). Scripture Sukhsagar describes his deeds.

Sixteen special powers (Kalas) of Lord Krishna

1. Sight power (Drashti Kala) - the power to see the things at far away places.
2. Invisible power (Adrashti Kala) - the power to become invisible to others.
3. Touch power (Saparshini Kala) - the power to enter into another's body and control his actions.
4. Attraction power (Akarshini Kala) - the powers to bring a distant object nearby.
5. Multi form power (Bahurupini Kala) - the power to assume any desired form of life.
6. Food power (Rasini Kala) - the power to have any food without having been prepared, as he produced the desired food at Draupdi's place and satisfied Rishi Durvasa's disciples.
7. Doing the impossible power (Karni Kala) - the power to do impossible things, like he danced on the hood of serpent Kaliya Nag and lifted Goverdhan Mountain on his finger.
8. Reaching power (Gamini Kala) - the power to reach instantly at any desired place, like he went to the courtroom to save Draupdi's honour.

9. Creation power (Udpadini Kala) - the power to create any thing in place of the existing things, as he created new cowherd and cow caretakers (Gavalas) to look after the cowherd.
10. Happening instantly power (Vachini Kala) - the power to instantly happen, what he desires.
11. Hearing power (Shravani Kala) - the power to hear a distant talk, like while sitting in Dwarka, he heard a distant call and ran to that place to render necessary help.
12. To work under water power (Jaltarangini Kala) - in Jamuna River below the water fought with serpent Kaliya Nag and came out victoriously.
13. To know before hand power (Anumanlnee Kala) - the power to know before an event happens, like with a resolution (Sankalpa) to know what had happened in the past, what is happening in the present and what will happen in the future?
14. Childhood power (Balni Kala) - the power to do big things in childhood, like: he killed Putna and overturned a bullock cart
15. To happen with resolution power (Satyasankalpni Kala) - the power of resolution by which a thing turns out to be true.
16. To make others tell a lie (Avantrinee Kala) - the power to enter into another's body and make him to tell a lie, as he made Udhishter to tell a lie.

Lord Krishna's end

Lord Krishna was resting under a Peepal tree at Bhalkatirth, at Somnath near Veraval in Saurashtra in Gujarat, a Bhil hunter named Jara by mistake shot an arrow from seashore, which hit him in the foot. He limped to a place called Golokdham at the confluence of Rivers Hiranya, Saraswati and Kapil, where Lord Krishna at the ripe age of 125 years died in Ashlesha constellation (Nakshatra) of Bhadra month of Vikram Samvat at 14:27:30 hours on Sunday on 18th February, 3,102 BC (5108 years ago). Kaliyuga began after his death.

9th Lord Buddha incarnation (567 BC – 487 BC, age 80 years) - in Kaliyuga devotion to Vedas get replaced by religious rituals and to enlighten humanity, Buddha's incarnation (Avatar) took place. He had 24 special powers (Kalas), which are the highest so far in the incarnation hood.

Lord Buddha was born to Maya Devi - the wife of Sakya King Shuddnodana in Lumbini forest. He was named Siddhartha, but later he became Buddha. He advocated middle path between extremes of self-indulgence and total abstinence. He offered a harmonious path in life. He said that to prevent suffering, one has to conquer craving and desire. This conquest leads to attainment of liberation (Nirvana).

10th Kalki incarnation (Kalki Avatar) - will take birth at the end of Kaliyuga. He will appear seated on a white horse with a drawn sword blazing like a comet. He will destroy the wicket, will start a new creation and will restore purity of conduct in people's lives.

11th Incarnation (Avatar) - not named. He will take birth at a very distant future and will have 64 special powers (Kalas). He will be super intelligent.

Incarnation hood gives the idea of evolution of soul from animal realms to spiritual perfection.

Four stages (Ashrams) in Hindu life

1. Brahmcharya stage (Childhood and adolescence) - begins from childhood, continues till one completes schooling with the aim is to acquire knowledge, build character and learn to shoulder responsibilities.

2. Grahasth stage (Adulthood) - begins with one's marriage and an individual discharges three debts: 1. Service to God, 2. Service to society, family, sages, saints and ancestors with aim to earn money (Artha), 3. Do reproductions (Kama) to maintain continuity of life and 4. Attain liberation (Moksha), but this is not so easily attainable, as such, my personal view is that one should stride for excellence in life.

3. Vamaprasth stage (Old age) - begins when one's children reach adulthood and the individual withdraws from active life. He begins to devote more time for study of scriptures and tries to follow spiritual life of meditation. Right from the age of 10 years or so, I have meditated on the advice of my father on different chapters of school books. This has helped me in remembering the things. I hope that meditation will benefit others, if done in the right way.

4. Sannyas stage (Final stage of life) - An individual mentally renounces all worldly ties, spends his time in spiritual pursuits and tries to attain some perfection in meditation. If asked and requested, renders help to others in solving their problems.

Hindu view on marks (Tilakas) - Hindus put a mark (Tilak) on their forehead between eyebrows, which represent a particular sect in Hindu society, like: 1. Vaishanavas - put 'V' shaped mark of white clay, 2. Shivaites - put three horizontal lines and 3. Red mark (Bindi) - indicate married women.

Hindu view on existence of worlds

1. Physical world - here we live.
2. Astral world - here spirits, devas and devis live.
3. Spiritual world - here Maha-devas live.

Hindu view on existence of body

1. Physical body - is the outer body, which gives us identity. Body consists of five elements: 1. Earth (Bhumi), 2. Sky (Gagan), 3. Air (Wayu), 4. Fire (Agni), and 5. Water (Nir), which on death decay, mix with their respective elements in nature and body looses its identity.

2. Astral body - is physical body's astral (Puranic) duplicate.

3. Intellectual body - can travel instantaneously from any place to the desired place. Every life form has brain to process the information as received from the sense organs, initiates action to save life from danger, but in addition to brain, human life has mind. Mind distinguishes us from animal life and operates at two levels: 1. Conscious level and 2. Subconscious level:

1. Conscious level of mind - is the place, where thoughts, feelings, likes and dislikes originate.
2. Subconscious level of mind - is the place, where previous life's traits (Sanskars) are stored and the tendencies, which form habits.

4. Soul body - is element of God (Brahman) and has physical body's identity. Soul body does not perish on death, on death passes from one body into another; soul tries to evolve from birth to birth, but in the process of re-birth forgets its past life. There are rare cases, where past-life is remembered and children speak of

their past life, but as time passes, the memories of past-life fade. Hindus believe that each soul chooses its family and home in its evolution from birth to birth.

Scientists, psychiatrists and parapsychologists have confirmed that there have been many cases of individuals remembering their past live. These cases have been verified and found to be true, but many religions do not believe in re-birth. Buddhism, Sikhism and Jews believe in re-birth.

Hindus believe that after death, soul leaves the physical body, lives in a subtle body form, which has non-physical dimension, remain in this state till it is re-born in another body. Medical observations show that at the instant of death, there is an instant loss of 21 gm of body weight; does it indicate that the soul weighs 21 gm?

Case of re-birth

A fact of re-birth of soul has been verified in a Hindu family, which was reported widely in Indian Newspapers on 02.10.2005. The reported case:

	PRESENT LIFE	*PREVIOUS LIFE*
Name	Manisha (Girl)	Suman (Girl)
Death		14.12.2000 at the age of 16 years in Delhi, while studying in 11th standard and the cause of death was fever.
Birth	23.03.2001	
Place of birth	Bhiwadi (Raj.)	
Mother's name	Khilli Devi	Santosh
Father's name	Rampal Gurjar	Kamal Gurjar

About two and a half years ago, Manisha started telling about her previous life that she was living in a double storied house, near a school in Delhi. As per her statement, previous life's house was traced; her statements were verified and found to be true.

5. Golden lights body - is the ultimate evolution of soul-body and is of golden light colour.

Astrological view on time of birth

Astrologically speaking human life begins eight months before our birth, when for the first time the tiny heart of the fetus beats independently of the mother's heart, though fetus' life remains completely dependent on mother for nutrition and sustenance. Independent human life begins after birth, when for the first time; the newly born baby cries and in the process breathes in air. The time of cry is the birth time on which calculations are done to cast a horoscope.

Hindu view on deeds (Karmas)

Hindus believe that deed is not fate, but is the result of actions, which one had performed in his previous life at physical, mental and spiritual level. This causes us to take birth. We lead a life as per our past deeds. This cycle of deeds keeps on repeating from birth to birth, till we learn the lesson of human life. After many births and rebirths, soul gets enlightenment. At this stage, all past deeds get exhausted and soul gets liberation (Moksha).

Hindu view on rituals (Samskars)

Hindu rituals (Sanskars) begin before a child is born and end at death with cremation. Traditionally there are 16 rituals, 11 rituals are connected with birth of a child. One of the major rituals is marriage, which completes, when a Hindu boy takes seven rounds around a holy fire along with the girl. Seven rounds represent: 1. Food, 2. Strength, 3. Prosperity, 4. Well-being, 5. Children, 6. Happiness and 7. Harmony in marriage.

Hindu view on liberation (Moksha)

Hindus believe that liberation is the ultimate goal of human life. Vedic astrology says that based on our past deeds, soul takes birth, adds some more deeds during the life and this keeps on repeating till one gets planet Jupiter (Guru) in the 12th house of ones horoscope. This birth becomes the last birth in the cycle of births and rebirths. After this soul gets liberation, which is merger of soul with God?

Four streams of worship in Hindu Religion

In the beginning of Hindu Religion, all worshipped one God (Eishwara), but India is a vast country, where with passage of time, four different streams of worship developed around four different Godheads, which are:

1. Shaivism stream - scripture Shiva Agama reveres the ultimate reality as Shiva. Worshippers worship Shiva in a temple, observe self-discipline, follow a divine teacher (Sat-guru), practice yoga and strive to be one with Shiva. Shiva is a symbol of love, wisdom, action, offers blessing of protection and fearlessness.

Scientists trace the roots of Shiva worship back to more than 8,000 years to the Indus Valley Civilization. There are six main schools of worship: 1. Shaivai-siddhanta, 2. Pashupatism, 3. Kashmir-shaivism, 4. Vira-shaivism, 5. Siddha-siddhanta and 6. Shiva-advaita. These schools follow the Mantra: 'Aum Namah Shivaya'. Temple Deity is Shiva, who is neither male nor female and along with him Ganesha and Karthikeya are also worshiped.

Shaivism is wide spread in South India, North India, Nepal and Sri Lanka. Shaivism is the path of attainment, which has four progressive stages of beliefs and practices: 1. Charya, 2. Kriya, 3. Yoga and 4. Jnana, through which soul evolves into virtuous living. Union with Shiva comes through the grace of divine teacher (Sat-guru) and culminates in soul's maturity in a state of attaining wisdom (Jnana).

2. Shaktism stream - scripture Shakti Agama venerates the ultimate reality as the divine mother. Worshippers worship Shakti, which has many forms, some are gentle, others are fierce. Worshippers use Mantras, Chants, Tantras, Yantras, Yogas, Holy-diagrams to invoke the divine mother, which awakens the Kundalini power, which is situated in the spine. Shakti radiates beauty, energy, compassion and provides protection to followers.

Shaktism arose in India around 1500 years ago in 5th century. Shaktism has four sub streams: 1. Devotional, 2. Shamanic, 3. Yogic and 4. Universal - all invoke the fierce power of Kali (Durga). Devotees in worship use Shri Chakra Yantra to establish intimacy with her.

Shamanics employ magic, trance-mediumship, fire-walking and animal sacrifice. These acts lead to healing, fertility, prophecy, power and awaken the sleeping Kundalini to unite with her through Sahasrara Chakra. Scriptures are: Vedas, Shakta Agamas and Puranas. They chant the Mantra: 'Aum Chandikayai Nama'. Temple Deity is Shakti Devi (Shri Devi), who is worshiped as Rajarajeshvari and includes Parvati, Sarasvati, Kali and Amman. Shaktism is wide spread in North East India, Bengal and Assam.

Shaktism is the path of attainment, with emphasis on Mantra, Yantra and involves left-hand tantric rites, which are somewhat occult in nature. Right-hand rites are more conservative in nature.

3. Vaishnavism stream - scripture Vaishnava Agama adores the ultimate reality as Vishnu. Worshippers worship Lord Vishnu and his two incarnations: 1. Lord Rama, 2. Lord Krishna. Worshipers are deeply devotional, revere the saints, perform worship (Puja) in temples and study scriptures.

Lord Vishnu resides on the coils of serpent Sheshnaga, whose has many heads, which shadow the Lord in the reclining pose. Sheshnaga floats over waves of ocean and the serpent represents agelessness. Worship of Lord Vishnu goes back to 7,000 years during the Vedic times. Vaishnava schools were founded by: 1. Ramanuja, 2. Madhva, 3. Nimbarka, 4. Vallabha and 5. Chaitanya.

Repetition of Lord's name (Japa) is the key devotional Sadhna and singing of devotional songs (Kirtana) involves dancing in temples. Festivals are elaborately celebrated. Vaishnavites chant the Mantra: 'Aum Namo Narayanaya'. Temple deity is Vishnu and his incarnations along with their spouses, like: Sita and Rama, Radha and Krishna. Vaishnavism is wide spread in whole of India.

Vaishnavism is the path of attainment and manifests in performance of devotion (Bhakti), practice (Sadhna) and through sight (Darshan) of Lord Vishnu, strive for liberation.

4. Smartism stream - is an ancient Brahminical tradition, which was reformed by Adi Guru Shankaracharya, who gave Hinduism a new liberal tradition called Smartism, which is non-sectarian and liberal. People follow a philosophical, meditative path, which emphasizes one's oneness with God (Eishwara). In Smartism, people worship their Lord in six forms: 1. Ganesha, 2. Shiva, 3. Shakti, 4. Vishnu, 5. Surya and 6. Skanda.

Smarta means a follower of classical scriptures, like: Vedas, Dharma-Shasta's, Puranas, Itihasas and Agamas. Temple deity is God in both male and female forms, like: Vishnu, Shiva, Shakti, Ganesha and Surya. Smartism is wide spread in North India and South India.

Smartism is the path of attainment, which believes that liberation is attainable through knowledge (Jnana-yoga) alone and not through Kundalini-yoga. Smartism has four attainment stages: 1. Scriptural study (Shravana), 2. Reflection (Manana), and 3. Meditation (Dhyana) and 4. Guidance from a realized teacher (Guru).

Adi Guru Shankara Charya (788 – 820 AD, age 32 years)

The great monk philosopher was known as Shanmata Sthapana Charya, the founder of six sect system. He campaigned through out India to consolidate the different Hindu faiths under the banner of Advaita Vedanta and to unify worship, he popularized ancient five deities: 1. Ganapati, 2. Surya, 3. Vishnu, 4. Shiva, 5. Shakti and added 6th Kumara. Out of these six deities, the devotee can choose any; call him his Ishta-Devta. Each deity is a reflection of one God (Saguna Brahman).

Adi Guru Shankara Charya re-organized hundreds of Hindu monasteries spread all over India into ten-order-system (Dashanami), with five pontifical centers. He wrote profuse commentaries on Upanishads, Brahma Sutras, Bhagavad Gita and proclaimed that it is one reality, which appears to our ignorance as a manifold of different names and forms. Reality remains unchanged, like the gold of which different ornaments are made, but gold itself remains unchanged and such is God (Brahman or Eishwara).

Adi Guru propagated the path of knowledge (Jnanayoga) and through it he re-established Hinduism with greater force in India. He founded four pilgrimage centers (Matts) in four corners of India: 1. Badrinath in North India, 2. Dwarka in West India, 3. Puri in East India, 4. Sringeri in South India and later established the 5th at Kanchi Kamakoti in South India. His main idea was that during pilgrimage, people will intermingle and will establish an uniform Hindu society.

I - Om Prakash Shukal, hereby bow to Adi Guru Shankra Charya for his greatness, thoughtfulness, leadership, wisdom in consolidating the diversity of worship practices as prevailed in different parts of India in the Hindu Religion and this he has done on foot, when there were no means of travel in olden days.

Three paths of worship

Hindus believe that evolution of soul takes place in human life only. Soul has a natural tendency to evolve itself from birth to birth, which leads to higher and higher level of existence. The higher level of existence is achieved through three paths - 1. Devotion path (Bhaktiyoga), 2. Knowledge path (Jnanayoga), 3. Deeds path (Karmyoga):

1. Devotion path (Bhaktiyoga) - is service to one's chosen godhead through thoughts, deeds, actions, exchanges of love between worshipper and his godhead. These acts lead the worshipper feel closeness with his godhead. In Vedas, God is known as Brahman, who has an Abstract Entity. This is also the present view of science. The physical forms of Lord Shiva, Lord Rama and Lord Krishna are very popular and worshipper tries to make his life an ideal one for his chosen Lord.

Devotion is expressed through chanting hymns, music, dancing and worship. An expression of devotion is also expressed through offering of flowers, fruits, rice, incense, sandal wood paste, milk, water and lighting of lamp (Arti) by burning Ghee or Kapoor. These acts produce vibrations in air, which purify mind, soul and develop deep love in the godhead. Devotional path is easier to follow and studies indicate that 80 % of population follows this path.

Scientifically speaking, the devotional path is equally applicable to other forms of religions, which involve visiting a place of worship, like: Church, Temple, Mosque, Gurudwara, Pagoda, etc. and prayer is offered in a language as prescribed by the religion. Devotional path begins, when a child accompanies his parents to the place of worship, there he watches with interest the proceedings going on. Slowly, he becomes familiar with his religion.

As the child grows, he acquires more knowledge about his religion; soon a condition arises, where he feels that salvation lies in following his religion's doctrines and dogmas. When he becomes an adult, he studies his religion's scriptures, which deepens his faith further. This condition soon leads him to the belief that his religion is the best in the world. This happens in respect of all religions.

Chaitanya Maha Prabhu - the great practitioner of devotional path, propagated it for mass adoption in the Hindu Religion. As one progress on the devotional path, a tendency arises to know more about the religion and this condition leads him to the 2nd path of knowledge.

2. Knowledge path (Jnanayoga) - is study of scriptures to know the truth and the philosophy of the religion. Studies raise the level of soul to a higher existence. Hindu Religion has 368 voluminous scriptures to study. Scriptures describe who is God (Eishwara), who is Lord (Bhagwan), who is male deity (Devta), who is female deity (Devi) and who is goddess mother (Mata).

Hindu scriptures

Hindu scriptures for the purpose of study fall into two categories: 1. Sruti scriptures and 2. Smriti scriptures:

1. **Sruti scriptures** - are of divine origin, whose truth was directly revealed to ancient Rishis (Sages) and they are:

Vedas - Veda means wisdom. Vedas contain sacred knowledge, which has been manifested in words, in human speech and reflects the divine powers, which have created us and rule over us. Vedas are considered to be the most ancient religious literary works in the world. Vedas are sacred in nature and are neither the creation of God nor of human beings, but are the sounds, which were directly revealed to the learned persons (Rishis) by the divine-beings. Veda's started in oral form about 7,000 years ago during Lord Krishna's time. Vedas are the highest religious authority in the Hindu Religion and contain 1, 00,000 verses.

Vedas are difficult to understand, are veiled in nature, are symbolic, are subtle and require vision to comprihend. Before the advent of written language, Vedas were committed to memory, were transmitted orally from generation to generation and this continued for centuries. Those who could recite Vedas, claimed to have inner-vision. They exerted tremendous fascination in the mind of others, as they were considered to be the first persons, who have arrived at the desired destination. Their teachings were cherished and acted upon with faith.

Vedas formed the first clear written tradition in Hindu Religion. Vedas emphasized the principles of incarnation (Avatar) and release from the cycle of birth and death. This principle is also popular in Jainism and Buddhism. Ancient Aryans were fire worshippers. Their beliefs and traditions got influenced by the beliefs held by the people of Indus Valley Civilization, where the earliest form of Hinduism Religion started developing. Ultimately, Aryan and Hindu philosophies merged together.

Vyasa Krishna Dwaipayana

He was the most learned person in the Hindu Religion. He was the 28th Vyasa in the chain of many Vyasas. He was older than Lord Krishna. He compiled Vedas and Puranas in Sanskrit language for the first time. Ved Vyas the great compiler of all the above scriptures and treaties is revered as the first teacher (Guru). In acknowledgement to Ved Vyas' contribution to Vedic knowledge (Vedanta), all religious teachers even to day, bow to him. He was born on Guru Purnima day in Asadh month of Hindu calendar. He was the grand son of Rishi Vasistha and son of Rishi Parashara. His mother was Satyavati - a fisherwoman.

Four Vedas are

1. Rigveda - is the oldest text of mankind and other Vedas are based upon it. Rigveda consists of 1,000 hymns of different seers and each hymn averages around ten verses. Rigveda is the book of hymns (Mantras). Rigveda is built around sound waves, which comprehend the meaning and power of each alphabet. Rigveda mentions about the path of worship (Yoga), meditation and hymn (Mantra), which includes Gayatri Mantra. Rig Veda contains 10,000 verses (Sutras), out of which 16 verses and 13 sub verses deal with Vedic mathematics. Rigveda considers numbers to have spatial and dynamic existence. Rigveda's abstract fundamental formulating principles extend beyond mathematics to astrological phenomenon.

Rigveda mentions about golden womb (Hiranya-garbha), which is viewed as Lord Brahma - the creator. Brahma was created by Brahman - the God Himself. Rigveda deals with Hindu gods, divine-beings (Devas) and rituals involving public ceremonies. Devas are: 1. Varuna - deity of water, 2. Indira - deity of rain, storm and war, 3. Agni - deity of fire, 4. Soma - deity of sacred plants, but none of these Devas are worshiped today, however Indira survives as weather god. Rigveda does not mention about the deities: 1. Rudra (Shiva), 2. Lakshmi, 3. Ganesha and 4. Vishnu, which are central to present day Hinduism.

2. Samveda - comprises of various hymns put in a musical chant. Samveda's musical annotation and rendering represents the ecstasy of spiritual knowledge. Samaveda is realization of Rigveda's knowledge in a musical form.

3. Yajurveda - is the ritual and sets forth worship practices. Worship practices purify the mind and awaken inner consciousness. The purpose of rituals is to put together and recreate the cosmic universe within our own psyche. Here individual feels unity with the divine. The series of sacrifices culminate in self knowledge (Atma Jnana) - where ego is surrendered to divine.

4. Atharvveda - has popular magic spells, which are outside of ritual knowledge and orientation of other Vedas. Atharvveda gives better idea of life of the common people during Vedic times. 'Athar' - is a Persian name for fire and 'Atharvan' - is fire priest. In Atharvaveda, Lord Shiva assumes a more visible role. Atharvveda's language is simple and deals with astrology.

Each of the four Vedas has four parts each, which are known as: 1. Samhita, 2. Brahmana, 3. Aranyaka - these three parts are collectively called Vedas and 4. Upanishads. Upanishads are eighteen and these are collectively called Vedanta.

Four Veda parts

1. Samhitas - are the collections of hymns, which are attached to each Veda. In ancient times, accessibility to Vedas was restricted to upper caste Hindus only and to spread the Vedic knowledge, Samhitas were compiled, which contain hymns (Mantras). Samhitas are oldest in the Hindu Religion. Samhita hymns are addressed to gods, which represent the forces of nature.

Hymns describe the rites and sacrifices, which are to be performed to propitiate the gods. Rigveda Samhita is the oldest.

In Samhitas, Vedic literature starts with a passion for truth, then grows in search of this truth through Brahmanas, then further grows through Aranyakas and ultimately grows through Upanishads to the truth, which is declared for follow up action.

2. Brahmanas - are priestly manuals, which were added to Samhitas by way of updating them. Brahmanas are not old, but are extensive in nature. Brahmanas show how to create the ritual of life and portray the cosmic rituals. These rituals proceed through speech, breath, mind and use chants (Mantra), which attunes one to the cosmic vibrations. Vibrations put one into tune with the forces in nature. Brahmanas are attachments to each Veda. Brahmanas were compiled to spread Vedic knowledge and teach the ritualistic proceedings in the religion. Satapatha Brahmana and Aitareya Brahmana are well known.

The above Samhitas and Brahmanas affirm that God is immanent (Present within and throughout), is transcendent (Based on intuition rather than on experience). Samhitas and Brahmanas describe worship rituals through hymns (Mantras), which establish communication and invoke the divinities of nature, loke: Sun, rain, wind, fire, prayer for matrimony, progeny, prosperity and protection.

3. Aranyakas - are forest treaties, which are the periodic additions to Vedas, made by way of growing with new knowledge and keeping pace with the changing times. Aranyakas are so named because they were composed in forests. During this period, sages and seers used to retire into the forests to contemplate and gain spiritual knowledge. Aranyakas combine ritual passages with philosophical texts and are the theological sections of the religion.

4. Upanishads - are the enlightened discourses. Upanishads are the periodic additions, made by way of growing with the changing time. Upanishad is a composite word of 'Upa' - near, 'Ni' - down and 'Shad' - to sit i.e. to sit down near by to listen to the divine knowledge (Brahm-gyan), which removes ignorance. Upanishads provide both spiritual vision and philosophical knowledge. Upanishads deal with doctrines, like: 1. self-realization, 2. path (Yoga), 3. meditation, 4. deed (Karma) and 5. reincarnation. Upanishads were popular few thousand years ago

before the advent of Lord Krishna. Main figure in Upanishad was Rishi Yajnavalkya - who taught the doctrine Neti-neti, which means that truth, can be found through negation of thoughts.

Aranyakas and Upanishads outline soul's evolutionary journey provide the philosophical training and propound realization of man's oneness with God, as the sole destiny of mankind. There is no neglect of truth, religion, welfare, prosperity, study and teaching. Knowledge as contained in Upanishads is called Vedanta.

Eighteen Upanishads

1. Aranyaka Upanishad - it consists of three sections (Kands), which are:

1. Madhu Kanda - expounds the teachings of basic identity of the individual and universal self.
2. Muni Kanda - provides the philosophical justification of the teachings of Knila Kanda.
3. Knila Kanda - deals with modes of worship and meditation.

2. Chandogya Upanishad - the first two chapters deal with sacrifices and other forms of worship. Further chapters discuss problems of public worship, doctrines and significance of 'Aum'.

3. Isavasya Upanishad - its main purpose is to teach the essential unity of God and life, where life is considered to be the same as divine-spirit is.

4. Aitareya Upanishad - the purpose is to lead the mind of the sacrificer away from the outer ceremonies to its inner meaning and points out that there are three classes of men, who desire to acquire wisdom. Three classes are:

1. Who have turned away from the world, their minds are free, they are eager to achieve freedom and for them Aitareya Aranyaka is intended.
2. Who wish to become free gradually, want to acquire knowledge and for them worship of breadth (Prana) is intended.
3. Who only care for the worldly possessions and for them meditative worship is intended.

5. Taittiriya Upanishad - is divided into three sections: 1. Siksa Valli - is the science of phonetic and pronunciation, 2. Brahmananda Valli and Bhrugu Valli - both deal with knowledge of the supreme (Paramatma Jnana).

6. Katha Upanishad - is the story, where Naciketa gets three gifts from Yama: 1. let me return alive to my father, 2. tell me how my good works may not be exhausted, 3. tell me the way to conquer death and enlighten me on the transition, which is called death.

7. Prasna (Question) Upanishad - has six sections, which deal with six questions, put to a sage by his disciples, who were intent to know: 1. nature of the ultimate cause, 2. power of 'Aum', 3. relation of the supreme, to the constituents of the world.

8. Kena Upanishad - has four sections, first two in verses and next two in prose. Verses deal with the absolute principle underlying the world of phenomenon and prose deals with the supreme-being (Eishwara), where:

Supernatural knowledge (Para Vidya) - secures immediate liberation (Sadyo-mukti) for those, who are able to withdraw their thoughts from worldly objects and concentrate on the ultimate fact of the universe.

Natural knowledge (Apara Vidya) - puts one on the pathway that leads to liberation through deeds (Karma-mukti) and soul gradually acquires higher wisdom, which results in consciousness of the identity with the Supreme-being.

9. Mundaka Upanishad - the name is derived from the root Mund (Shave). One, who comprehends the teachings of Upanishads, is shaved and is liberated from ignorance. Upanishad states the distinction between the higher knowledge of the Supreme-being (Brahman) and the lower knowledge of the world. It is the higher wisdom, not sacrifices or worship through which one can reach the Supre-being (Brahman).

10. Mundukya Upanishad - it is an exposition of the principle of 'Aum', which refers to three states: 1. walking, 2. dream and 3. dreamless sleep. Four states of consciousness: 1. wakefulness, 2. dream, 3. dreamless sleep and 4. transcendental consciousnesses.

11. Svetasvatara Upanishad - its name is derived from the sage, who taught it. It is theistic in character and identifies the Supreme-being (Brahman) with Rudra. Rudra is conceived as the material and cause of the world. Here the emphasis is not on Supreme-being (Brahman) - the absolute, whose perfection does not admit of any change or evolution, but on the personal Godhead

(Eishwara) - who is omniscient and omnipotent. Upanishad is an attempt to reconcile the different philosophical views, which prevailed at the time of its composition.

12. Kausitaki Brahmana Upanishad - has thirty chapters and forms part of Aranyaka.

13. Maitrayaniya Upanishad - it contains seven chapters of which the last two are comparatively modern and has reference to the Trimurti concept: 1. Brahma, 2. Vishnu and 3. Mahesh, who have three attributes (Gunas): 1. Rajas, 2. Sattva and 3. Tamas.

14. Subala Upanishad - is in the form of a dialogue between the sage Subala and Brahma - the creator. It discusses the nature of universe and character of the absolute.

15. Jabala Upanishad - discusses the important questions regarding renunciation.

16. Paingala Upanishad - is in the form of a dialogue between Yajnavalkya and his pupil Paingala. Upanishad discusses meditation on Supreme-being and nature of release.

17. Kaivalya Upanishad - is the study and practice, which leads to the state of aloneness (Kaivalya).

18. Vajra Sucika Upanishad - describes the true character of Supreme-being (Brahmana) and offers comments on the nature of Supreme reality. It undermines the caste distinction based on birth.

The knowledge as contained in Upanishads unfolds spiritual and philosophic truths in story and anecdote form. Knowledge heralds the decline of sacrificial rituals and advocates shift towards more personal, internal style of religious practices. Here concept of re-incarnation, rebirth of soul developed. In this new concept Vedic sacrifices lost their importance. Upanishads advocate the concept of liberation.

Six great sentences (Maha-vakyas) of Upanishads

1. I am Brahman (Aham Brahmasmi) - is the identity of an individual with the Supreme Divine. Ultimate truth of Vedic knowledge is not that some savior is God or that such and such is God or form of particular God is supreme, it is not the worship of a person, book, image, or idea, but what ever we worship as truth apart from our self, destroys us or in other words, they teach that our own self is true divinity.

2. The self is Brahman (Ayam Atma Brahma) - not only is our self the divine, but the same self is in all beings, which is the absolute truth.

3. That thou art (Tat Tvamasi) - what ever we see or think, we are that and not only I, but you also is that.

4. Intelligence is Brahman (Prajnanam Brahma) - that divine intelligence is present within us and has the power to return us back to the divine. Our inner most intelligence is that supreme intelligence through which we can merge in the absolute.

5. The universe is Brahman (Sarvan Khalvidam Brahma) - entire universe is divine, which includes our self, the divine is not only the consciousness principle in us, it is also the principle in all beings. It is one in all and all are in one.

6. He am I (Soham) - shows the identity of the self with the divine, who is inherent within the natural movement of our breadth, 'So' is the natural sound of inhalation and 'Ham' is the natural sound of exhalation.

All the above six statements are the identity of an individual's consciousness with the divine reality and ultimately merges into Him.

Three Veda chapters (Kands)

1. Three Veda chapters (Kands) - are the subject wise chapters of Vedas, which comprise of 1, 00,000 hymns (Shruties). Karmkand - has 80,000 hymns, which deal with rituals. Upasnakand - has 16,000 hymns, which deal in the art of worship through hearing (Sravana), through teaching (Upadesha) and through logical reflection (Manana). Gyankand - has 4,000 hymns, which deal with knowledge.

2. **Smriti scriptures** - are to be remembered. They are of human origin, which guide individuals in their daily conduct of rituals, according to time. They list the codes, rules, which govern the actions of individuals, community, society and nation. They were written to explain the Sruti writings to make them understandable and meaningful to the common people. Smriti scriptures fall into five groups of writings: 1. Itihas - historical epics, 2. Puranas - are mythological in nature, 3. Dharma Shastras - are law codes, 4. Agamas and Tantras - are sectarian scriptures and 5. Darshanas - are manuals of philosophy·

1. Itihas (Historical epics) - these are three and are historical in nature. Hindus believe that most of the events in Itihas (History) did take place, but were written much afterwards. Three Itihas (Histories) are: 1. Ramayana, 2. Mahabharata and 3. Bhagavad-Gita:

1. Ramayana - Lord Rama is also mentioned in Persian literature. Hanuman is the monkey head-devta, who was companion of Rama. Hanuman is the devta of air (Vayu), Sita was Rama's wife and Prathvi is the godess of Earth. Ramayana has been written in three versions:

(1) Valmiki Ramayana - written by the great sage Valmiki in a biographical form. He treats Ram as a king. Valmiki Ramayana is referred to as Adi Kavya and is popular as a folk story in India and in the Far East. Valmiki was the contemporary of Ram. Once upon a time, Valmiki was thief and hunter, but later he became a saint. He wrote Ramayana for the first time in Sanskrit language and gave the planetary configurations, which existed during Ram's life. Planetary configurations have been back calculated with the help of computer software and reckonings of dates are:

King Ram's birth - took place in Uttarayana, 9th day of Chaitra month, bright fortnight (Shukal Paksha) in Punarvasu constellation (Nakshatra) on Monday under Karka sign ascendant (Lagna). This configuration brings the birth date to 4th December 7323 BC, but due to continuous precession of Earth, Ram's birth day on Ram Navami has shifted by almost four months over the last 9,300 years.

1. Lord Ram's birth——— 04.12.7323 BC
2. Lord Ram's marriage with Sita——— 07.04.7307 BC
3. Lord Ram's exile——— 29.11.7306 BC
4. Hanuman's entry into Lanka——— 01.09.7292 BC
5. Hanuman's meeting with Sita——— 02.09.7292 BC
6. Construction of Setu (Bridge) — 26 - 30.10.7292 BC (Five days)
7. Beginning of War in Lanka——— 03.11.7292 BC
8. Kumbha Karan's death——— 07.11.7292 BC
9. Ravana's death——— 15.11.7292 BC
10. Lord Ram's return to Ayodhya——— 06.12.7292 BC

Valmiki Ramayana has seven chapters (Kands): 1. Balkand, 2. Ayodhiyakand, 3. Aranyakand, 4. Kishkindhakand, 5. Sunderkand (Most popular and is recited at the time of death, 6. Yuddhakand and 7. Uttrakand.

King Ram's horoscope - he was Manglik, as planet Mars was in 7th house, which made Sita a courageous lady, but sharp-tongued. This led Lakshmana leave her in a jungle, while she was pregnant; planet Venus (Shukar) was in 9th house of travel and destiny, which gave Rama the company of Sita during exile period; planet Jupiter (Guru) and Moon (Chander) is in the ascent (Lagna), which forms Gajakesari Yog, which blessed Rama with simplicity, honesty, religious belief, fame and Sun (Surya) in 10th house of deeds (Karma) made him King of Ayodhiya.

(2) Tulsi Ramayana - Tulsidas wrote Ramayana as a religious scripture in a devotional form. He treated Ram as Lord and the scripture is known as Shri Ram Charit Manas. Goswami Tulsidas (1526 - 1617 AD, age 91 years) started writing the epic at the age of 43 years in Hindi and completed it In 2 years, 7 months and 21 days. Tulsi Ramayan has 24,000 verses (Shalokas). Tulsidas was born at Rajapur in Banda district in Uttar Pradesh. He expired at the ripe age of 91 years at Asighat in UP. His wife's name was Ratnawali, who had instigated him to write Ramayana. The epic is a great source of religious inspiration. Ramayan is made familiar through readings, re-enactments, plays, films and works of art. Tulsidas was a devotee of Lord Ram.

Ramayana is the story of Lord Rama, who is an ideal model for Hindu life. Ram is seen as an ideal example of honour, strength and obedience to his father's will. Sita is depicted as an ideal model of Hindu womanhood. In 1020 AD, Ramayana appeared in Nepali language (Nevari Bhasha) for the first time.

(3) Kamban Ramayana - poet Kamban wrote Ramayana in a literary form in Tamil language in his own style. He treats Ram as a great man. This version of Ramayana is known as Kambar's Kamba Raamayanam.

Legendary bridge (Setu) - the bridge as mentioned in Ramayana, connects India with Sri Lanka. It is believed that Ram built the bridge to invade Lanka (Sri Lanka) to rescue his wife Sita from the captivity of Ravana. Recent studies by NASA [USA] through remote sensing revealed that a 30 km long prehistoric bridge exists in a submerged condition from Rameswaram in Tamilnadu to Sri Lanka (Ceylon). The bridge is known as Adam's Bridge and is estimated to be 17, 00,000 year old. The bridge structure is not natural. This finding has created a doubt, as to who built the bridge originally, as the time period of Lord Ram, who was husband of Sita and king of Ayodhiya, lived around 9,300 year back?

2. Mahabharata War- Maharishi Veda Vyas dictated it to Lord Ganesh in a cave, which is still named as Vyas Gufa (Cave). This is situated in a village named Mana, which is 4 km away from the famous shrine of Badrinath in Uttarakhand State in India. This great epic contains 1, 20,000 verses (Shalokas) and is the largest scripture ever written in human history.

Vyas mentioned that there was Solar and Lunar eclipse at the time of Mahabharata War. A comet was seen beyond Pushya constellation (Nakshatra), which is named as Haley's Comet. This comet appears every 77 years and was seen in 1910 and 1987. Eighteen different calculations give the start of Mahabharata War as 16.10.5561 BC. This cosmic configuration will repeat after 2,229 crore years and the present age of Earth is 465, 00, 00,000 year (465 crore year). As such, the devastating configuration of planets will never repeat in the life of Earth.

Mahabharata War was fought on the battlefield at Kurukshetra, Haryana between Pandavas - the five sons of king Pandu and their allies on one side including Lord Krishna. On the other side were Kauravas – the hundred sons of king Dhritarashtra and their allies. It seems that virtually every tribal king in Central and Northern India had joined the war.

King Dhritarashtra was born blind, as such, he was not eligible to assume the throne of Hastinapur State, so his younger brother Pandu - assumed the throne. Pandu stepped down from the throne and with his wives went to live in the forest. Pandu left the kingdom under the stewardship of blind king Dhritarashtra.

Pandu's senior wife Kunti had five sons, known as Pandavas. The eldest son was Yudhistra, who was the wisest chariot warrior, second son was Bhima, who was enormously strong warrior and third son was Arjuna, who was the master archer. Pandu's second wife was Madri, who had two sons Nakula and Sahadeva. They were expert swordsmen. In the forest, Pandu and his second wife Madri died. Pandu's senior wife Kunti, who was cousin of Lord Krishna, took the five boys to Hastinapur. She said to Dhritarashtra that these are the sons of Pandu.

Duryodhana's attempt to burn the Pandavas in the resin house (Laksha-grah) failed. Pandavas escaped. The legendary resin house still exists at Brava in Bagpat in Hariana State. Draupadi the wife of Pandavas and Lord Krishna joined hands. Blind king Dhritarashtra and his wife Gandhari with her hundred sons joined hands. Their eldest son Duryodhana assumed the role of crown prince in Hastinapur. Blind king Dhritarashtra split the kingdom in half and remained king of Hastinapur.

Pandavas established their capital at Indraprasta. Their fortunes flourished, while the kingdom of Kauravas stagnated. King Yudhistra conducted a Vedic ritual, which would make him the lawful king of the known world. These rituals required thousands of Brahmins and many years to perform. Yudhistra invited all the kings in his dominion to celebrate the occasion of becoming the great king (Maharaja). Duryodhana came, but he was jealous because Pandavas have every thing, while he had nothing.

Sakuni, the uncle of Duryodhana and younger brother of Gandhari (Wife of Dhritarashtra) was an expert dice-player. He invited the Pandavas to a game of dice. Duryodhana said that my uncle Sakuni would cast the dice for me. Yudhistra started playing the dice and lost every thing including his palaces, lands, herds, chariots, servants, clothes, brothers and even his wife.

Duryodhana called his brother Duhsasana to bring Draupadi. She was dragged to the assembly hall. She was weeping with shame, as Duhsasana tried to rip her to expose her nakedness. She could not be exposed as her sari kept on lengthening due to intervention of Lord Krishna. Bhima vowed that Duhsasana, I will tear your chest open; I will drink your blood; I will crush your thigh, before I kill you. Blind king Dhritarashtra said to Draupadi that you are free. King granted her three boons: 1st Boon - Yudhistra you are free, 2nd Boon - Nakula, Sahadeva, Bhima and Arjuna along with your chariot and armour are free, 3rd Boon - at this point, Draupadi said that this is enough and I need no further assistance.

Duryodhana settled the dice-game with the promise that Padavas spend twelve years in exile in forest; they be clothed as hermits; they spend the thirteenth year among the people in disguise; if discovered, they would have to spend another twelve years in exile. If Pandavas are able to escape detection, then the kingdom becomes theirs, but when the exile punishment was over, Pandavas asked for return of five villages: 1. Panipat, 2. Sonipat, 3. Bagpat, 4. Maripat and 5. Indraprasta from Kauravas, but Duryodhana refused to relinguish the kingdom, which lead to Mahabharata War. Lord Krishna offered a compromise, which Duryodhana refused. Both sides started recruiting allies and prepared for the War.

Mahabharata War was held on the field of Kurukshatra, on the side of Kauravas, were Duryodhana, Dhritarashtra and 18 armies including the army of Lord Krishna. On the opposite side Pandavas had 12 armies and Lord Krishna became the Charioteer of Arjuna. War lasted for 18 days and 36, 00,000 people were killed, while the population of India at that time was 2.5 crore. After the War, Pandavas with handful of others survived, but they felt guilty.

Five Pandava brothers, Draupadi and Yudhistra's faithful dog went on their last journey to the Himalayas, where one by one, they died: first Draupadi died, and then Sahadeva, Nakula, Arjuna, and Bhima died. Yudhistra along with his faithful dog continued the journey, Indira devta's chariot welcomed Yudhistra to take him to heavens, but as the dog was not allowed in the heaven, so Yudhistra along with his dog stepped down from the Chariot and continued the journey to perish.

Lord Krishna's time - National Institute of Oceanography at Goa in India has discovered the legendary Dwarka submerged under sea water near the port of Dwarka, Gulf of Kachchh in West India. The site is dated from 5000 BC to 6000 BC, but due to discrepancies in the Indian System of calendars, the seasons move one month backwards every two thousand years, presently rainy season starts in Jeshtha month, but two thousand years ago at the time of Kalidas - the great writer, rainy season used to start in Ashadha month. At the time of Lord Krishna's birth, summer was in the month of Shravan month, now it is in Vaishaka, as such, summer has shifted by four months, and hence Krishna's time comes to around 4 x 2,000 = 8,000 years, which is 6000 BC.

Reckoning of Mahabharata War events (Date wise):

1. Pandavas going to forest ——— 04.09.5574 BC
2. Pandavas going underground ——— 19.05.5562 BC
3. Pandavas end of secret life ——— 09.04.5561 BC
4. Cows stolen ——— 15.04.5561 BC
5. Arjuna exposed ——— 16.04.5561 BC
6. All Pandavas exposed ——— 19.04.5561 BC
7. Marriage of Abhimanyu with Uttara — 04.05.5561 BC
8. Lord Krishna tried for a treaty ——— 27.09.5561 BC
9. Mahabharata War started ——— 16.10.5561 BC
10. Abhimanyu killed ——— 28.10.5561 BC
11. Mahabharata War ended ——— 02.11.5561 BC
12. Yudhishtra crowned ——— 16.11.5561 BC
13. Bhishma Pitamaha expired ——— 22.12.5561 BC

3. Bhagavad-Gita (Song of Lord) - is a section in Mahabharata, which is most famous, most popular and most sacred scripture of the Hindu Religion. Gita contains 700 hymns (Shlokas) in 18 chapters. At the beginning of Mahabharata War, when Arjuna saw his relatives and teacher (Guru) standing opposite to him on the battlefield, he faltered to fight the impending war. Lord Krishna at the age of 98 years gave the preaching (Upadesh) of Gita to Arjuna on 16.10.5561 BC.

Lord Krishna said to Arjuna that the knowledge of Gita, which he is giving, had been given by him in his previous birth to Vivasvan, who in turn gave it to Manu. Manu in turn gave it further to Echvaku, but since then the knowledge of Gita has faded, as such, he is repeating it again. Gita is the record of the conversation, which had taken place between Lord Krishna and Arjuna. Lord Krishna said to Arjuna, that you may kill the bodies of the enemies, but their souls are immortal and indestructible, so Arjuna accept your duty to fight, if you seek no rewards from fighting, your mind will remain as calm and detached, as that of a Yogi in meditation.

Lord Krishna in Gita describes his own nature as that of God and explains that love (Bhakti) is more desirable than even liberation (Moksha). Gita is a complex piece of philosophical writing, but has influenced all later developments in Hindu thought and belief. Gita's central message is that one should discharge his duty, however hard and unpleasant it may be with selfless dedication (Sva-dharma), which pleases the God and serves to repay one's debt to society.

2. Puranas

Puranas are mythological in nature and are the ancient history. They assert that universe gets created, destroys itself and is re-created again in an eternally repetitive series of cycles. It is a wonder of wonders that how this concept got developed about three thousand years back in the Hindu Religion, as the present scientific observations tend to prove this concept to be correct, though one cycle may take millions of year to complete. Puranas are the richest collection of Hindu mythology and in ancient times they were passed orally from generation to generation. Puranas attained their final form around 560 AD.

Puranas describe the deeds of Lord Vishnu and Shiva with emphasis on devotion to personal devta. Puranas are the narratives of ancient times and were compiled by Ved Vyasa. There are eighteen Puranas; each one is a long book containing various stories of gods, goddesses and hymns, which outline ancient history, cosmology, rules of life, rituals, and instructions on spiritual knowledge. Puranas are like encyclopedia of the Hindu Religion and culture. They act like guide books on life and society.

Hindu religion is philosophical in nature and to teach it to the less educated persons; the religion is taught through dance, plays and story telling around fires. In olden days, there were few books, as such; the religion was conveyed orally through stories and parables. Puranas contain myths, legends and Lord Krishna's life is the most dwelt upon subject. Each Puran glorifies his own deity and considers him or her to be supreme amongst all the other deities.

Eighteen Puranas

1. Brahm-puran - contains 10,000 verses (Shalokas).
2. Padma-puran - contains 55,000 verses and describe existence of 84,00,000 life forms.
3. Vishnu-puran - contains 23,000 verses and at the time of Bore incarnation (Varah Avtar), many Manus existed and one of the Manu wrote Manu memories (Smreti).

4. Shiv-puran (Vayu-puran) - contains 24,000 verses.
5. Bhagwat-puran (Shrimad Bhagavatam) - contains 18,000 verses and is considered to be superior to other Puranas and narrates the activities of Lord Krishna. It is traditionally recited in the course of one week, in emulation of Sukudeva Goswami, who narrated it to Maharaja Parikshit, while he was awaiting death.
6. Narad-puran - contains 25,000 verses.
7. Markandai-puran - contains 9,000 verses.
8. Agni-puran - contains 15,400 verses.
9. Bhavishya-puran - contains 14,500 verses.
10. Brahm-Vaivart-puran - contains 18,000 verses.
11. Ling-puran - contains 11,000 verses.
12. Varah-puran - contains 24,000 verses.
13. Skand-puran - contains 81,100 verses.
14. Vaman-puran - contains 10,000 verses.
15. Kurm-puran - contains 17,000 verses.
16. Matsay-puran - contains 14,000 verses.
17. Garud-puran - contains 19,000 verses and is traditionally recited on death of a person.
18. Brahmand-puran - contains 12,000 verses.

In addition to 18 Puranas, there are 18 subsidiary Puranas (Up-purans).

3. Six religious treaties (Dharma Shastras) - are law codes and are different schools of philosophy, which systematize and co-relate the various parts of the Vedas and are:

1. Purv-Mimansa treatise (Shastra) - was written by Maharshi Gemini. It narrates the importance of deeds (Karmas) in life, on which human life depends. Shastra deals with philosophy of rites and rituals.

2. Uttar-Mimansa treatise - was written by Maharshi Ved Vyas. It narrates the importance of Lord Brahma and deals with the Vedanta philosophy.

3. Niyai treatise - was written by Maharshi Gautam. It narrates the prime importance of God (Eishwara), on whom every thing depends. Shastra deals with logical analysis of Hindu philosophy.

4. Vaishaishik treatise - was written by Maharshi Kanad. It narrates the importance of time (Kal), according to which every thing happens, like day and night, seasons, childhood, youth, and old age. Shastra deals with atomic school of philosophy. It is again a wonder, as at that time modern science was unaware about it.

5. Sankhya treatise - was written by Maharshi Kapil. It narrates the dependence upon nature and Hindu philosophy.

6. Yoga treatise - was written by Maharshi Patanjali about 3,000 years ago. This was the last Shastra, which was written in the Hindu Religion. Shastra deals with spirituality, meditation, spiritual philosophy and is the base of spiritual aspect of human life.

4. Agamas and Tantras - are sectarian scriptures, which deal with worship of a particular godhead, prescribe a discipline for worship and each Agama has four parts:

1st Part deals with philosophy and spiritual knowledge.

2nd Part deals with Yoga and mental discipline.

3rd Part deals with rules for construction of temples, sculpture and carving of the figures of deities for worship in the temples.

4th Part deals with rules pertaining to the observance of religious rites, rituals and festivals.

5 . Tirukural - is considered to be the world's greatest ethical scripture and is sworn on in South Indian law courts. It was written in Tamil language by Saint Thiruvalluvar - who was a weaver. He wrote the scripture in a village near Chennai about 2,000 years ago. The scripture is divided into three sections: 1 Section - deals with religion (Dharma) and morals, 2 Section – deals with teachings on ones duties and 3 Section - teaches divine love.

6. Purusarthas - deal in the objective to be attained in human life. Four Purusarthas, are:

1. Dharma Purusartha - deals in righteousness.
2. Artha Purusartha - deals in money matter.
3. Kama Purusartha - deals with reproduction.
4. Moksha Purusartha - deals in liberation.

7. Prastana Traya - is a scripture of the Hindu Religion. It is a three-fold movement based on post-vedic literature particularly Upanishads and Gita. Prastana Traya has a self-perpetuating spirit and mechanism by which it adopts itself to the periodic re-

interpretations of scriptures based on development of new knowledge. This fits the scriptures to the changing times. This periodic re-interpretation of scripture is called Bhashya. This is a unique system in the evolution of Hindu Religion, while other religions are static in nature and do not change their scriptures with the new knowledge acquired.

Shankra, Ramanuja and Madhwa wrote Bhashyas to the Prastana Traya, but these Bhashyas have now lost their edge with the passage of time. Hindu Religion needs a new Bhashya to be written in tune with the present scientific development and awaits the arrival of a new Shankra to do.

All religions await:

1. Buddhists await - the arrival of Amitabha.
2. Christians await - the arrival of a new Jesus.
3. Hindus await - the arrival of Kalki incarnation - the inaugurator of Satyuga.
4. Jews await - the arrival of Messiah.
5. Muslims await - the arrival of Imam Mihdi.
6. Zoroastrians await- the arrival of manifestation of Hooshidar and Shah Bahram.

Arya Samaj

Arya Samaj was founded in Mumbai in 1875. The founder was Mool Shanker Tewari (1824 – 1883), who became famous as Dayanand Saraswati and the movement flourished in Lahore (Pakistan). He re-interpreted Vedas, re-emphasized their universal application, propagated a rational religion based on monotheism, introduced the doctrine of equality of males and females, rejection of idol worship, advocated that caste system be based on vocation, not on birth as at present, any person can practice any profession and none of the profession to be considered derogatory.

In olden days, Varanasi was the stronghold of Hindu Religion's Brahmanism. Dayanand Saraswati worked over there against idol worship; some persons started plotting against him and a dozen attempts were made on his life. He remained steadfast in his convictions, but his enemies poisoned him. He died in 1883. Arya Samaj has spread all over India, East Africa, South Africa, Mauritius, Guyana, Trinidad, Singapore and Bangkok. Arya Samaj runs hundreds of schools, technical institutes, gymnasiums, hostels, publishes newspapers, periodicals and maintains large libraries.

3. Deeds path (Karmayoga) - is the path of dutiful life, where one performs his normal work as his duty towards his godhead, family, society, and nation. He does not desire any thing in return. This attitude leads him to lead a life of contentment. He performs good deeds with the hope to counteract the past life deeds. The doctrine believes that each soul is divine and goal of human life is to realize divinity within through psychic control.

Good deeds (Sukarmas) can be offered in worship, while bad deeds (Kukarmas) cannot. Good deeds make a person pious; he becomes an incorruptible person in life. Swami Vivekananda - the great learned person, followed this path and said that religious doctrines, dogmas, rituals, books, places of worship are of secondary nature. The prime goal of human life is to do good deeds (Sukarmas) and offer them to God in worship. Lord Krishna in Gita said that do your duty, but do not desire to take reward for it, as it depends upon him.

1.5. Studies on religious activities

Studies reveal that a child when participates in his religion's activities, the percentages of devotional path activities slowly increase from 20 % to 60 %. When he studies his religion's scriptures, knowledge path activities increase from 20 % to 60 %. This increases ones understanding of philosophies of his religion. The understanding thus developed, leads one to adopt the deeds path activities, which makes him an ideal person. He performs his work as his duty, but expects anything in return. He becomes dutiful towards his family, society, nation and finally realization dawns on the limitations of his religion.

Scientific experiment

Religious beliefs are usually regarded as beyond scientific explanation. Neurologists have located an area in the temporal lobe of human brain, which appears to produce intense feelings of religious tendencies and sense of mystical presence. Neurologists have managed to reproduce peculiar feelings in otherwise non-religious people by stimulating the temporal lobe area. Some people reported the presence of some one else in their body, some experienced god visiting them. When their EEG was analysed, it showed slow wave seizure over the temporal lobe area, at the very instant of peculiar experiences, while other parts of the brain remained normal.

During experiments, many people claimed that god spoke to them directly; some reported that divine light illuminated all things. It was established that the concerned person's state of consciousness and his personality was the same as before the experiment. This proves that brain integrates the working of its highly specialized parts and creates apparent perceptions of peculiar experiences.

SPIRITUAL ASPECT

As one progresses in his religion, he realizes the limits of the religion, beyond which he cannot progress and at this stage, his behaviour changes. He starts to loose interest in the outward religious activitie. He prefers to offer prayer in his house instead of going to the place of worship. He undertakes fasts on health grounds rather than on religious grounds. He prefers to go on a pleasure trip to relax instead of going on a pilgrimage. This is the stage, where spirituality begins.

1.6. Comparison between religion and spirituality

Religion

Religion believes in creation and is based on the belief that God is an External-being. One has to seek him outside in a place of worship. He goes there for worship and prays, which create vibrations. Vibrations purify mind and create a feeling that ones soul has achieved a higher level of existence. This belief strengthens one's faith in his religion.

Spirituality

Spirituality belives in evolution and is based on the belief that God is an Internal-being. One has to seek him internally through meditation and for this visit to a place of worship is not necessary. As such, spiritual path (Ashtangayoga) is not influenced by any religion; however different religions have produced certain minor variations, like: Buddhist-yoga, Christian-yoga, Jain-yoga and Hindu-yoga. One is free to follow any of the spiritual paths, as it depends upon thought processes, which are organized in three layers:

1. Outer layer - has influence on the immediate happenings, which one has experienced and during meditation these thoughts are to be ignored.
2. Secondary layer - has subjectivity, but meditation is not done on them.
3. Inner layer - has objectivity and contemplation is done on the inner thoughts, which help one to attain objectivity and when this is attained, it is called advancement in spiritual life, where powers of the mind are directed upon the mind itself, to reveal the secrets of life.

Spiritual path (Ashtangayoga)

Ashtangayoga is based on Maharishi Patanjali's treatise (Sutra), which was written 3,000 years ago. Treatise has four chapters to show the eight stage spiritual practices:

Chapter 1 - has 51 aphorisms (Sutras), which teach the technique of meditation (Dhyan) on an object of interest, which can be either outer or inner.

Outer object - can be a candle or tip of nose or forehead portion between the eyes.

Inner object - can be either the mental presence of divine light or image of a divine person in the heart.

In the initial stage of meditation, many thoughts arise in mind, which are to be ignored and contemplation has to be done on a single thought, on which meditation is being done. When stage of meditation on a single thought is achieved, it is called Samadhi. Highest Samadhi is called Nirvikalpa Samadhi, which is the highest stage, where one experiences the presence of divinity within himself.

Chapter 2 - has 51 aphorisms, which teach the technique of process (Kriya), which enables one to gain control over self. This is an eight-fold system, which comprises of:

1. Behaviour control process (Yama Kriya) - is development of five moral and ethical values in life: 1. Non-violence (Ahinsa), 2.

Truthfulness (Satya), 3. Celibacy (Brahm-charya), 4. Non-stealing (Asteya) and 5. Non-covetousness (Aparigraha).

2. Rules and regulations process (Niyama Kriya) - is adherence to strict time schedule in life and comprises of: 1. cleanliness of body and speech, 2. studies of scriptures, 3. surrender every action to the universal spirit, 4. be content with what one has and 5. performances of austerities.

3. Body posture process (Asana Kriya) – is to keep the body still in a posture, which is comfortable to maintain calmness in mind and in the posture keep the spinal cord straight.

4. Breadth control process (Pranayama Kriya) - breathing affects mental state. Mental state affects breathing. Breathing is deep, slow and rhythmic, which is: breathe in deeply for few seconds, hold the breath for few seconds, breathe out for few seconds, wait for few seconds and repeat the process. Rhythmic breathing provides constant control over senses, induces the feeling of relaxation, improve mental concentration, but it is better, if the process is learnt from an experienced teacher.

5. Control of senses process (Pratyahara Kriya) - is achieved through: 1. absence of desire for worldly objects, 2. sense of detachment and 3. absence of undue awareness of the coming event. It is better, if the process is learnt from an experienced teacher.

6. Concentration process (Dhaaranaa Kriya) - is unbroken contemplation, where body, mind and breath are under control. Meditate at a place and requirements are: 1. sit in a quiet place, 2. focus the mind on an object, 3. repeatedly bring the mind back to the object of contemplation, as natural tendency of the mind is to wander away from an object of contemplation. This is the point in spiritual life, where a practitioner (Abhyasi) joins Sahaj Marg System of meditation under Master or his nominated preceptor.

7. Meditation process (Dhyana Kriya) - is a process, where the eyes are closed, single thought prevails during the session and when it is achieved, it is called advancement in Sahaj Marg System.

8. Mergence process (Samadhi Kriya) - is realization of union of an individual's soul with the universal spirit. At this stage, one forgets his individuality, external environment and gets deeply absorbed into the cosmic wholeness with intensity, which

encompasses every thing. This is the highest attainment in Sahaj Marg System

Chapter 3 - has 56 aphorisms teach the technique of divine power (Sidhi), which can be attained through meditation.

Chapter 4 - has 33 aphorisms teach the technique to get liberation (Moksha) from the cycle of birth and death.

Spiritual path (Asthangayoga) is based on self-introspection, in which one stands outside his own body, tries to analyze with detached objectivity, the tendencies, motives, responses of mind, cause of one's existence and deliberates on the complexities of human life. Progress in spiritual path depends upon SQ.

Spiritual Quotient (SQ)

SQ is a measure of one's spiritual intelligence on which progress in spiritual life depends. SQ increases with age, with study of spiritual books and depends upon:

1. Egoism - to be discarded at the very beginning in spiritual life.
2. Aptitude - towards life change and interest in spiritual life begins.
3. Aspiration - increase to achieve advancement in spiritual life.
4. Attitude - change towards putting more efforts in following the spiritual life.
5. Compassion – increase to have sympathy for those, who believe in spiritual life.
6. Confidence - increase that success will be attained in spiritual life.
7. Dedication - increase to devote more time in following spiritual life.
8. Ability - increase to follow spiritual life.
9. Faith - increase that enlightenment in the spiritual life will be obtained.
10. Gratitude - increase towards the teacher (Guru) for his guidance in spiritual life.
11. Meditation - enhance the chance of success in leading spiritual life.
12. Self-esteem - increase, which generate courage to follow spiritual life.

13. Service - is rendered in helping others, to follow spiritual life.
14. Study - more time is devoted to gain knowledge in spiritual life.
15. Ultimately - surrender to spiritual teacher (Guru) occurs and all worries are left to him.

Meditation

Meditation is a technique, which help in maintaining a single thought during a meditation session. The technique has proved its worth over many centuries. Technique does not require a mountain to be climbed or one to sit in an odd position for long period of time.

Four types of meditation (Any one can be adopted)

1. Hymn meditation - is mental repetition of a phrase, which aids in concentration during meditation session (15 to 20 minutes). This keeps the mind busy and one does not think about anything else.
2. Scanning meditation - is mental scanning of body from tip of toes to top of head. During scanning, attention for some time can be paid to an area of pain in the body or part of body suffering from any illness, like: lungs for asthma, pancreas for diabetes, heart for heart-patients etc. This form of meditation is called Vipassna in Buddhist Religion, but is not part of the religion.
3. Breadth meditation - is concentration on the process of inhaling and exhaling. This is an art to be learnt to achieve concentration.
4. Divine meditation - is a thought process, where divine light is assumed to be present in one's heart and the light is illuminating the whole body. This type of meditation is practiced in Sahaj Marg System and is easiest to follow.

Meditation pre-requisites

1. Environment - be quiet, where one does not get disturbed.
2. Position - sit crossed legged on floor or sit on a chair with preferably straight back, if one feels comfortable.

3. Wear - comfortable clothes.
4. Breathing - slow and rhythmic.
5. Eyes - closed, as it avoids distraction and enhances concentration.
6. Mental focus - is directed on one's breathing or on any symbol, which pleases one or on a flower or on a candle or on any word or any phrase (Mantra), which is repeated mentally.
7. Stay - still, as far as possible depending upon one's comfort, where mind becomes calm and body achieves a state of rest.

Meditation process

Process involves focusing on breathing in the beginning, as it is easy to follow, is consistent and one need not react physically or emotionally to any out side stimuli. One has to slip into a state of tranquility and the following things help:

1. Quite place - away from noise and telephone.
2. Sitting down- in a comfortable position in dim light.
3. Straighten spine - elongate neck and lower the chin.
4. Spend first few minutes - in trying to relax every body part.
5. Concentrate on each - inhalation and exhalation.
6. If mind wander - bring it back on the original thought.
7. Meditate - for at least 10 minutes every day in the morning.
8. After meditation - wait for few minutes to normalize the body and then start moving slowly.

Meditation benefits

Meditation removes stress, fatigue and tension. It balances spiritual aspect and material aspect of life. It increases creativity, induces enthusiasm in life and prepares one to face the life with confidence. It induces calmness in the mind. This state leads to good health and improves self-healing power. It stops internal dialogue in mind, opens the door to inner intelligence. This awakens the infinite potentiality for self-improvement. It improves power of concentration in studies and significant improvement in memory take place. It has enabled many to work at a higher level of efficiency in life. It enhances the power of intuition and one learns to live in the present, treats his past as an experience and develops faith to do better in future life.

Scientific experiments in meditation

Experiments have revealed that when eyes are open, brain produces Beta Waves of high frequency, which get dissipated in short distance. When eyes are closed, as in meditation, brain produces Alpha Waves of low frequency, which travel long distances and are capable of establishing contact over there. As such, one must close his eyes in meditation and has to learn to control these waves through mental discipline.

Programming of an individual's mind

Every individual is programmed to do certain things in a better way. This programming takes place during pregnancy stage. Programming depends upon the variations, which have occurred in the Earth's magnetic field. Variations depend upon the position of planets, which have occurred in the zodiac during pregnancy. Even after birth, the programming continues up to the age of seven years, when intelligence peaks. After this age, further programming slows down, as such; it becomes difficult for a person to learn a new language. Meditation gives control over this programming, but the control comes slowly and lot of patience is required.

Three stages in meditation

1st Stage - one gains conscious control over mid-brain's ascending reticular formation, which controls the limbic system. Limbic system control thoughts, emotions and secretes hormones, as follows:

1. Brain - secretes serotonin, which give relief from depression and mental tension.
2. Pineal glands - secrete melatonin, which has connection with hypothalamus part of brain. Hypothalamus control body's biological clock and give relief from insomnia, jet lag, and headache. Hypothalamus also increases body's resistance against diseases.
3. Thymus glands - secrete hormone, which strengths immune system and is very useful during childhood period.

2nd Stage - heartbeats become steady and regular; breathing become slower and deeper; digestive system improve due to better liver function and hormone secretion from glands improve, which make one feel relaxed.

3rd Stage - brain produces neuro-chemicals, Neuro-transmitters give feeling of extreme pleasure, happiness, one lives in peace and harmony with nature. Brain produces another chemical called Endorphin, which suppresses the feeling of pain and is similar to morphine (Opium derivative), which reduces pain. Mr. J. Krishnamurthy - the 3rd stage meditationer gave permission to doctors to perform operation on him without the use of anesthesia and the operation was painless.

Scientific observation during meditation

Meditation is suspension of self-consciousness that occupies the mind all the time. It improves concentration, induces tranquility, provides physical relaxation and based on these observations, doctors recommend that meditation even for 5 minutes refreshes one, fills him with energy and enables him to face the challenge of life. Meditation is secular in nature, is not aligned with any religion and is self-development through virtual reality. It is like dreams under control of mind, and with repeated practice, the nature of experiences improve. There is no danger directly or indirectly in practicing meditation.

Positron Emission Tomography (PET)

PET studies indicate that pleasure giving activities, like eating tasty food, listening to good music or experiencing happiness of any kind. These activities establish neural pathways in brain, which are similar to those, which get established during meditation session. Meditation is pleasurable and enjoyable. After meditation, one experiences lightness and sleepiness, which vanish within few minutes.

Vipassna meditation

This meditation is a technique in Buddhism. Gautam Buddha made it part of Buddhist tradition, but is not related to the religion. During Vipassna, one realizes various sensations in body, but they disappear after some practice. The technique purifies the mind from cravings and aversions, but habit pattern of mind changes slowly. One no longer reacts to body's sensations. Vipassna helps to overcome negative qualities, like: anger, greed, hatred and selfishness through self-realization. Before start of Vipassna, one has to follow the code of conduct, which is:

1. Do not - take intoxicants, do not kill animals, do not tell lies, do not indulge in sexual misconduct, do not steal and this prepares one mentally to do Vipassna.
2. Anapana Sati - is a process of meditation, where one learns to concentrate on incoming and outgoing breaths. This gives control over the thought process, as mind is ever active in thinking about the past, present and future. If thoughts are pleasant, one enjoys them and develops a craving for them. If thoughts are unpleasant; one unnecessarily worries about them. It is better to ignore both.

Meditainment

Meditainment is a blend of traditional meditation with audio-entertainment. It is enjoyable and has been Introduced on some of trans-atlantic air flights. It was observed that when passengers alighted from aircraft, they felt refreshed. Practice of meditainment has number of psychological benefits, like increased calmness, happiness, reduction in tension, removal of anxiety, reduction in blood pressure and enhancement of immune system.

1.7. Sahaj Marg System

It is the simplified system of Rajayoga system of meditation. The system helps one to realize his potential, which lies dormant within oneself. The system balances one's material aspect and spiritual aspect. System fosters universal love, brotherhood through common spiritual goal, is based on philosophy that God is an Internal-being and can be experienced internally through meditation. System neither disturbs one's household life nor career. One can join the system irrespective of his religion and political views.

Master is the spiritual head of the system. He guides the practitioners (Abhyasis) to lead the life at a higher level of existence.

This he does as guided and instructed by the previous Masters. There is only one living Master at a time, who accepts the responsibilities as President of Shri Ram Chandra Mission (SRCM). Master leads a life of utter orderliness, is full of playfulness, has genuine humility and is a person, who has mastered himself. He has an ability to transmit from his own centre of existence to the centre of Abhyasi's existence and strives to make him like himself.

System tries to minimize previous life's inherited traits (Sanskars) through cleaning (Safai) and preaches that sinful traits are not added in the present life. System tries to develop body, mind and soul through meditation (Dhyan). As one advances in the system, he experiences divine transmission (Pranahuti), which is available to the practitioners only. It is a gift from Master, which can be experienced anywhere in the world, irrespective of distance and time. Master transmits Pranahuti in four ways: 1. through speech, 2. through touch, 3. through sight and 4. through mind, when one meditates. This makes advancement in the system easier, speedier and one can grow without any limitation.

Shri Ram Chandra Mission (SRCM) - is a registered body in India since 1945. It is non-religious, non-profit, spiritual organization and has more than 1,000 centres in India and 90 centres abroad. The mission does not charge any fee of any kind for its services and training. Chennai is headquartering the mission, where Master resides. Regional centers are at Chennai in India for Asia, at Ogrance in France for Europe and at Molena in USA for North America. Master has appointed 1,783 Preceptors (952 in India, 62 in Africa, 90 in Asia, 453 in Europe, 182 in North America, 19 in Oceania and 25 in South America), who act on his behalf and give sittings to Abhyasis.

SRCM has research and training institute in Chennai, which conducts courses, gives training, is involved in research and development, arranges classes, develops study materials, conducts youth programs, publishes books and periodicals, researches into benefits of meditation, arranges conferences and seminars. These activities develop a practitioner's mind, as in the mind everything originates, first as thought and later as action.

Masters of Shri Ram Chandra Mission:

1st Master - was Shri Ram Chandra (1873 - 1931). He was fondly called Lala Ji and was born on 02.02.1873 on Basant Panchami day at Fatehgarh, in Uttar Pradesh, in India. Lala Ji modified Raja Yoga of Patanjali Rishi. He made the system suitable for present day household life, where a practitioner can lead his / her normal family life and still practice meditation. Lala Ji attained perfection in transmitting divine energy (Pranahuti) in seven months. In the beginning, he had a small band of disciples. He passed away on 14.08.1931, but before his death said that he will continue to guide the mission.

2nd Master - was Shri Ram Chandra (1899 - 1983). He was affectionately called Babu Ji. He was born on 30.04.1899 at Shahjahanpur, in Uttar Pradesh, in India. His wife was Bhagwati, she expired in 1947 and they had two daughters and four sons. He met Lala Ji for the first time in June 1922. He further developed the system and registered it as Society in 1945. He under took extensive tours in India and abroad. He established centers many centres in India and all over the world. He passed away on 19.04.1983

3rd Master - is the present Master Shri Parthasarathi Rajagopalachari (1927). He is respectfully called Chari Ji. He is born on 24.07.1927 at Vayalur near Chennai, in Tamilnadu, India. He married Sulochana in 1945 and they have one son Krishna (1957). He has done BE in chemical engineering and joined M/S T.T.Krishnamachari as Executive Director in 1955. He met Babu Ji for the first time in 1964 and joined the mission as an ordinary practitioner (Abhyasi). His life style is so perfect and exemplary that he is an example for others to follow. He is very much loved in India and abroad.

Shri Ram Chandra Mission practices

1. Meditation (Dhyan)

Meditation requires own efforts, where an Abhyasi (Practitioner) sits in any convenient position, closes his eyes; meditates on the thought that divine light is present in his heart, which is illuminating his whole body system. This thought is maintained for half an hour, but in the initial stage, unwanted thoughts arise, which are to be ignored. Soon a stage arrives, where unwanted thoughts subside and positive thoughts prevail. This is called advancement in the system.

2. Cleaning (Safai)

Cleaning requires own efforts, where a practitioner sits in any convenient position at the end of day's work. He brings the thought that his complexities, impurities, grossness, darkness are going out from his body in the form of smoke and vapor from back side. Divinity from Master's heart is flowing into his heart and with his grace, heart is getting filled up. At the end of cleaning, one feels fresh and light.

3. Prayer: O, Master!

Thou art the real goal of human life,
we are yet but slaves of wishes,
putting bar to our advancement,
Thou art the only God and power,
to bring us up to that stage.

Meaning of prayer

Thou art the real goal of human life - Master refers to God, as the real Master and he alone is, while Master is only his representative and he is the only goal.

We are yet but slaves of wishes, putting bar to our advancement - our wishes are the impediments to our progress.

Thou art the only God and power to bring us up that stage - God himself has to assist us to reach to Him.

Prayer has no element of begging, demanding, requesting, but simply describes the present state of one's mind. Prayer is offered after getting up in the morning; before going to bed in the night and before start of meditation. We remember what we love, when we remember Master, we create love for him. When this happens, our love knocks at Master's door step and his heart opens for our love (Union with Master).

4. Universal prayer - is offered at 9 pm in every time zone of the world for 15 minutes, with the thought that divine love and devotion is developing amongst all brothers and sisters, true faith is developing in them. Practitioner does the prayer once, but it gets repeated many times, as time zones differ.

1.8. My experience in meditation

When I was just 10 years old in 1940s, my father used to meditate. I used to wonder as to what he is doing? One day, I asked him and he said that he was meditating. Further he said that I can also meditate even on different topics of science and mathematics. If this can be done even for five minutes, it improves memory. This I tried and it helped me in remembering the facts in the form of a picture. Further, it improved my self confidence to do the things. My classmates made me monitor of the class and the position continued right up to matriculation.

Meditation helped me in clearing all India competition examination for entry into the engineering college of Indian Navy. In 1956, at the end of final examination, I topped the list of successful candidates and I was deputed for higher studies to Liverpool in England UK. In 1966, I joined the department of Atomic Energy as Senior Scientific Officer and I still continued with my meditation for 10 minutes only. In a senior position, when I started controlling a large number of engineers and technicians, I found that it was difficult to control intelligent persons. Meditation helped me in creating the necessary self-confidence and soon, I establishing a good rapport with them.

The above is my personal experience, and I hope that if meditation is taken in the right spirit; it may help the readers in their career development.

1.9. Scientific religion

Mankind is one through out the world, though it may differ in colour and stature. Sooner or later, it has to seek unity in diversity of religions. Scientific aspect will help in this direction. The so called miracles are to be subjected to scientific investigations to establish the truth. Material just cannot be created; wish cannot be fulfilled unless adequate efforts are put in the right direction. Every religion has to emphasize that each human-being is a ray of the Divine-being. Every one deserves respect irrespective of his religion or country of origin. It is not something new; it already exists in many religions, but requires to be implemented.

Science is advancing at a fast rate, soon a stage will reach, where it will be able to solve mysteries associated with religious practices, provided the followers co-operate with the right spirit. Before 21st century ends, there will be a blending of science and religion to such an extent, that a scientific religion will come into being.

2

Scientific Aspect

2.0. Evolution

Beginning of universe is not in the realm of religion, but lies in science.

2.1. Galaxy

Galaxy is a unit of the visible universe. Our Milky Way Galaxy is a unit of the universe. Star system is a subunit of the galaxy. Our Solar System is a subunit of Milky Way Galaxy. Planet system is a sub-subunit of a star system. Our Earth is a sub-subunit of Solar System and a moon orbits a planet. Our Moon orbits the Earth - the planet where we live. Galaxy is a band of luminous stars, stretching across the sky and stars have evolved from clumps of matter, which was thrown out after Big Bang. Galaxies are of four types: 1 Spiral arm, 2 Barrel spiral, 3 Elliptical and 4 Irregular. The visible universe has around 10,000 crore galaxies (I crore = 1, 00, 00,000). These galaxies exist in clusters, clusters are arranged into groups and each group consists of many galaxies.

Milky Way Galaxy - is a spiral arm galaxy, which belongs to the group called Local Group, which consists of 30 galaxies. The galaxy is situated on the edge of Virgo Super Cluster and had taken 50 crore years to form. The present age of Milky Way Galaxy is 1,200 crore years, diameter is 1 laky light-year (1 lakh = 1, 00,000), depth at the central bulge is 6,000 light-year, number of stars contained are 20,000 crore. Most of the stars are situated on the curved spiral arms, but few are situated between the arms also. The number of stars taper towards the edge of the spiral.

Sun - is situated on Orion arm and is 30,000 light-year from the center of Milky Way Galaxy. The galaxy is revolving round a Black-hole, which has a mass one lakh times the mass of Sun and takes 22.5 crore years to revolve once round the Black-hole. This period is known as one cosmic-year.

Satellite galaxy - Milky Way Galaxy has a satellite galaxy called Sagittarius Dwarf Elliptical Galaxy, which is currently being eaten up by the Milky Way Galaxy. Local Group Milky Way Galaxy and M 31 (Andromeda Galaxy) are gravitationally locked and are approaching each other at high speed. If these two galaxies meet, they will pass through each other and gravity will distort both the galaxies. This will eject some gas; dust and stars into inter galactic space. Eventually both the galaxies will merge together, but this will take crores of years to happen.

Smallest galaxy - in the universe is 42 crore light-year away from us. This galaxy has collided with Tadpole Galaxy, which has a tail of stars extending up to 2.8 lakh light-year.

Largest galaxy - in the universe is Abell 2029 Central Galaxy, which has a diameter 56 lakh light-year. It is 107 crore light-year away from us.

Nearest galaxy - is Andromeda Galaxy, which is 25 lakh light-year away from us and the next nearest galaxy is M 101.

Most distant galaxy - in the visible universe so far discovered, has a red shift of 6.58, which indicates that the galaxy is 1,280 crore light-year away from us.

Big Crunch theory - states that cooling of visible universe is still going on. The visible universe is expanding in all directions, it may reach an optimum size and after that, the visible universe may start collapsing under its own gravity. This phenomenon is known as Big Crunch theory

Doppler effect - wavelength of light from an object, as it moves away from us, causes red-shift to occur in the light-spectrum, where shift towards the red end of the spectrum occurs. This is known as red shift. Scientist Edwin Hubble in 1929 showed that the farthest galaxies were fleeing away from each other. This observation was based on the measurement of red- shift of 24 galaxies. He discovered that farther a galaxy is, the faster it is moving away from us. This fact of observation established that all the galaxies are receding away from us at high speeds. This phenomenon proves that the visible universe is still expanding in all directions. On the other hand, blue shift occurs when an object is coming nearer to us.

Matter - is what, can be perceived through the five human senses. Matter can exist in five states: 1. Solid, 2. Liquid, 3. Gaseous, 4. Plasma and 5. Bosone particles. In Bosone particle state, the independent atomic identity vanishes, atoms merge to form a super atom and the gas is so cold and dense that the atomic particles almost become stationary. This transformation is known as Bose Einstein concentration. It was discovered in 1924 for the first time, when Indian scientist Satyendra Nath Bose wrote a letter to Einstein about his observation on this state of matter. In this state of matter, the atomic particles can be grouped into two categories: 1. Particles - electrons, protons and neutrons are called Fermiyans and 2. Particle photons are called Bosones.

Matter has inertia, the tendency to stay at rest or keep on moving, if in motion, unless and until acted upon by an external force. Matter exerts gravitational pull on all other matter and the gravitational pull is called weight of the matter.

Dark-matter - cannot be perceived by the five human senses, but it exists in the universe and does not emit any form of electromagnetic radiation, but its gravitational effect reveals its presence.

Electro-magnetic spectrum - objects in space give off radiation in the form of electric and magnetic waves, which are of varying length. This radiation is called Electromagnetic spectrum, which range from Gamma rays (Shortest wave length) to 'X'-rays to Ultraviolet rays to Visible light to Infrared rays to Micro-waves and to Radio waves (Longest wave length).

Cosmic units - cosmic distances involved are so large that new units have been devised to measure them:

1 light-year = distance traveled by light in one year @ 3 lakh km per second (Accurate 2, 99,776 km per second)

astronomical unit (au) = distance from Earth to Sun = 15 crore km and au is used in measuring the distances in the Solar System.

1 light-year = 63,000 au
1 parsec = distance of star nearest to Earth = 4.23 light-year and parsec is used in measuring the distances in the Milky Way Galaxy.

Geological time scale - geology is the study of Earth's origin, structure and composition. Geologists refer to: Eon = 55 crore year long period, which is the largest subdivision of time on the geological time scale. Eon is composed of several geological Eras, Eras are composed of geological Periods, and Periods are composed of geological Epochs. We are currently living in: Phanerozoic Eon, Cenozoic Era, Neogene Period and Holocene Epoch.

Unit of time- the smallest unit of time is known as Planck's time, which is 10^{-43} seconds and is the period of time, which light takes traveling @ 3×10^{8} m / s to cross the Planck length of 1.6×10^{-35} m

2.2. Birth of Universe

1,370 crore-year ago - at the instant of Big Bang, the universe had infinite temperature as it existed as a single infinitely small, infinitely dense as a point and just 10^{-43} seconds later (Planck time), it cooled to 10^{32} k and expanded to a size of 10^{-33} cm across.

Big Bang theory - on creation of universe was propagated by the great scientist Einstein in 1931, which stated that matter, energy, time and space were created in an instant by **intelligence** outside of space and time. Big Bang explosion took place 1,370 crore-year ago and the sequence of events:

0 second - instant of Black-hole explosion, with this time and space came into being. This happened when a Black-hole sucked in enough matter from the surrounding areas, it became Super-critical and exploded (Big Bang theory). Explosion released tremendous amount of energy and radiation. Black-hole matter was thrown out in a highly compressed state.

1-second later - the temperature of the exploded matter was 1,000 crore degrees centigrade (10 times hotter than the core of the Sun).

1-minute later - subatomic particles formed and gravity appeared as a force.

5 lakh-year later - complex atoms got formed.

100 crore-year later - temperature was in lakhs of degrees and clouds of matter started gathering together under the force of gravity.

200 crore-year later - universe continued to expand, cooling process was continuing, clouds of gases came nearer and formation of galaxies started. As such, galaxy is unit of the universe and star system is the unit of a galaxy. At this stage, galaxy matter was in the form of superheated gases, the temperature ranged in lakhs of degrees. At these elevated temperatures hydrogen atoms fused into helium atoms, superheated gases formed into clouds of matter and the increased force of gravity brought gas clouds closer to form huge gas clouds.

300 crore-year later - expansion and cooling of the universe was continuing and during this period, complete darkness prevailed in the universe, as no star had formed, but the formation of galaxies continued.

360 crore-year later - cooling process of the universe continued, which lead to condensation of super heated gases into semi-solid matter. This further increased the force of gravity and bigger junks of solid matter got formed. Increased force of gravity brought bigger junks of solid matter still together and huge masses of cosmic bodies formed.

Birth of star - gravity in a cosmic body increases the internal pressure, which heats the cosmic body. Heating continues, increased temperature initiates nuclear-fusion-reaction, hydrogen gas starts converting itself into helium gas. This releases enormous amounts of energy, which heats the cosmic-body to two lakh degrees centigrade. This turns the cosmic-body into star. Star shines with its own source of light like Sun. Star size depends upon the amount of hydrogen gas contained in the core. Stars formed at this time and they lighted the universe for the first time.

460 crore-year later - visible universe consisted of crores of galaxies and formation of Milky Way Galaxy started. There are galaxies, which are older than our Milky Way Galaxy and formation of new galaxies continued, as such there are galaxies, which are younger than Milky Way Galaxy.

760 crore-year later - Milky Way Galaxy started taking the present spiral arm form. Formation of Sun and Solar System started taking the present shape.

1,370 crore-year later - Milky Way Galaxy is 610 crore-year old. Sun is 460 crore-year old. (Present age of universe)

455 crore-year from now - Sun will start becoming hotter and hotter, will start expanding, will engulf the planets Mercury and Venus, Sun's periphery in likely to touch Earth, but much before this happens, Earth will become terribly hot and life on Earth would have vanished much before this happens.

535 crore-year from now - Sun's death process would be completed, Solar System would collapse and Sun would meet it's own natural death after having lived for 995 crore-year.

2.3. Nine Types of Stars

1. Brown Dwarf star - is a small size star, but is bigger than a planet and due to insufficient hydrogen gas contained in its core, the nuclear fusion reaction takes place very slowly. The star radiates dull light.
2. White Dwarf star - is a medium size star, which shines very brightly and continues to collapse under its own force of gravity, till the very end of its life. Then the cooling process starts, expansion takes place and it become a red giant
3. Supernova star - is a giant size star, which becomes hotter and hotter at the core, cooler and cooler at the surface. In the end it explodes and the exploding star is known as Supernova. Then it may follow any one of the following three courses:

(1) Birth of new star - supernova material may be thrown out in the form of super heated inter stellar dust and in course of

time may form a new star. Then it may have its own system of planets, like the Solar system.

(2) Birth of Black-hole - supernova materials may collapse under its own force of gravity. It may form a Black-hole, which is an invisible object in space. When a star completes its life cycle (Consumes its hydrogen) and implodes (Opposite of explosion) on itself. It crushes the stellar matter to an extreme degree. This gives rise to extreme gravity, as such, Black-hole matter is so dense that a matchbox size may weigh up to 1,000 crore tonnes.

Black-hole matter has super gravity, which does not allow even light and radio waves to escape from it. As such Black-hole remains invisible, but its presence can be detected through extreme gravity. Chandrasekhar limit gives the possible mass of a cold stable star, above which it must collapse to form a Black-hole.

(3) Birth of Neutron star - Supernova materials may keep on collapsing under its own force of gravity and in the end it may form a Neutron Star, which does not shine, but radiates neutrons. Neutron star mass may weigh up to 125 ton / cubic cm due to crammed up neutrons. Supernova spectacle was observed from the Chinese sky in the early part of 20th century. The spectacle lasted for few months.

4. Pulsar star - is a neutron star, which at the end of its life becomes a Pulsar Star and rotates, but does not shine. Star has a very powerful magnetic field and gives out radio signals at precise intervals. One exception has been traced out, where the Pulsar star is still giving out feeble visible light.

5. Nebula - is a cloud of dust, which surrounds a faint star. Nearest Nebula to Earth is 5,000 light-year away.

6. Quasar star - is one, which gives out radio signals and emits tremendous amount of energy due to the existence of Black-hole in the center. Quasar star shines 200 times brighter than Sun. These are the brightest objects in the visible universe and 200 such stars have been traced out. Surprisingly, they all are receding away from us @ 2.832 lakh km / second and the farthest star is 145 crore light-year away from us.

7. Quark star - is one, which emits X-rays and free quarks are huddled up in it. Quark star is unimaginably dense and one cubic cm may weigh up to crores of tones. So far only two Quark stars have been discovered. One is designated as: RJX 1856 (Diameter 16 km and 400 light-year away from us), which is situated in the constellation Corona Australis. Other Quark star is designated as: 3 C 58 (10,000 light-year away from us) in the constellation Cassiopeia
8. Shooting star - is a misnomer, as it is a meteoroid, which is a fragment of rock of 1 m length or so. When it enters into Earth's atmosphere, due to frictional heat, it glows in a straight line for few seconds, but some bigger pieces may remain unburnt and fall on the surface of Earth as Meteorites. Many such meteorites have been picked up for scientific research. Meteoroid showers also occur, when Earth passes through the meteoroid belt.
9. Comet - looks like a star shining with a long tail of light, but it is not a star. Comets are the oldest and smallest objects, which revolve around the Sun. They go nearest to Sun and then travel farthest away from Sun in a highly elliptical orbit. Comet is a shining body of ice, gas, dust and originate at the very edge of the Solar System. Comet does not have its own source of light, but reflects the light of Sun.

   Comet when approaches the Sun, heats up and a tail of lighted gas gets formed, which always points away from the Sun. Comet tail may streach to a length of 10 crore km. Comet takes many years to complete one orbit around the Sun. Famous comet Halley takes 76 years and comet Hale-Bopp takes 18,000 years to go once around the Sun.

Life of Star

Normal life of star is about 1,000 crore years and present age of star is revealed by the colour of shine it emits, like:

1. Star shining with increasing and decreasing brightness - new star is being born.
2. Star shining with constant brightness - star has just been born.
3. Star shining blue - star is young in age.

4. star shining yellow - star is in the middle of its age. Sun is presently in this age group.
5. Star shining red - star is old in age.
6. Star Shining white - star is about to die.
7. Star not shining - star is dead, but emit gamma and X-rays to reveal its presence.

Luminosity and Brightness of a Star

Luminosity of a star is a measure of how bright a star is in real terms and is independent of distance from Earth. Brightness is a measure of how much light, we see with our eyes and is dependent upon distance from Earth, as well as, how much light the star is actually producing. Grading scale has been devised to measure the brightness of a star. Brightest star is assigned a grade 1.0, but later the grading scale was extended on both ends of the scale. Negative side of scale was devised for brighter stars and grades more than 1.0 were devised for fainter stars, as described below:

Grade (–) 27 – Sun shines at this brightness.
Grade (–) 13 - Full Moon shines at this brightness.
Grade (–) 1.4 - Star Sirius shines at this brightness.
Grade 0.0 - Star Vega shines at this brightness.
Grade 0.04 - Star Rohini shines at this brightness.
Grade 0.1 - Star Abhijeet shines at this brightness.
Grade 1.0 - No star shines at this standard brightness.
Grade 1.1 - Star Rohini shines at this brightness (Fainter than Abhijeet).
Grade 1.3 - Eighteen stars shine at this brightness (Fainter than Rohini).
Grade 6.0 - 3,000 Stars shine at this brightness (Faintest stars visible to naked eye).
Grade 29 - Faintest star visible through telescope.

Guide Star Catalog (GSC)

GSC lists the location of 1, 51, 69,873 stars in the Milky Way Galaxy. Typical star is designated as: GSC 1234 1132, first four digits specify one of the 9,537 small regions of the sky and the last four digits specify star's serial number within the region.

Well known Stars

1. Pistol star - the brightest star in the visible universe and is one crore times brighter than the Sun.
2. Sirius 'A' star - brightest star in the night sky and is 24 times brighter than Sun.
3. Proxima Centauri star - is the nearest star to us and is 4.23 light-year away.
4. Betelgeuse star - biggest known star in the visible universe (Diameter 100 crore km)
5. PSR B 1937 + 214 star - fastest spinning star, rotates at 642 revolutions / second.
6. Alpha Star (Dhruv Tara) - is situated at the tail end of Ursa Minor group of seven stars (Laghu Sapt Rishi Tara Mandal) and is in line with the outer two stars of Big Dipper (Sapt Rishi Tara Mandal). Three thousand years ago, Dhruv Tara was the Bita Star in the Ursa Minor group and three thousand years from now, another star will occupy this position, as the stars in the seven-star constellations are revolving at different speeds with the Milky Way Galaxy, which is revolving around a Black-hole.
7. The famous seven star constellation (Saptrishi) in the Northern sky is known as: Ursa Major and the last star in the tail is called Alpha star (Dhruv Tara), which always points to the Celestial North Pole and Earth's axis of rotation is directly below it.
8. Constellation (Nakshatra) - is a group of stars. These stars maintain their relative position to each other and 27 Nakshatras are famous in Indian astrology. However, other constellations also exist in the Milky Way Galaxy and 88 constellations have been identified so far.

Twinkle of a Star

Twinkle of a star is caused when light from the star passes through Earth's atmosphere, which has many layers of air at different temperatures. These layers bend the light producing a wavering effect, which is called twinkle of a star.

Blue Sky

Dust particles and gas molecules are present in the atmosphere, which scatter Sunlight in all directions. Shorter wave length light at the blue end of the spectrum get scattered more effectively than the longer wave length light at the red end of spectrum. Scattered blue rays against the dark black background of space, makes the sky appear blue.

Hindu Religion's View on Creation

During Vedic period about 7,000 years ago, Hindu Rishis visualized that the universe came into being as a result of point-explosion (Bindu-Visphot). It is a surprise that how Rishis came to this conclusion, when there was no trace of science evidence about it. This is the present scientific view on the creation of universe (Big Bang theory). Further, the Rishis said that point-explosion (Bindu-Visphot) produced the sound waves (Nada), which is the monosyllable 'Aum'. As such, all Hindu Religion hymns (Mantras) begin with the word 'Aum'. Lord Krishna in Bhagavad Gita said that I am 'Aum' in all the Vedas and in sky (Akash).

Two types of sounds (Nadas)

1. Struck sound (Ahat Nada) - we hear it, if sound has rhythm; it is called music (Sangeetam). Samveda traces the origin of Indian musical system and in Gita Lord Krishna said, that in all the Vedas, I am Samveda. Vedic chants in the beginning had three note (Swar) system, but later seven note (Swar) system developed in Indian musical system.
2. Un-struck sound (An-ahat Nada) - we do not hear it, but is the internal sound, which meditaters (Yogis) hear, when they go into deep meditation.

Indian Music System

Musicians of Indira Devta excelled in all the three forms of music, like: Apasaras - excelled in dancing, Kinnars - excelled in musical instruments and Gandharvas - excelled in singing. Hindu Godheads have identified themselves with musical instruments, like: Lord Shiva - with Damru, Lord Vishnu - with Shankh, Devi Sarasvati - with Veena, Lord Ganesha - with Mridang, Lord Krishna

- with Bansuri and Narad - with Ektara. Lord Shiva is considered to be the originator of five Ragas: 1. Bhairav, 2. Shri, 3. Vasant, 4. Pancham and 5. Megh and his concert Parvati originated 6. Nat-narayana. Indian musical system has two parts: 1. Vedic - is sung to please the Lords and deal with Vedas and 2. Laukik - is sung for recreation and entertainment for common people to enjoy.

2.4. Solar system

Solar system lies between Milky Way Galaxy's spiral arms: Sagittarius and Perseus. This mid portion between the arms is considered to be a safe zone and is far away from the galaxy's core, which is most dangerous due to cosmic activities going on there. At the same time spiral arms are also considered to be most dangerous, because arms are the places, where active star formations are taking place, due to higher rate of supernova explosions.

Sun

Sun's diameter is 14 lakh km. It will continue to live for another 455 crore-year, after this death process will start, which will take another 80 crore-year. (Present life of Sun 460 crore-year + Future life of Sun 455 crore-year + Sun's death process 80 crore-year = 995 crore-year total age of Sun). There are stars in the Milky Way Galaxy, which are older than our Sun. There are stars, which are younger than our Sun and formation of new stars is still going on. Sun is a medium sized star and is in the middle of its age. Light from the Sun takes 8.3 minutes to reach to us. Sun has 11-year cycle of Sunspot activity and during this period, magnetic field gets affected.

Sun consists of: 71 % hydrogen, 27 % helium, 2 % heavier elements, like: carbon, oxygen, nitrogen, iron and neon. Extreme heat and pressure in the Sun causes hydrogen atoms to fuse into helium atoms. This nuclear fusion-reaction releases enormous amounts of energy in the form of heat, light and radiation. Sun's energy on Earth is absorbed in the following manner: Surface absorbs 51 % energy, clouds reflect back 30 % energy and atmosphere absorbs 19 % energy.

Sun is at the center of Solar system, planets, asteroids and comets orbit around the Sun. At the same time, planets rotate on their own axis like Earth and moons orbit round the planets like our Moon. All planets orbit the Sun in the anticlockwise direction, while planet Pluto orbits in the clockwise direction.

Planets - their diameter and distance from Sun in km and in au are as follows:

<table>
<tr><th>S/N</th><th>Planet</th><th>Diameter</th><th>Distance</th><th>Distance</th></tr>
<tr><td>1.</td><td>Mercury (Budh)</td><td>4,878 km</td><td>5.8 crore km</td><td>0.38 au</td></tr>
<tr><td></td><td colspan="4">Mercury is the nearest planet to Sun, moves 48 km / second. It takes 88 days to orbit the Sun and the day temperature is 425° C</td></tr>
<tr><td>2.</td><td>Venus (Shukr)</td><td>12,104 km</td><td>10.8 crore km</td><td>0.72 au</td></tr>
<tr><td></td><td colspan="4">Venus rotates East to West; as such Sun rises in the West and sets in the East. It is the hottest planet in the Solar System, day temperature rises to 480° C. It has the longest day equal to 243 Earth days and takes 225 Earth days to orbit the Sun. Venus has poisonous atmosphere and is known as Evening / Morning star, as it is visible during this time.
Sun is the right size star. Star bigger than our Sun, burns its fuel more rapidly and erratically. Star smaller than our Sun, are more stable than our Sun, but they do not burn as hot to keep the planets at the right temperature to sustain life. If a planet is near the star, the tidal forces would be strong enough to break its rotational period. This has happened in the case of two Mercury and Venus planets in our Solar system, where the rotational periods have been broken from several hours to several months.</td></tr>
<tr><td>3</td><td>Earth (Prathvi)</td><td>12,756 km
(Equator)</td><td>15.0 crore km
(Av) = 1.00 au</td><td>12,711km
(Poles)</td></tr>
<tr><td></td><td colspan="4">Earth is the only planet in the Solar System, which has surface water and life-supporting oxygen in the atmosphere to sustain different forms of life. Earth's orbit is elliptical (Farthest 15.21 crore km in July and nearest 14.71 crore km in January), distance from Sun is 8.3 light-minute. It is tilted 23.5° on its axis and looks blue from space.</td></tr>
</table>

4 Mars (Mangal) 6,794 km 22.8 crore km 1.52 au
Mars looks red due to red-iron-oxide in its soil. It has 2 Moons.
+ Asteroid Belt - consists of lakhs of hurtling rock pieces, orbiting the Sun between the planets Mars (Mangal) and Mercury (Budh). These pieces of rock pose a threat to life on Earth and hazard to astronauts going beyond Mars (Mangal). Asteroid Impact Hazard (AIH) - asteroid belt pieces burn out to ashes in the Earth's atmosphere, but sometimes bigger pieces remain unburned. They fall on the surface causing danger to life and property. This hazard is known as Asteroid Impact Hazard (AIH). Each hurtling piece is assigned a number from 0 to 10 and have a color code, like: 0 White zone - unlikely to collide with Earth (Likely to break up in the atmosphere), 10 Red zone - mean certain collision and may cause global climatic catastrophe.
On 16.05.1996, a rock piece measuring 0.5 km width passed the Earth from a distance of 4.12 lakh km, which is hair like distance in cosmic terms. These rock pieces measuring 220 to 490 m travel almost at the velocity of light and 2,000 such rock pieces have been identified through a number system, like 2001 YB 5, 1999 AN 10, which cross Earth's orbit each year and pose a threat.

5 Jupiter (Guru) 1,42,800 km 77.8 crore km 5.20 au
Jupiter is the largest planet in the Solar System (1,300 x Earth) and is the fastest spinning planet.

6 Saturn (Shani) 1,20,000 km 142.6 crore km 9.53 au
Saturn planet is made up of gas. Planet orbits the Sun in 29 years. Planet has three main rings and four fainter rings. Planet has 30 Moons. Jupiter and Saturn with their strong gravitational pulls act as vacuum cleaners and sweep the Solar system of dangerous asteroids.

7 Uranus (Harshal) 51,000 km 287.1 crore km 19.10 au
Uranus orbits the Sun in 84 years, rotates on its side, surface temperature – 220° C. Planet has 21 Moons and was discovered in 1781 AD. Planet was discovered by Harshal for the first time.

8 Neptune (Varun) 48,000 km 4,498.8 crore km 30.00 au
Neptune planet looks blue, has methane atmosphere, which absorbs red light. Planet has the strongest winds (2,000 km /

hour), orbits the Sun in 165 years and has eight Moons. Triton Moon is the coldest place in the Solar System (Tempt. – 236° C) and was discovered in 1846 AD

9 Pluto 2,274 km 5,906.0 crore km 39.48 au

Pluto is the smallest planet in the Solar system and is the farthest planet from the Sun. Light from Sun takes 5.5 light-hour to reach it. Pluto orbits the Sun in 288 years and was discovered in 1930 AD

Earth

Astronomy has leaped from the primitive Earth centered universe to the modern scientific view that shows that Earth is a tiny insignificant speck in an infinitely large universe. Basically Earth is a space ship, which is hurtling through space at the speed of 1, 04,000 km / hr and is spinning at 1,600 km / hr. Earth has two engines: 1. Sun's gravitational force and 2. Earth's spinning, as described below:

1. Earth moves forward due to Sun's gravitational force. Sun also keeps the Earth on its elliptical path. The centripetal force caused by gravity, keeps the Earth on its orbit. Earth has a particular speed and is spun by centripetal force. Earth stays in a stable orbit around the Sun. Earth's distance from the Sun is ideal to sustain life. If the distance had been closer, it would have burnt us. if the distance had been longer, it would have frozen us.
2. Earth's spinning - fuels its interior and heats the Earth's core deep inside, where the radioactive fuel is decaying, which heats the Earth and drives the tectonic plates due to the convection of the liquid iron in the Earth's core. This acts like a dynamo, which generates Earth's magnetic field.

Earth's Tilt

Earth has an optimum tilt of 23.5°, which has created ideal seasons to sustain life. If the Earth's axis had a tilt of 45°, temperatures would have been very hot in summer and freezing cold in winter. If the axis had been vertical to the plane of its orbit, January and July would have the same temperature and ice would keep on accumulating at the Poles. The present ideal tilt permits the Sun's rays to uniformly heat the Earth.

Earth's Time Scale

Earth was formed out of the dust and materials, left over after the formation of Sun. Time scale for the formation of Earth had been, as follows:

460 crore-year ago - formation of Solar System started. Earth was in a gaseous state, but it's cooling process was continuing.

457 crore-year ago - as per Radiometric-dating system our Earth was formed. It is most surprising that about 7,000 years ago, Hindu Religion's time counting (Kalganna) System of Creation calendar (Sarishti Kalpa) calculated the age of Earth to be 432 crore-year, which is very close to the present day scientific calculation.

420 crore-year ago - gaseous state of Earth cooled to a molten state. Heavier elements, like: iron sank inside the Earth to form the Core, while lighter elements remained floating on the surface.

350 crore-year ago - Earth's atmosphere consisted of: ammonia, methane, hydrogen, water vapour. Earth was surrounded with clouds, where lightning used to take place quite often. This led to formation of Proteins.

45 crore-year ago - all the landmasses of the Earth were joined together and were huddled in the Southern Hemisphere.

25 crore-year ago - in Paleozoic and Mesozoic Eras, a super continent existed and was named Pangaea (All Earth landmass), which existed before the process of tectonic-plate movement began. Pangaea was the 'C' shaped landmass, which spread across the equator.

18 crore-year ago - in the Jurassic Period, the super continent Pangaea broke up into two huge continents, as described below:

1. Laurasia (Asia and North America) started drifting towards the Northern Hemisphere of the Earth.
2. Gondvana- the huge continent comprised of: Madagascar, New Guinea, New Zealand, South America, Africa, Australia, Antarctica, Atlantic Ocean, Arabia and India (Now Arabia and India are in the Northern Hemisphere). The Gondvana continent started drifting towards Southern Hemisphere and

the drifts in the continents is still going on, like: Australia is drifting in the Northern direction, Africa is splitting along the Rift Valley and Atlantic Ocean is widening.

16.7 crore-year ago - in mid Jurassic Period, East Gondvana comprising of Antarctica, Madagascar, India and Australia began to separate from Africa.

13 crore-year ago - South America began to drift slowly westward from Africa.

12 crore-year ago - East Gondvana began to split. India began to move northward and the drift is still continuing in the North East direction.

8 crore-year ago - Australia began to separate from Antarctica continent.

6.5 crore-year ago - Indian subcontinent started drifting in the Northeast direction and began to collide with the Asian continent. The collision started raising the Asian continent to form the Himalayan Ranges.

5.7 crore-year ago - Australian and New Guinea began separating and ice caps started forming on the Poles.

4.5 crore-year ago - South America separated from West Antarctica

3.4 crore-year ago - Red Sea emerged. Indian subcontinent's collision with Asian continent forced the Earth's crust to buckle to form the Himalayas, as we see it now. The mountain has the world's highest peak Mount Everest (Height 8,848 m), which emerged on the Nepal / China border and the second highest peak K2 (Height 8,611 m) emerged on the Pakistan / China border.

0.5 crore-year ago - North American and South American continents got joined together (Panama). South America and Africa are moving apart at an average of 5.7 cm / year.

Continents - once upon a time, all the continents of the world existed as a single landmass, but gradually the landmasses started splitting and drifted to the present positions, where we see them now. If the continents as shown in the atlas are cut, they will fit into the opposite side of the ocean's landmass and will form a single landmass. The seven continents of the world with their land surface areas in percentage are:

1. Africa	20.1 %	5. North America	16.1 %
2. Antarctica	9.3 %	6. Oceania	6.0 %
3. Asia	29.6 %	7. South America	12.1 %
4. Europe	6.8 %	Total Earth's surface – 100 %	

10 lakh-year ago - formation of ice sheet started on the Antarctica continent, which covered an area of 139 lakh square km and presently the ice sheet at places is 4.3 km thick. World's 66 % of fresh water is locked up here.

10 thousand-year ago - Sea level rose to the present levels. Dead Sea on the border of Israel / Jordan remains 400 m below the Mean Sea Level.

5 thousand-year ago - Sarasvati River (Mentioned in Rig Veda) was flowing parallel to the East of Indus River from Himalayas to the Arabian Sea through the Thar Desert in Rajasthan. The river started disappearing from the surface of Earth due to Tectonic Plate movement.

3 thousand-year ago - Saraswati River disappeared. The present Luni Rivulet flowing into the Rann of Kachchh, is the remnant of the Saraswati River.

Earth's Rotational Period

Earth's rotational period is 24 hours, but the rotational period is slowing down. In course of time, this period will increase from the present 24 hours to 26 hours and further to 28 hours. Once upon a time, Earth was rotating every 20 hours. If Earth rotates too quickly, there will be more tornadoes and hurricanes. If Earth rotates too slowly, it will get too cold at night and too hot during the day. Earth's mass is ideal. If Earth had been more massive, it would have retained lighter gases, like: ammonia, methane, hydrogen and helium in the atmosphere, which are harmful to life. If Earth had been lighter, it would not retain water, which is essential for life.

Earth's Features

Earth's diameter - 12,756 km (Equator), circumference 40,076 km (Equator), water covers 71 % of land area and the remaining surface area 29 % is where we live.

Earth spins - at the speed of 1,600 km / hour at the Equator and slower at the Poles. It takes 23 hours and 56 minutes to spin once on its axis. It takes 365.2419 days to orbit once round the Sun.

Earth's axis - had pointed to different places in the sky over the last 26,000 years. This is called Precession and presently, the axis is tilted 23.5° on the plane of orbit around the Sun.

Earth's inner core - Earth is a sphere. Its inner core is at the central part of the sphere, which is solid, is 2,740 km wide, core is made up of iron, nickel and the temperature is 4,500° C.

Earth's outer core - inner core of Earth is surrounded by an outer core, which is 2,000 km thick and is semi-liquid. It is made up of iron and nickel.

Earth's mantle - outer core of the Earth is surrounded by a layer called Mantle. It is a layer of rock of 2,900 km thickness and the temperature is 3,700° C at the bottom of the mantle, but high pressure keeps these layers of rocks solid, while at the top of the mantle, the layer of rocks are relatively soft due to less pressure.

Earth's crust - soft mantle of the Earth is surrounded by a Crust, which is a layer of rock, which is 70 km deep. Crust is made up of segments, called Plates. Earthquakes happen, when these plates move against each other at weak spots, called Faults.

Earth's tectonic plates - are the outer most segments of the Earth's crust, which is generally 7 km thick at the bottom of oceans and 35 km thick beneath the continents. Seven tectonic plates are: 1. North America, 2. South America, 3. Pacific, 4. Africa, 5. Eurasian, 6. Australia and 7. Antarctica. These plates are interlocked, but are not fixed in position, as such, they keep on moving slowly @ 5 cm / year and over the past crores of years, have moved to their present positions.

Earth's Magnetism

Earth's magnetism may be either due to the presence of charged molten metallic fluid of dia. 7,000 km at the Core, which rotates along with the Earth, which may be generating electric current to magnetize the Earth or the cause of magnetism may be the presence of ionized layer in the atmosphere, which may be inducing electric current, as the Earth rotates in it. Earth's magnetic field is generated in the inner Core and the field extends up to 60,000 km into space. Magnetic field provides protection against harmful radiation coming from the Sun.

Earth's Poles

Earth's magnetic poles and geographical poles do not coincide. Magnetic North Pole is currently drifting Westwards @ 0.2 % per year. Every 5 lakh years, the magnetic poles reverse their polarity and the reversing process takes 1,000 years to settle down. Earth's magnetic North Pole and geographical North Pole are situated in the Arctic Ocean. Magnetic North Pole is 1,000 km away towards Canada from the geographical North Pole. Earth's magnetic South Pole and geographical South Pole are situated on landmass in the Antarctica continent.

Earth's Oceans

1. Pacific Ocean - is the largest ocean and covers 33 % of Earth's surface. It contains half the water of the planet and the deepest point on Earth is known as Challenger Deep in the Marina Trench, which is 10,911 m deep near the Guam Island in the Pacific Ocean. Marina Trench is 2,500 km long and 69 km wide.
2. Ocean depth zones - as Ocean depths increase, Sun light penetration gets reduced and zones get created, which are known as:
   (1) Sun lit zone - micros-copic plants grow due to photosynthesis. These plants provide food to fish life and the zone extends from surface up to 200 m depth.
   (2) Twill light zone - is dimly lit area, water is quite cold and the zone extends from 200 m up to 1 km depth.
   (3) Abyssal zone - lights come from the signals generated by the creatures to attract prey, water temperature is 5° to 6° C and the zone extends from 1 km to 5 km depth.
   (4) Dark zone - complete darkness prevails, temperature is 1° to 2° C and the zone extends from 5 km depth to the bottom of the ocean.

3 Waves - derives their energy from the winds. Highest point of wave is called Crest and the crests are separated with low-level water called Trough. Wave height is measured from trough to crest and the maximum height recorded is 34 m in the Pacific Ocean during a hurricane. Waves contain energy

and the energy moves through the water, while the water itself does not move, but just moves up and down. Wavelength is measured from crest to crest and when the crest collapses, the resultant turbulent water is called Surf. In 2004 Tsunami tidal waves in the Bay of Bengal had caused 2.8 lakh casualties

Level Marking on Ships

Salinity and temperature affect the density of water, which in turn affect the level at which a ship floats, as such, ship's hulls are marked with Level markings to show at which level the ship will float, when passing through different density waters, which is illustrated below:

TF	Tropical fresh warm water
F	Fresh water
T	Tropical warm water
S	Summer sea
W	Winter sea
	WN Winter North Atlantic (Salty and cold water)

Shipping Canals

1. Suez Canal - connects Red Sea with Mediterranean Sea. The canal was opened to traffic in 1869 AD. I have passed through this canal, when I was serving on board I.N.S.Magar.
2. Panama canal- connects Atlantic Ocean with Pacific Ocean. The canal was opened to traffic in 1914 AD.

Water Courses

1. Longest river - is Missouri Mississippi in USA and the length is 6,680 km
2. Largest flows in a river - takes place through Amazon River in South America. Tthe river is 50 km wide at the mouth, where it joins the Atlantic Ocean.
3. Largest flow in an ocean current - takes place through Gulf Stream, which is 80 km wide, 450 m deep and moves @ 7.4 km / hour through the Atlantic Ocean from East Coast of North America to West Coast of United Kingdom. Gulf Stream makes the climate pleasurable in Europe.

4. Water trapped - in Oceans 97.2 %, in Polar Ice Caps 2.15 % and in the ground from 4.8 km to 11.2 km depth 0.65 % Floods - worst floods, which have occurred:

Year	*River*	*Casualties*
1931	Flood in Yangtze-Kiang River in China	37 lakh
1971	Flood in Red River in Vietnam	1 lakh
1975	Flood in Yangtze-Kiang River in China	2 lakh

2.5. Atmosphere

Atmosphere came into existence from the gases spewed out by the volcanoes and is roughly 2,000 km thick. Atmosphere exists in layers and the different layers of the atmosphere are:

1. Troposphere - extends from sea level up to 12 km up and consists of 77.03 % Nitrogen, 21.91 % Oxygen, 0.93 % Organ, 0.03 % Carbon-di-oxide and 0.1 % other gases, like: Neon, Helium, Methane, Krypton, Hydrogen, Xenon, Ozone, etc. Temperature falls by 7° C / km up to – 58° C, while the temperature at the surface remains near about 20° C. Weather turbulence prevails up to 11 km height, as such, airplanes fly at 12 km height, where the temperature at 9 km height is – 32° C and at 12 km height – 60° C.
2. Ozone layer - extends from 15 km to 35 km height. Layer gets formed over the tropics, where Sun's radiation is strongest and high level winds distribute the Ozone gas. Ozone layer absorbs harmful ultra-violet rays, has few dust particles and the humidity is extremely low. Release of CFCS (Refrigerant gas) has depleted the Ozone layer and has caused big holes in the layer. These holes were first noticed over the Antarctica in 1980. Depletion of Ozone layer may give rise to more cancer cases. Releases of refrigerant gases are being phased out. Concord Airliner flies at 18 km height, which disturbs the Ozone layer; as such, the airliner has been phased out.
3. Stratosphere - extends from 16 km to 50 km height and the temperature practically remains constant from 12 km to 18 km height. Interceptor fighter planes fly at 20 km height, where the temperature is – 54° C and at 24.5 km temperature is – 51° C.

4. Mesosphere - extends from 50 km to 80 km height and the temperature keeps on falling, reaches up to – 100° C. This is the limit of the rise of weather monitoring balloons and the meteors burn up in this layer.
5. Mesopause belt- is situated at 80 km height and at the top of this layer meteor showers occur.
6. Ionosphere - extends from 80 km to 500 km. Here atoms and molecules get ionized (Electrically charged) and temperature goes up to 1,700° C due to Solar Radiation, which generates heat. Radio signals from Earth get reflected back, Northern Lights (Aurora) appear and magnetic disturbances occur in this layer. American space shuttle travels at 300 km height, where the temperature is – 63° C.
7. Thermosphere - extends from 80 km to 600 km height and temperature keeps on rising.
8. Exosphere - extends from 600 km to 1,500 km height and beyond, until it merges with the interplanetary gases of outer space, where temperature ranges from 300° C to 1,700° C. Helium and hydrogen molecules are very thinly present over here and almost vacuum prevails. Short radio waves get reflected back to Earth from here. Hubble space telescope orbits in this layer.

Weather

Weather is a condition of atmosphere with respect to wind, fog, mist, rain, temperature, cloudiness, air pressure and humidity.

1. Wind - is created by difference in air pressure; as hot air rises, it creates low-pressure area at the surface, cold air sinks in to create high-pressure, this creates wind and the wind is known from the direction, it is coming from. Wind speed - is measured in km / hr and has many names, as given below and its effect:

Wind speed	Name	Effect
0 – 5	Circulation	Smoke rises and drifts
5 – 10	Wind	Smoke indicates wind direction
10 – 20	Gentle breeze	Tree leaves rustle

20 – 30	Breeze	Dust blows
30 – 50	Strong breeze	Papers blow away
50 – 70	Gale	Tree branches sway
70 – 90	Strong gale	Trees sway, branches break & roof tiles blow off
90 – 120	Storm	Trees get uprooted & rooftops get damaged
120 & Above	Cyclone	Cause severe destruction

2. Tropical storm - is known as Hurricanes in America, Typhoon in China, Cyclone in India and Australia. Worst cyclone occurred in 1970, which killed 3 lakh people in Bangladesh
3. Monsoon - is seasonal wind, which brings rain to the Indian subcontinent. Hot air as it rises from the tropics, spreads towards to the Poles and Earth' rotation deflects this wind in clockwise direction in Northern Hemisphere and anti-clockwise in Southern Hemisphere.
4. Jet stream - develop in the higher reaches of the atmosphere between 10 to 15 km height, where large difference in temperature and pressure occur. This gives rise to high speed winds of 130 km / hour (Average).
5. Tornado - is a rapidly rotating column of air that extends from clouds to ground level and dust whirlwind occurs over dusty ground.
6. Moisture in air - when moisture in air condenses into water droplets, clouds are formed, which have different names:
   (1) Alto (Altus) clouds - form from 2 km to 6 km height.
   (2) Cirro (Cirrus) clouds - form above 6 km height.
   (3) Nimbus clouds - are rain bearing and when air temperature inside a cloud is above freezing point, water droplets merge to grow until they are heavy enough to fall to ground as rain.
   (4) Cumulus clouds - occur below 2 km height and indicate unstable weather condition.
   (5) Status clouds - indicate stable weather conditions.
   (6) Snow - if ice crystals are present in the clouds, they bond together, until large enough, which fall as snow.

(7) Hailstones - when several layers of ice build up on super cooled water droplets, they grow in size, until large enough to fall as hailstones.

(8) Dew - forms from condensation of moist air, when it comes into contact with cold surface of plants, grass and flower petals.

(9) Frost - occur, when moist air comes into contact with colder surfaces. Frost is of two types:

1. Air frost - when air temperature is 0° C or below, as measured 1.2 m above the ground.
2. Ground frost - forms on the ground or in the top layers of soil, which cause damage to plants.

(10) Mist - is tiny droplets of water, which are suspended, in cold air.

(11) Fog - if mist is denser and visibility is less than 200 m, then it is classified into fog. Fog is a ground level cloud. The amount of moisture air can hold depends upon its temperature, as Sunrises, it heats the air and the fog disappears.

(12) Smog - is combination of smoke and fog. It is of two types:

1. Sulfurous smog - is formed, when fossil fuels burn and smoke combines with damp air.
2. Photochemical smog - is formed, when hydrocarbon and nitrous oxide fumes from vehicles and industrial processes combine.

Smog reacts with Sun light to create toxic gases, which affect city life and cause respiratory, skin and eye irritation and lung diseases.

7 Rainbow - when Sun light passes through suspended raindrops, the light splits into seven colors due to prism effect of raindrops. Sun light has different wavelengths, which bend at different angles after emerging from the raindrop. Rainbow spectrum has colors in the sequence: VIBGYOR (Violet-short wave length, which appears on the inner side of the rainbow, I- Indigo, B- Blue, G- Green, O- Orange and R-Red, longest wave length, which appear on the outer side at top of the rainbow)

8. Acid rain - Sulfur-dioxide and Nitrogen-dioxides as released from the industrial processes, when combine with water vapor in the atmosphere, the reaction produces Sulfuric-acid (H_2SO_4) and Nitric-acid (HNO_3) of 5.6 pH value. When it precipitates, it falls as Acid-rain and cause damage to plant life, fresh water creatures and to buildings.
9. Aurora - spectacular show of light, which appears when, charged Solar-wind particles enter the upper atmosphere and get deflected towards the Earth's magnetic Poles. The particles spiral down the magnetic lines of force; they bombard gas molecules and cause them to emit colored light.
10. Mirage - when Sun light passes through different density and temperature air layers, the light bends. This happens on hot surfaces as found in deserts, the light is refracted upwards and this produces a false image that a sheet of water is just ahead. Deer's run after this sheet of water in vain.
11. Green house effect - carbon-di-oxide gas is produced when coal and fuel burn; nitrogen-oxide gas, methane gas and water vapors are emitted from vehicle exhaust. As the quantity of these gases increase in the atmosphere, they reflect back Solar heat and trap the heat, which increase the temperature and through this process the temperature rise has taken place by 0.5° C since 1905 and by another 1.5° C is expected to take place by 2025. This will slowly increase the level of oceans and rise in level will inundate the low lying areas of the world.
12. UVI (Ultra Violet Index) - Ultraviolet rays cause damage to human skin. This damage is measured on an UVI Scale, which ranges from 0 to 11+ Level, but the damage level differs from place to place, depending upon: 1 Cloud cover, 2 Visibility, 3 Atmospheric Ozone gas concentrations, 4 Sun elevation, 5 Weather condition and 6 Altitude above sea level. UVI Scale categories the skin damaging effect, as follows:

UVI	*Risk*	*Level*	*City*
0 to 2-	Minimum		
3 to 4-	Low	3	London

5 to 6-	Moderate		
7 to 9-	High	9	Delhi
10 -	Very high ...	10+	Chennai, Kolkatta
11+ -	Extreme		

13. Lightning flash - strong up drafts and down drafts cause separation of electrical charges inside the clouds, positive charge appear at the top and negative charge appear at the bottom of the clouds. As the potential difference increases between them, a point is reached where electrical discharge takes place within the clouds or between bottom of cloud and the Earth's surface and a lightning flash occurs, which raises the temperature of the surrounding air up to 22,000° C. This causes the surrounding air molecules to expand instantly, producing the thunder. This thunder we hear after few seconds from the instant of seeing the flash. The time interval depends upon the distance the clouds are from us. This distance can be calculated, as follows:
    Distance in m = Elapsed time in seconds x 330 velocity of sound in m / sec
14. Extreme weather:
    1. Hottest place 57.8° C recorded at Al'Aziziyah in Libya on 13.09.1922
    2. Coldest place (–) 89.22° C at Vostak Station in Antarctica on 21.07.1983
    3. Coldest regions- temperature (–) 80° C at the North and South Poles
    4. Highest rainfall 1869.9 mm in 24 hours on La Reunion Island in the Indian Ocean on 15 / 16 March, 1952
    5. Highest annual rainfall 11874.5 mm at Cherrapunji in East India
    6. Highest casualty 10 lakh caused by cyclone in the Ganges Delta of Bangladesh on 12 / 13 November, 1970
    7. Highest Tsunami (Harbour wave) was 524 m high and was caused by a giant land slip in Alaska, USA on 09.07.1958

2.6. Earthquake

Earthquake is shaking of Earth's crust, as a result of release of locked up energy beneath the ground rocks, where pressure builts up due to tectonic plate movement or due to weight of water behind a dam or sometimes the tremors get triggered due to meteorite impact. Most Earthquakes occur at tectonic plate boundaries, where fault lines lie. The center of Earthquake is called Focus, which is buried, much below the ground level, from where the Earthquake waves originate. The point directly above the focus at the ground level is called Epicenter, from where the shock waves blast out. These waves may cause tidal waves and volcanic explosions.

Earth's Crust

Earth's crust is roughly 50 km deep and mostly Earthquakes originate between 30 km to 100 km depth, where the tectonic plate movement occurs. The movement can take place in three ways:

1. Tectonic plate moving - like: the Indian sub continental tectonic plate is moving in the North East direction @ 3 to 5 cm / year. The movement builds up stress at certain places, which get released suddenly and Earth tremors occur on the surface.
2. Tectonic plates sliding - like: the Indian sub continental tectonic plate is slowly sliding underneath the Asian tectonic plate, which has raised the Asian plate to form the great Himalayan Ranges and the Tibetan Plateau.
3. Tectonic plates colliding - like: the Indian sub continental tectonic plate has collided with the Asian tectonic plate and has formed the fault zones, where frequently Earthquakes occur.

Earthquake Symptoms

Earthquake symptoms appear much before an Earthquake strikes and symptoms are:

1. Radon gas- starts oozing out from water wells.
2. Chemical changes- occur in water wells.
3. Sudden rise or fall- in water level occurs in water wells.

Earthquake Tremors

Earthquake tremors occur in three phases, as given below:

1. Primary phase tremors - occur before the main Earthquake strikes.
2. Main phase - tremors occur during the main Earthquake, which cause extensive damage.
3. After phase - tremors occur for few days more, after the main Earthquake has occurred and during this phase damaged buildings collapse.

Richter Scale

Richter scale has been devised, which indicates ten fold increases in ground tremors from one scale division to the next division. Increase of each scale division corresponds to 32 fold increase In the amount of energy released. The scale has no upper limit and is logarithmic in nature. This has been done, as the relative magnitude of larger seismic waves are thousands of times greater than the weak waves, as such to accommodate this large variation in magnitude, Richter Scale has been devised. Richter scale and its consequences:

Richter	*Consequences*
1.	Can be detectable by instruments only.
2.	Not felt by man, but sensed by cows, buffaloes, horses, donkeys and hares and these animals become restless and start running here and there. Mice and serpents come out of their holes. Crows and pigeons start flying in panic.
3.	Sensed by man and buildings may develop cracks.
4.	Sensed within 32 km of the epicenter and cause light damage to property.
5.	Shock waves cause damage to life and property in the localized area.
6.	Shock waves cause heavy damage over wide areas.
7.	Shock waves cause extensive damage over very wide areas and is classified as Major Earthquake.
8.	Shock waves cause havoc over extensive areas and is classified as Great Earthquake.

9. Shock waves cause unprecedented damage and is classified as Catastrophic Earthquake. If an Earthquake of this magnitude occurs in the ocean / sea or near the island, it produces Tsunami tidal waves, which cause great loss to life and property in the coastal areas.

Indian astrology - on Earthquakes and its classification:

Indian astrologer Varahmihir predicted that Earthquakes are likely to occur after 3, 5, 16, 17, 28, 37, 48, 59 and 71 days after an eclipse has occurred and said that Earthquakes are of four types, as given below:

1. Varun Earthquake- changes the course of river, fall in water level occurs in water wells and animals, birds and insects change their behavior, before an Earthquake strikes a region.
2. Vayava Earthquake- river flows become wayward and people become agitated, which lead to accidents and fires on a large scale. Unusual changes occur, like: In 1994- speed of trains increased suddenly in California in USA, petrol pipelines burst and fires killed many people.
3. Agneya Earthquake- is caused by emission of lava from volcanoes, wide fluctuations occur in temperatures, cracks occur in Earth's surface and unprecedented uneasiness prevails in the behaviour of birds and animals, as they are more sensitive to ground tremors.
4. Indra Earthquake- monkeys become restless, dogs bark, cows hay, mice run out from their holes, birds break their nests and under ground creatures, like: ants, mice show unusual behavior for periods ranging from two months to few hours before an Earthquake strikes, followed by torrential rains.

Major Earthquakes: (RS- Richter Scale magnitude)

Date	*Casualties*	*Place*	*Country*	*Time (Remark)*
02.02.1556	8,30,000	Shanshi	China	Midnight (Highest death toll)
11.10.1737	3,00,000	Kolkata	India	Midnight

01.11.1755	7,00,000	Lisbon	Portugal	(RS- 8.7 & lasted 10 minutes)
1793	53,000	Unsen	Japan (Island sank beneath Satsuma Sea)	
1899	———	Yakatut Bay,	Alaska, USA (Coast rose 14.5 m at places)	
1923	1,42,800	Tokyo	Japan	
1950	———	Assam	India	(RS- 9.0, highest in India)
1960	———	Coast	Chile	(RS- 9.5, highest ever recorded)
02.09.1962	thousands	Munduzara		Iran Midnight
10.12.1967	thousands	Koyna Nagar	India	Morning
27.07.1976	6,55,000	Tangshan	China	Midnight (RS- 8.0)
30.09.1993	30,000	Latur	India	(Richter scale 6.0)
1995	6,400	Kobe	Japan	
17.08.1999	17,000	Istanbul	Turkey	
26.01.2001	1,00,000	Bhuj	India	Morning (Richter scale 7.9)
26.12.2003	41,000	Bam	Iran	
26.12.2004	2,85,000	Sumatra	Indonesia,	Richter scale 8.9,

it unleashed tidal waves, called Tsunami and inundated the coastlines of 12 countries around the Indian Ocean and Earth wobbled on its axis and permanently shifted Sumatra to the South West by 36 m.

Earthquake Proof Construction

Earthquake proof construction can minimize the casualties and reduce the damages in the following manner:

1. Multistory building - to have pile foundations.
2. Beams - to be constructed in the house above the plinth and on top of windows, doors and all the beams be inter-connected.

3. Concrete proportion - 1 Cement: 2 Rubble: 4 Sand and Sweet Water, as required for the mixture and wetting are done sufficiently to get the strength 40 kg / cm.
4. Estimation of load = Twice of actual load + Estimated load of structure + Wind load.
5. Balcony projection - be limited to 1.25 m

2.7. Volcano

Earth's crust is made up of plates, which move @ 10 cm / year. The plates are propelled by convection currents in the upper mantle of the Earth and the areas along the edges of plates are prone to geological upheaval. Molten rock and magma is normally situated about 250 km deep inside the Earth. If it reaches the surface of Earth, it becomes a Volcano. Most of the 550 active volcanoes are found along the edges of plates and more than half of these encircle the Pacific Ocean in the so-called 'Ring of fire'.

Volcanic eruption is caused by the dissolved gases getting released and building up pressure in the magma. When the pressure becomes greater than the surface can hold, the volcano erupts and usually a cone shaped mountain gets formed, which has a crater, through which lava, rocks, hot ash and smoke are thrown out. Volcanic lava is molten rock and has a temperature of 1,000° C, which flows slowly and burns anything in its path. Volcano can cause cracks, swelling and subsidence on the volcano's flanks or dome.

Tilt meter - monitors change in the slope angle on the volcano's flanks or dome and are used as an Earthquake warning device.

Volcanic cloud - consists of smoke, ash and toxic gases including sulphur-dioxide, which pollute the atmosphere over a wide area.

Volcanic lahar - is mud, which flows swiftly, silently and engulfs houses many kilometres away from the volcano.

Five types of volcano: 1. Caldera type, 2. Strato type, 3. Complex type, 4. Shield type and 5. Lava dome type.

Volcanic Eruptions

1. Thera volcano - Thera Island is in the Aegean Sea area of Mediterranean, which got blasted with a force of 150

hydrogen bombs going off simultaneously. This created a gap of 13 km width x 1.5 km depth on the seabed. Dense cloud and smoke covered the Earth for months. In China Sun was dimmed, ice was formed in summer months and crops withered away. In California, USA, the core of a 5,000 year old pine tree showed a ring of dark cells dating back to this year. In Greenland, each year a fresh snowfall builds up a distinct layer in the ice. When the glacier was drilled into, there were traces of Thera sulphur and ash for this year.

2. Tambora volcano - Volume of matter discharged in April 1815 from the eruption of Tamora volcano on the Indonesian Island of Sumbawa was 180 km^3. Tamora also holds the record for the highest death toll of 92,000 people directly and 82,000 people indirectly due to starvation. Volcanic eruption created an ash column of 44 km height.

3. Krakatoa volcano (Caldera type) - Krakatoa Island in the Sundra Strait of Indonesia exploded, when a volcano erupted with a force of 10,000 times of Hiroshima Atom Bomb. The island disappeared in smoke and dust. Earth tremors caused tidal waves, called Tsunami wave 40 m high, which carried a steamship a distance of 2.5 km away, killed 36,000 people and destroyed 165 villages on the coast of Java and Sumatra on 27.08.1883.

   Volcanic ash blocked the Sun for 280 km around Krakatoa for three days and dust from the explosion rose 80 km high, which stopped the Sun warming up the Earth and temperatures returned to normal in 1888. The explosion sound was the loudest sound ever-recorded in human history, which was heard 4,653 km away by the people on Rodriguez Island.

4. Mount Pelee - a volcano erupted, which killed 29,000 people in the seaport of St. Pierre in Caribbean Island on 08.05.1902

VEI (Volcano Explosivity Index)

VEI describes the relative size of a volcanic eruption and is based on factors, such as, volume of material erupted, height of ash cloud and activity is measured on a scale from 0 to 8 and the scale is based on past eruptions and indicates potential for future eruptions and the state 0 is non-explosive and 8 is colossal.

Geysers - are found in the volcanic regions of the world, where pools of water in underground caverns are heated up by Magma and the water boils, steam is formed, pressure is built up, which is forced up through a crevice to the surface of the Earth. There are 1,000 Geysers in the world and their spout can reach a height of 100 m.

2.8. Threat to Earth

25 crore year BC- an asteroid hit the Earth and this was the 1st Mass destruction of life, which destroyed 90 % of all plant and animal life.

6.5 crore year BC- an asteroid 15 km wide hit the Earth and released energy equivalent to 10 crore megaton and this caused a sudden change in climate and this was the 2nd Mass destruction of life on Earth, which destroyed 90 % of ocean life, 70 % of land life and the mighty dinosaurs weighing more than 100 tonnes vanished.

1908 AD- an asteroid of 60 m length exploded over Siberia in Russia with a force of 600 Atomic Bombs (Hiroshima type), which reduced 40 km wide stretch of forestland into ashes.

1937 AD- on 30th October, danger hung over Earth, as sub planet Hermes traveling at the speed of light, missed the Earth by mere 3 seconds, which is a hair like distance in cosmic terms, if it had struck, great havoc might have been caused.

2019 AD- on 1st February an asteroid, called 2002 NT7 may possibly strike the Earth and is 15 km wide and is large enough to release energy with an explosive strength of 10 lakh megaton and can destroy a continent. NASA in USA has reported this.

2027 AD- on 7th August, an asteroid rock called 1999 AN 10, is likely to come very close to Earth and it may miss the Earth by few seconds.

2.9. Moon

Moon 45 crore years ago, planet of the size of Mars collided with the Earth and the debris collected together under its own gravity, which formed the Moon. Moon orbits the Earth from East to West. Moon's distance from the Earth varies from 3.63 lakh km to 4.05 lakh km (1.3 light-second). Moon has no source of its own light, but reflects Sun's light to Earth.

Moon's diameter is 3,380 km, travels in space @ 3,60,000 km / hour, takes 27.3 days to go once round the Earth and spins on its own axis in 27.3 days. This makes the same side of Moon always visible from the Earth. Moon's temperature during daytime goes up to 100° C and during the night falls to (–) 100° C. Moon's half portion facing the Sun is always lighted, but we see only Moon's phases from Earth. Moon rises every day with a difference of 48 minutes.

Moon shields the Earth from meteorite hits and stabilizes Earth's tilt, just as clock has counter balancing weights. Moon's distance from the Earth is ideal and this regulates the tides, which circulate water in the oceans and sweeps away the waste products from the shores. If the Moon had been closer to Earth, it would have caused great tides, which would wreck the harbours. If the Moon had been further away, it would not cause the tides to rejuvenate the waters of the oceans with oxygen.

2.10. Mystery of the Visible Universe

Man's most powerful Hubble space telescope was focused, which looked through a tube, the diameter of a human hair and was focused on the spot near the Big Dipper Star, where the light emanating was 400 crore times fainter than detectable with human eye. This was done to know the vastness of the visible universe and to know how far we can see in the universe. Astronomers were amazed to see 1,500 galaxies of various shapes, sizes and colours. It is estimated that around 10,000 crore galaxies exist in the universe. The farthest galaxy was 1,000 crore light-year away from us.

Big Bang theory as we study it today is merely one of a series of Big Bangs, which are occurring ever since time infinite, where the present visible universe has come into being after a massive explosion; after this massive explosion, matter was thrown out into the space; the thrown matter accelerated; this acceleration phase of the universe is still going on, as such, the distance between galaxies is increasing in all directions.

It is scientifically estimated that the acceleration phase of the universe will stabilize after some timed in the very distant future; at that time the universe will occupy an optimal size in the space; the universe will stabilize for some time; gravity will initiate the deceleration phase of the universe, galaxies will start collapsing on each other; matter will be concentrate; one day the concentrated matter will have critical mass; another Big Bang will occur; this cycle seems to be repeating ever since time infinite.

The present age of the universe gets confirmed through three methods: 1. Burning of stars, 2. Age of stars, 3. Radio-metric elements, which we have on Earth, like: uranium and thorium. If the universe had been very old, then these two elements would have decayed to the element lead metal, but the very presence of uranium and thorium elements prove that the universe is relatively young in age. This conclusion is based on the present lavel of scientific knowledge and the time cycle of acceleration and deceleration phases of the universe will be got calculated in future, as science advances.

Greatest human effort in the history of mankind based on scientific knowledge had been utilized in building the Great Wall of China; construction took place from 221 BC to 210 BC; Wall length 3,460 km; height varies from 4.5 m to 12 m; thickness 9.8 m. This is the only man made structure on the surface of Earth, which is visible from Moon through naked eye.

3

Life

Earth is the only planet in the Solar System, which supports life, better respect life in all its forms.

1st and 2nd Generation stars - in the universe, the stars of these two generations do not have heavy elements necessary for life. There is a narrow window of time in the history of the universe, where life can exist on late born star systems, like our Sun, which have planets like our Earth to support life. Spiral galaxies produce stars late enough in their history that they can take advantage of the elements that are essential for life and only 6 % galaxies in the universe fall under this category.

Life is feasible - at a distance of 2 / 3 from the center of our Milky Way Galaxy. Sun is roughly situated at this distance. Life is impossible at the center and at the outer edges of our galaxy, because stars at the center of the Milky Way Galaxy are so jam-packed together that the mutual gravity destroys the planetary orbits and the high radiation level destroys the life.

Fluorine - if the stars are too far away, there would not be heavy elements left over from the exploded remains of supernova. Heavy element fluorine is an essential element of life, which supernova does not make. Fluorine is made on the surface of white-dwarf-star, which is a burned out star, glowing like a cinder in a fire place. Orbiting the white-dwarf-star is another star like our Sun, which has not exhausted its nuclear fuel. Sun like star pulls the fluorine from the surface of the white-dwarf-star, drags the fluorine down to it and this initiates nuclear reaction that produces fluorine. Then gravitational interactions produce strong stellar winds, which blow the fluorine from the surface of the white-dwarf-star and blast the fluorine into outer space, which the future stars absorb to sustain life.

Origin of life - chemical evolution theory suggests that initially our planet Earth was covered with a warm, slightly alkaline ocean. Ultra-violet light from Sun, geothermal energy from volcanoes, shock waves from thunder and cosmic radiation acted upon the gases of the primitive atmosphere to cause the formation of amino-acids, sugars, proteins, nucleic-acids and cell membranes. Randomly, these compounds came together into the first protocell, which in course of time became more complex, until the first living cell came into existence. Living cells had the molecule, which carryed the vital information that defines life, its nature and its functions. Thus from inanimate things, life originated on Earth

Plant life - appeared first. Plant life slowly enriched the atmosphere with oxygen through photo-synthesis process. The process converted carbon-di-oxide from the volcanoes into oxygen. Oxygon enriched the atmosphere to support bacterial life forms. In 1953, researchers synthesized amino-acids and proteins in a simulated primitive Earth environment.

Seven characteristics of living things:

1. Adaptation - living things adapt to the environmental changes in a short term by changing the behavior pattern and adapts itself in the long term through evolution cycle.
2. Growth - living things show inherited and controlled structural growths, like animals grow up to their maturity.
3. Metabolism - living things break down the food into energy and create complex substances, like proteins in animals.
4. Movement - living things move freely, while plants move by growth.
5. Reproduction - living things ensure continuation of the species.
6. Responsiveness - living things respond to external stimuli.
7. Consciousness - living things are aware of their environment and they try to save themselves from danger.

Five types of organism (Smaller living thing):

1. Virus - lie on the borderline between living and non-living thing. They do not have all the characteristics of life. Virus do not have cell wall and cannot move by itself, but contain genetic material, which has the ability to reproduce by taking part of living cell from other living organism, like plant and animal. Virus is the smallest microorganism that causes infection and disease in human.
2. Bacterium - is a single celled organism, which is found in every environment. They cause disease in humans. Bacterium is the smallest living thing that can be seen through a powerful microscope. Some bacteria cause food poisoning, while others break down the food to release nutrients.
3. Protozoan – is a single celled organism that feeds by scavenging other microorganisms, like: bacteria.
4. Fungus - grow as branching threads. They are capable of remaining dormant for years before causing disease.
5. Worm - is a small limbless invertebrate animal and is a complex organism that range in size from microscopic to several meters long. They are capable of infecting humans.

Species

Species include plants, animals, birds, and insects and so far 17.5 lakh species have been scientifically identified. Efforts are going on to identify the remaining 111 lakh species, which are believed to exist. It is estimated that more than 99 % of all plant and animal species are extinct and during the last 200 years 1,600 animals and 700 types of plants have gone extinct.

Life span - is roughly four times the childhood period of a species:

Life form	*Childhood*	*Times*	*Life span*
Insects			1day (Fly round a lamp).
Ant	1 yr	1 x 4	3 yrs.
Rabbit	1.5 yrs	1.5 x 4	6 yrs.
Cat	3 yrs	3 x 4	13 yrs.

(Contd.)

(Contd. Table)

Life form	*Childhood*	*Times*	*Life span*
Man	20 yrs.	20 x 4	80 yrs (Normal).
Dog	3 yrs.	3 x 4	12 yrs.
Horse	3 yrs.	3 x 4	12 yrs.
Camel	6 yrs.	6 x 4	24 yrs.

Fossils - are the remains of animals and vegetation, which have turned into stony substances. Based on the half-life of potassium, uranium and carbon-14, which are found in the fossils, the age of the fossils, have been reckoned, as to when the fossils were living. Potassium and uranium isotopes have much higher half-lives and are used for reckoning the life of fossils in millions of years. Carbon-14 decays to nitrogen-14 with a half-life of 5,730 years. This method is used for reckoning the life of fossils up to 50,000 years. Every living thing has Carbon-14, when it was living, but soon after death, carbon-14 starts decaying and the present count of carbon-14 gives the age, when the living thing was alive.

Fossil records testify that life sprang on Earth 380 crore years ago and 36 lakh years ago, mankind evolved on Earth. Fossils indicate that there were 30,000 land animals, but today only 15,000 species of animals are found on Earth. This shows that the rest of the species have gone extinct.

3.1. Time Scale of Evolution of Life

380 crore-year BC - Earth's outer surfaces cooled, hardened, vapours condensed to form water and weather system got established.

350 crore-year BC - Earth's atmosphere consisted of Ammonia, Methane, Hydrogen and Water vapour, but the Earth was still quite hot and the cooling process was continuing. Earth was surrounded with clouds and lightning was taking place.

250 crore-year BC - vegetation life form evolved on land. Plant life through the process of photosynthesis produced oxygen,

which has affinity with water. This process enriched the ocean waters with oxygen.

196 crore-year BC - through a process of mutation from bacterial life forms, multi cellular life forms evolved.

194 crore-year BC - from the multi cellular life forms, invertebrate life forms evolved.

192 crore-year BC - from invertebrate life forms, fish life forms evolved.

190 crore-year BC - from the fish life forms, amphibian life forms evolved. These amphibian life forms could live both on land and in water.

180 crore-year BC - from the amphibian life forms, reptile life forms evolved. They lived on land and as well as in water.

150 crore-year BC - from reptile life forms, mammal life forms evolved.

140 crore-year BC - from amphibian life forms, insect life forms evolved. Insects adapted themselves to the terrain, where they lived in different parts of the world.

135 crore-year BC - from the insect life forms, bird life forms evolved. They have the instinct to build nests and in search of food, some birds developed an instinct to migrate to other lands, as seasons changed.

100 crore-year BC - Earth's atmosphere got rich in oxygen, ozone layer developed, which protected the life on Earth from Sun's harmful radiation and through a process of mutation from mammal life form ape-like creatures evolved.

25 crore-year BC - an asteroid hit the Earth. This was the 1st Mass destruction of life on Earth, which destroyed 90 % of all plant and animal life forms.

22 crore-year BC - Late Triassic Period, dinosaurs first appeared and were the biggest animals ever evolved. They roamed for the next 18 crore years. Dinosaurs had the ability to walk at 6.5 km / hour and could sprint at 30 km / hour.

15 crore-year BC - Late Jurassic Period saw the arrival of bigger dinosaurs. The plant eating dinosaur Plodocus was 26 m long and weighed 100 tonnes; longest dinosaur was 41 m long; heaviest dinosaur weighed 100 tonnes. Dinosaur

named Brachiosaurus was the largest dinosaur that ever lived on Earth, was 16 m tall, 26 m long and weighed 80 tonnes.

Wonders of Vegetation Life Forms

1 Fastest growing plant - bamboo vulgaris, can grow at the rate of 5 cm / hr (5 feet / day)

Wonders of Animal Life Forms

1. Dam builder-beaver - through instinct the beaver builds same type of dams' generation after generation, which impounds large quantities of water.
2. Fastest running animal - cheetah is the fastest running animal, can run at 110 km / hour and weighs 72 kg.
3. Largest, heaviest mammal and animal - blue whale, 24 m long, weighs up to 160 tonnes, has the slowest heartbeat of 4 to 8 beats / minute, makes the loudest sound at 188 dB at low frequency, which was measured 8 km away with special instruments.

Wonders of Bird Life Forms

1. Fastest flying bird - peregrine falcon, can reach speeds in excess of 300 km / hr and weighs 900 gm.

   Bird migration - is the ability of some birds to navigate accurately across thousands of kilometers over unknown territory. They land at the right regions at the right time of the year to feed and to breed. Scientific experiments have revealed that the migrating birds have inherited this ability and they use stars at night and Sun during daytime. Migratory birds subconsciously process altitude, latitude and longitude to fly unerringly to a predetermined place on Earth. They have an internal clock and calendar to let them know, when to start and finish their migration. Most wonderful thing is that they are able to reach their destination even on their very first trip.

   (1) Longest migration - bird golden plyover, nests in Canada and Alaska in North America; undertakes the

longest nonstop migration flight from North Eastern tip of Canada; circumnavigates across the Atlantic Ocean down to Brazil and Argentina in South America; a journey of 3,800 km. When the season is over; they travel back Northwards; take a different route through South and Central America; up the Mississippi River basin all the way back to their nesting grounds in Canada and Alaska. They do this flawlessly year after year during winter season in Northern hemisphere and return back in summer season. Thus they remain in Sunlight through out the year.

(2) Reunion migration - bird white throated warbler, migrates from Germany to Africa. When the adult birds migrate; they leave their offspring's behind, but several weeks later, when the young birds are strong enough; they instinctively fly across thousands of kilometers over unknown lands and seas. They arrive at the same spot, where their parents are waiting for them.

Wonders of Fish Life Forms

1. Amazing life cycle of salmon fish – they hatch from eggs in streams, spend few years of life in fresh water lakes and rivers, grow to several centimeters, swim down the stream to the ocean, where they adapt to saltwater life, spend the next few years there, eventually towards the end of their life, they leave the ocean, swim upriver, upstream against the current until they reach the same very stretch of stream, where they were hatched years ago, here they die, the decaying bodies provide nutrients for the newly laid eggs, the eggs hatch to start a new generation, repeating the same cycle all over again.
2. Decoy fish - swim in Hawaiian waters. When hunting, it raises its dorsal fin, which appears like a small fish complete with mouth and eyes. It then stays motionless, except for the dorsal fin, which moves side to side to make the decoy-fish appear to open and close its mouth. This creates an optical illusion to an incoming fish. The incoming fish lands directly into the jaws of the waiting fish.

3.2. Evolution of Human Life

Apes do not have tails, which make them different from monkeys, who have tails. Apes see the things in colour. They are able to spot the ripe fruits. Apes belong to two different families: 1. Lesser apes - are gibbons and 2. Greater apes - are gorillas, chimpanzees and humans. Chimpanzees make their own tools including shaping sticks to dig up termites. Humans and chimps share 98 % of the same genes, while 2 % genes are different.

Time Scale of Evolution of Human Life

15 crore-year BC - Late Jurasic Period, mutation occurred in an apelike creature in Tanzania in Central Africa and apelike-looking-mouse appeared, who has 16 pairs of chromosomes.

12.7 crore-year BC - Early Cretaceous Period, predator dinosaurs appeared.

9.0 crore-year BC - Cretaceous Period, from apelike-looking-mouse through a process of mutation, evolution of human life form began, who has 23 pairs of chromosomes. Genetically speaking, we are not very much different from mouse life form, as 97.1 % genes are common to both human beings and mouse, while 2.9 % of genes are unique to humans and 2.9 % genes are unique to mouse life.

6.5 crore-year BC - Late Cretaceous Period, saw the end of dinosaurs, when an asteroid 10 km wide smashed into Mexico's Yucatan Peninsula. This released energy equivalent to 10 lakh times the energy required to cause a powerful earthquake. This energy activated many volcanoes around the Earth, volcanic smoke and dust engulfed the Earth. Sunrays were blocked for many years. This caused sudden change in climate, 90 % of ocean life, 70 % of land life was destroyed and the mighty dinosaurs weighing more than 100 tonnes vanished from Earth for ever. This was the 2nd Mass destruction of life on Earth.

6.5 crore-year BC - common ancestor of monkey and ape named Primate evolved, who had some resemblance to human beings.

3.0 crore-year BC - from Primate Life, a species known as Anthropoid evolved, who had more resemblance to human beings. This happened in Tanzania in Central Africa.

70 lakh-year BC - from Anthropoid, a species known as Gorilla evolved, who had still more resemblance to human being. He became a common ancestor to human being and to chimpanzee.

50 lakh-year BC - from chimpanzee, Australopithecus evolved, who had Human looking like features and had more intelligence than a chimpanzee.

39 lakh-year BC - from Australopithecus, Afarensis evolved, who had human physical characteristics in respect of bone structure and had protruding jaw, like that of a chimpanzee. Afarensis was biped (Walking on two legs), had a small brain, like that of a chimpanzee and lived in Tanzania, Central Africa.

An Afarensis's upright skeleton was found and was named Lucy. She is considered to be the mother of all mankind and her skeleton remains as a reference point with which other human fossils are compared. Her brain size was 450 – 500 cc, which is mid-way between apes and humans.

33.6 lakh-year BC - from Afarensis, Hominid evolved, who had more intelligence. He was living in Tanzania, Central Africa. During this time, a volcano erupted, lava flowed ou, a Hominid ran for safety and in the processing of running made 57 footprints on a hot lava bed, which contained plaster of Paris. As it was raining then, the footprints soon got solidified. These 57 footprints are still preserved and are a great tourist attraction. Anthropologist Mr. Marry Lekay estimated the height of this Hominid to be 122 cm. Hominids from Tanzania migrated to other parts of the world.

25 lakh-year BC - from Hominids, Parathropus Boisei evolved, whose remains had been discovered in East Africa. He had a skull, which was adopted for chewing tough vegetation, had large molar and premolar teeth. He pelted stones to drive away the wild animals. He developed hand held stone tools for hunting.

22 lakh-year BC - from Parathropus Boisei, Homo habilis (Handy man) evolved. He had 500 - 800 cc brain, about half the size of a present day human being and increase in brain size lead to development of better tools. This marked the beginning of human civilization. Homo habilis had more human like features. He lived in Tanzania, Central Africa.

19 lakh-year BC- from Homo habilis, Homo Ergas evolved, who had large brain. He improvised his hand held stone tools into axes. He used rudimentary form of language for communication. He lived in families and in search of food migrated from Africa to other continents of the world.

18 lakh-year BC - from Homo Ergas, Homo erectus (Upright man) evolved. He looked more like the present day man. He is considered to be the direct ancestor of modern mankind. He migrated from Africa to other continents of the world. He used a developed language and gestures for communication. He was eating cooked food. This developed his brain to 1,000 cubic cm.

14 lakh-year BC - from Homo erectus, Homo Sapien (Modern man) evolved. He looked similar to us, used fire for warmth, prepared tasty foods, lit fires to drive away predator animals and from here, it is considered that modern human life started.

Scientific Classification of Human Life

Anthropology is the science of mankind and is concerned with all humans at all times. Science explores the biological, linguistic and symbolic dimensions of mankind. Taxonomy is the classification of plants and animals, which gives the classification of human life in seven stages from most general to most specific:

1. Kingdom: Animalia - having cell membrane, but lacking cell walls.
2. Phylum: Animals - with a vertebrate column.
3. Class: Mammalia - warm blooded animals with mammary glands and females secrete milk to nourish their young ones.
4. Order: Primates - have collarbones, eyes face forward, grasping hand with fingers and thumb and have two types of teeth (Incisors and Molars).

5. Family: Hominidae - have upright posture, large brain, and stereoscopic vision and have flat face.
6. Genus: Homo - have curved spine.
7. Species: Homosapiens - have high forehead, developed chin and skull bones.

Human Evolution on a Straight Line

Molecular biology provides a new kind of data, which adds to the knowledge of our past life. Fossil evidence suggests that anatomically modern humans evolved in Africa in the last 2 lakh

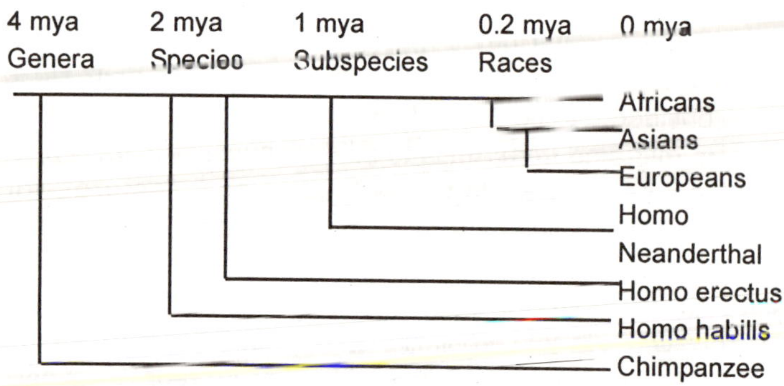

years. Our physical characteristic makes us different from Apes. We have high round skull and facial retraction. Human evolution can be represented on a straight line in mya (Million year ago):

Human Migration

DNA studies reveal that ancestors to present-day human race had migrated from Central African region to other continents of the world in two waves: 1st Wave human migration and 2nd Wave human migration:

1st Wave Human Migration

8.4 lakh-year BC - human migration took place from Africa to other continents of the world.

5 lakh-year BC - human settlements at Kanker in Chhattisharh State in India took place. People ate natural foods, like: fruits and roots of trees.

2.3 lakh-year BC - Homo Neanderthal settlements near the town of Heidelberg in Germany, France and Greece in Europe, Zambia in Africa took place. People used javelins for haunting. Ice-age prevailed on Earth. Homo Neanderthalensis developed burial rites for their dead persons.

2.0 lakh years ago, from Homo Neanderthalensis, Human race developed. People looked much similar to us. Rudiments of religious activities started in different parts of the world and burial rites became common. Human remains of a modern man has been discovered in Ethiopia in Africa, which is 1.6 lakh year old. This is the oldest human remain of a person so far discovered in the world.

2nd Wave Human Race Migration

1.5 lakh-year BC - Human migration took place from Central African region to other continents of the world.

1.4 lakh-years BC - Homo sapiens in search of food moved to other continents of the world. They inhabited different parts of the world. They lived in caves for protection against wild animals and weather. They domesticated wild cows and buffaloes for milk.

3.3. Human Life

Human life dependent on mother - begins eight months before birth, when for the first time the tiny heart of the fetus begins to beat, independently of the mother's heart beat, while brain and other parts of the fetus are still developing. At this stage of development, the fetus is completely dependent on mother for sustenance.

Human life independent of mother - begins when a baby cries after birth for the first time and in the process, breathes in air for the first time to sustain an independent life. The time of cry of the baby is taken as the time of birth in Indian astrology.

Human Cell

Cell is the smallest unit of human body, which has life. Each cell has thousands of structural components and Chromosomes control cell's processes in the nucleus. We are unconscious of the incomprehensible complexity of our own creation. We are not aware of what goes on in our own cells. Human Genome directs the cells to convert amino-acids into proteins, proteins to make cell walls, cell walls to split and divide to form another cell. It is amazing as to how crores of atoms in each DNA molecule arrange themselves perfectly for the self-perpetuation, which we call life.

Self-replicating cells exist, due to inherent intelligent system, which involves crores of functions, interact perfectly; otherwise the cells would become dead. Heart tissue cells, liver tissue cells, skin cells and blood cells are so distinctly different and perform different functions, but each cell has the same DNA. It is a wonder that how a cell knows its identity, function and position in the body.

Cells are nature's building blocks. Animals and plants are all made up of cells and each cell has four parts:

1. Nucleus - the inner body of the cell, which acts as cell's brain.
2. Membrane - the thin wall of the cell, which acts as cell's skin.
3. Cytoplasm - soft stuff, which fills the space between cell's nucleus and membrane.
4. Mitochondria - these meet the energy needs of the cell.

Cells carry out all the functions of life. Most of the cells are so small that they can be seen only through a microscope. In the cells, different chemical reactions take place to produce proteins, enzymes, carbohydrates, lipids, amino acids and nucleic acids (DNA) and RNA. They control heredity. All cells have the same basic component, but vary in shape, form and function. A collection of similar cells with a specific function is called a Tissue. Groups of tissues form an organ. Normal size of animal cell is 0.01 mm, but human brain cell is 0.005 mm, while nerve cells are as long as 1.2 mm, but are narrower than a hair.

DNA (Deoxyribo Nucleic Acid)

DNA is the chemical parent of all the cells in our body. DNA is found in each cell's nucleus and is the command center of the cell. DNA acts at the molecular level. DNA is both a substance and an instructional blueprint for every cell, which makes our body. DNA is structured in a ladder like formation of two strands with rungs creating a double helix shape. The ladder forms a continuous giant molecule called chromosome, which has a diameter of 2 nano-meters.

DNA's two long intertwined strands appear like stilts made of an alternating phosphate and sugar. The step like rungs between the strands are made up of paired bases of nitrogen compounds identified by the letters: G, C, A and T (First letters of four kinds of bases: Guanine, Cytosine, Adenine and Thymine). These are the only substances in DNA, hence the Genome consists of only these four alphabets, but they are in seemingly endless sequence. These compounds tell every cell of our body, what to do and communicate through certain sequences on the genome and the bands of these compounds are the genes.

DNA carries the genetic information from generation to generation and has self-replicating mechanism. Molecules of DNA multiply, as we grow from infancy to maturity and every cell continues to carry every trait and characteristic, with which we began our life. Humans share 98.7 % of DNA with chimpanzees, the closest living creature to us in the evolution cycle.

Chromosomes

Chromosomes are reproductive cells, which contain a long thread like substance, called Chromosome, which controls heredity. The sperm cell from a male parent, when unites with an egg cell from a female parent, the result is a third cell, which is a combination of chromosomes from each parent. This combination can take place in crores and crores of ways and on account of this unlimited variation; no two human beings are born alike.

Chromosomes carry human body formation information from one generation to the next generation. They are made out of DNA and Histon Protein. Human body has 23 pairs of chromosomes; out of which 22 pairs are similar in man and woman and are called Autosom, which determine the formation of human body. The 23rd Pair of chromosome is different in man and in woman; woman has XX chromosome, while man has XY chromosome, as such, man can only give XY Chromosome in reproduction for a male child to born.

Chromosomes carry information in bunches and bunch portion of chromosome is called Gene. DNA finger printing is to identify the order of genes present in a chromosome, which establishes one's identity and inheritance. Chromosomes get transferred from parents to their children. Children get half chromosomes from their mother and half from their father, as such; children are close to their parents in appearance.

Genes

Genes are paired on each chromosome with sequences that account for specific traits and physical characteristics. Each body trait requires one or more pairs of genes. Traits are: eye colour, shape of body parts and susceptibility to diseases, all these are found within the gene pairs of the genome. There are 80,000 to 1, 00,000 genes in the human genome. Every activity of each cell is controlled by the production of proteins. There are 35,000 pairs of genes in each human body cell.

Several plant life forms have far greater number of genes than us, like: rice has 50,000 genes and each gene has sections of tightly coiled DNA Strands. DNA strand is self-replicating and consists of units called Bases. The sequence of Bases spells out a chemical code, called: Genetic Code, which carries the inherited characteristics from parent to baby. The inherited characteristics further get passed down to the next generation.

Human Genome Project (HGP)

US National Institute of health, the world's largest institute funding medical research has announced that they have deciphered 90 % of human genome and the decade old project is churning out 12,000 letters of genetic code every minute of every day from the last 10 years; creating a list that will total more than 300 crore, when completed. About 1,100 biologists, computer scientists and analysts in six countries are working to complete the HGP, which will be the biology's version of human life. One in every 1,300 DNA letters, are what make us an individual, except for the identical twins, no one has the same combination. Thus we are genetically distinct from every other human being.

Start of Human Life

Every living thing we see is made up of atoms. Atoms combine to make molecules, which make a single cell. We start our life as a single cell and molecules combine, breakdown, recombine into the same type or other molecules. This process keeps on going, day in and day out to provide energy and cell maintenance for our body. We developed from a single cell into a fetus, cells multiplied to form a baby, after birth from baby into infancy, from infancy into childhood, from childhood into adolescence and from adolescence into adulthood of age 18 years. During this process from single cell to adulthood, we have been adding10 crore cells every minute.

Human Body

We have 50 lakh hairs, which have an average life of 3 years. Our body has enough fat to make a soap cake, enough lime to white wash a shed, enough phosphorus to make 2,000 match sticks, enough iron to make a long nail, enough sulphur to fill one spoon and enough carbon to make 12.7 kg coke. Our saliva and tears are slightly antiseptic; stomach acids digest food and kill dangerous bacteria and viruses, which invade us from time to time.

We have 305 bones at birth and as we grow, the bones fuse together to become 206 bones. We have 100 joints, 650 muscles, 1.85 square meter of skin surface and the top layer skin has an average life of five days. Our muscles anchor to bones and can withstand a stress of 1.25 tonnes / sq. cm. When we walk, the thighbones can take a strain of 0.15 tonnes / sq. cm. In our life, we walk around 11,000 km in urban areas and 45,000 km in rural areas. We can sprint at 40 km / hour, can throw at 160 km / hr and are capable of jumping 2.1 m.

Three Types of Human Immunity System

1. Active immunity - germs are introduced artificially in the body. They release a poisonous substance called antigen, which stimulate production of a different type of white cells, which have a defensive chemical called antibody. These antibodies after their victory over poisonous substances get disbanded, but some persist in the blood stream for a long time and act

as natural defense against second attack. In active immunity, cowpox germs are injected to develop resistance against a more dangerous disease called smallpox.

2. Passive immunity - the unborn baby acquires it from the blood stream of mother and after birth; the baby acquires it through breast-feeding in the first few days and the function of white cells in the blood stream is to fight diseases.
3. Lymphatic immunity - protects the body by fighting out and destroying foreign bodies, like infection causing organisms and the system collects excess fluid from the tissues.

Six Types of Human Adaptation

With time, changes take place in human body to make it more suitable to a particular climate, which prevails in different parts of the world. This is called adaptation and the changes, which have taken place, are:

1. Eyes - Eskimos living in extremely cold climates, have a heavy layer of fat on their eyes, which acts as insulation against freezing temperatures. The eyelid folds are so heavy, that they open to a slit to protect against Sun-glare, which gets reflected from the snow. Eskimos have eyes, which are quite different from ours.

   Seeing - when we look at an object, our eyes send information about the object's color, shape, depth, distance and movement to our brain. Brain puts all the information together to identify the whole object. Process of seeing involves: light falls on an object, gets reflected, enters our eyes through the pupil, iris changes the size of the pupil depending how bright is the light, lens focuses the light on to retina, which has photo-receptors (Light sensitive nerve cells), which change light signals into electrical signals, which are carried to the brain for interpretation.

   When we look at an object, each of our eyes sees a slightly different picture, which helps us to know how far the object is. When we look at a moving object, signals go to a special part of the brain, which enables us to see the object moving, but any damage to this part of brain, results in the object to be seen as a still object, which changes positions constantly, like moving car, is perceived as a still car, which changes positions, but not actually the movement.

Eye is a most remarkable organ and electrical signals from each retina pass along the optic nerve, which meet at a junction and from here, half of the nerve fibers from left eye cross to the right side and vice versa. Fibers continue along the optic tract to the brain, where the image is interpreted as an upright object. Light sensitive retina at the back of the eye, has three types of cone cells, each of which is sensitive to the primary colors: BGR (Blue, Green, Red) and brain interprets the combination of these primary colors into thousands of hues. If the cones are faulty, this may lead to color blindness, which is an inherited disease.

We have visual abilities of judging speed, distance and integrate the movements to catch a flying ball and can thread a needle. Eyes have a remarkable power of accommodation, like: Instantly shifting sight from a close object to a distant object, which requires re-adjustment of lens and from dim light condition to bright-light condition, which requires adjustment of pupil.

2. Nose - people living in higher altitudes have prominent nose bridges, which lengthens the nasal passage to heat up the cold air for breathing, as cold air is harmful to health and may prove fatal in some cases.

Smelling - different smells, trigger different receptor cells in the lining of our nose and most smells are a mixture of several odorants. Smell receptors in the roof of the nasal cavity are stimulated by odors and nerve impulses carry them to the brain for interpretation. We can detect 2,000 different smelling substances or odorants.

Pheromones the chemicals carrying sexual signals to members of the same species, are detected in the VNO (Vomero Nasal Organ) in the nose, which are separate from smell receptor cells, but we no longer use VNO.

3. Tongue - we have around 4,000 taste buds on our tongue, mouth and throat. Each bud contains up to 100 taste receptors, which respond to different substances in our food. Taste buds send information about the type and amount of substance to our brain.

Six basic types of tastes:

1. Astringent taste - is given by beans, pulses, and fruits like pomegranate.
2. Bitter taste - is given by green and yellow vegetables, such as cauliflower, cabbage and spinach. Our ability to taste bitter substances protects us from swallowing harmful substances, as many poisonous plants taste bitter.
3. Pungent taste - is given by spices like ginger, garlic, onion, pepper, mustard, cloves and cumin seeds and the acquired taste of chilli and pepper makes them hot, which is liked by many people.
4. Salty taste - is given by pickles and rock salt.
5. Sour taste - is given by yoghurt, buttermilk and fruits like oranges and lime.
6. Sweet taste - is given by sugar, ripe fleshy fruits like mangoes.

   Tongue and nose - detect certain chemicals in the environment and both these senses are closely linked. These two senses are less developed in humans than in some animals. Information about taste and smell is sent to a number of areas in our brain, which give emotional reactions.

4. Skin - people get varying amounts of exposure to Sunrays in different parts of the world, which turns the skin brown in Asia, yellow in China, white in Europe and black near the equator, which gives protection against summer heat.

Our skin receptors detect touch, pressure, vibration, temperature, pain and pleasure. We have 40 lakh receptors in the skin to feel comfort, pain, hotness and coldness. Our fingertips and lips have 202 touch receptors in every one sq. cm of surface. These are the most sensitive parts of the human body. Our skin sensory receptors respond to stimuli and transmit data to the brain, which processes the data, to let us know, as to what is happening with us.

When we touch something, we detect it through Mechano-receptors situated below the skin. These send information to the brain. The distance between two close pin-points, is sensed as one touch and the distance varies from part to part of the body, like: it is 2 mm on finger tips and lips, varies from 10 to 40 mm at other points of the body. Human body's normal temperature is 36.9° C.

5. Seven Types of Rhythmic Cycles

1. Sleep - after every 16 hours of work, we sleep for eight hours and for one third of our life we sleep. During sleep our heart rate drops, muscles relax, breathing slows and we respond less to out side world. Sleep restores body's energy. EEG (Electro Encephalo Graphy) measure electrical brain activity, which show that we pass through five stages of sleep:

   Stage 1 to 4 - shows deepest level of sleep and brain becomes less active.

   Stage 5- is level of REM (Rapid Eye Movement), which lasts for 5 - 15 minutes. Our brain becomes active and we dream during this stage.

   The whole cycle of 5 stages lasts about 90 minutes and this cycle keeps on repeating through out the night.

   Human body clock regulates waking, sleeping cycle and is usually 24 hours long. The body clock regulation is related to an area of our brain, called Hypothalamus - the part that is directly connected to our eyes. Baby sleeps for 16 hours a day, adult sleeps for 8 hours a day and an old man above 60 years of age sleeps for 7 hours or less a day. Manual workers go to bed early and rise early, while brainworkers go to bed late and rise late in the morning.
2. Blink - we blink once after every 20 to 30 seconds.
3. Breathing - after every three hours, each nostril is changed automatically for breathing.
4. Hunger - we feel hungry after every 3 to 4 hours.
5. Mental tiredness - every 2 to 3 hours of mental activity, we feel tired, better give some rest to brain cells for some time.
6. Body temperature, blood pressure, pulse, breathing, hormone activity all rise and fall in a rhythmic cycle of 24 hours (Earth's rotation).

7. Menstruation - women follow a 27 day cycle and men too have a monthly cycle, but the effects are less perceptible and cannot be easily noticed.

   Hypothalamus gland, a knob of tissue about the size of a sugar lump, situated at the base of our brain produces a chemical, called Cortisol, which controls the rhythmic cycle.

6. Serotonin - is a naturally produced chemical in our brain, which controls our mood. If the chemical's quantity is more, it induces sleep, increases hunger and develops positive thinking. If the chemical's quantity is less, it produces depression.

3.4. Ages of Mankind

35,000 BC: Old Stone Age - things started getting definite only after this age.

30,000 BC: Early Human Civilizations - developed on the riverbanks in different parts of the world and they used pottery.

25,000 BC: Early Stone Age - hunting scenes of this age are found on cave-walls in geometric and non-geometric forms. Men used fire for cooking and developed improved stone tools.

20,000 BC: Middle Stone Age - men started living in colonies and domesticated wild cattle for milk. Last Ice Age prevailed from 20,000 BC to 10,000 BC. Polar ice caps extended up to 52° latitude North and South.

15,000 BC: Late Stone Age - nomadic hunting was abandoned and people adopted agricultural life style.

10,000 BC: Early Human Civilizations - flourished and people started living in villages and towns. Human race developed concept on the existence of God and based on these concepts, different religions appeared in different parts of the world. People started believing in the existence of heavon (Swarga) and hell (Narka), which an individual's soul may get after death, but the fear of hell goaded the people to behave well in the society. Nationhood concept developed.

7,500 BC: Gujarat Coast Civilization - developed, but later the coastal areas got submerged, the civilization was destroyed and presently Gulf of Khambhat is situated over here.

7,000 BC: New Stone Age - human civilizations framed their own rules to govern themselves. Agriculture developed on scientific lines. People worshiped God in different ways to get his blessings. Lord Rama ruled over Ayodhya during the Age. Wheel was invented and chariots (Raths) were made to go to places.

5,000 BC: Copper Age - copper was used extensively for making utensils, tools and implements for hunting. Lord Krishna migrated from Mathura to Dwarka and established his kingdom over there. Presently, Dwarka is submerged in seawater and Gulf of Kachchh is situated over here.

3,500 BC: Sumerian Civilization - developed.

3,300 BC: Egyptian Civilization - developed in the Nile delta.

3,000 BC: Bronze Age - bronze (Alloy of copper and tin) was used extensively for making knives, daggers and arrowheads.

2,500 BC: Indus (Sindh) Valley Civilization - developed on the banks of Indus River. Scientific knowledge grew in various fields of human activity, rudimentary calendar was developed, based on this calendar, records of floods in the Indus River were maintained and land measuring units were used for land records. Villages and towns developed, which had drainage system.

1,500 BC: Aryan tribes - from the Northwest invaded Indus Valley Civilization and with passage of time, Aryan tribes got merged into the Indus Valley Civilization.

1,000 BC: Iron Age – is the present age and extensive use of iron is made. Scientific and technical knowledge developed. Human population increased by leaps and bounds. Territorial claims became an issue.

800 AD: Arabs - invaded India.

1200 AD: Turks - invaded India.

1500 AD: European traders - came to India.

1800 AD: Britain - assumed political control over India.

1947 AD: India - got independence on 15th August and Pakistan on 14th August.

1957 AD: Russia - launched Sputnik satellite.

1969 AD: USA - launched Apollo Mission to Moon. Neil Armstrong was the first man to put his foot on the surface of Moon on

11th July at 02:56:15 GMT. It is an outstanding achievement in the development of mankind.

1971 AD: India and Pakistan - fought a war. Bangladesh was liberated and 93,000 Pakistani troops surrendered to Indian Forces and this is a record surrender in human history.

2003 AD: India's present ethnic composition - Indo-Aryan 72 %, Dravidian 25 % and Mongoloid 3 %.

3.5. Human Blood

Blood flows through 1, 00,000 km of blood vessels that pack our body. Blood contains four types of cells:

1. Red blood cell - imparts red color to the blood and constitutes 41 % of blood volume. Our blood contains 2 million million red cells, which carry oxygen to different parts of the body. Red cells have an average life of 120 days.
2. White blood cell - destroys bacteria and constitute 4 % of blood volume. Our blood contains 300 crore white cells, which fight infection by engulfing invading organisms. White blood cells have a life of 12 hours. White cells are the main components of the immune system and protect the body against infection, toxins (Produced by bacteria) and cancer.
3. Platelets - are tiny cells and number in billions and billions. They clot together to seal the injured blood vessels and stop bleeding.
4. Plasma - is the fluid part of blood, which contains antibodies that react with antigens of a different blood group, causing the red blood cells to stick together and clumps of red cells are then attacked by the immune system. This immune system response may lead to internal bleeding. Plasma constitutes 55 % of blood volume and carries the nutrients.

Blood Group

Blood group is based on proteins called antigens, which are present on the surface of red blood cells. These determine a person's blood group. Antibodies in the blood are produced against any type of antigens, foreign to the red cells. Proteins are identified through blood test and four blood groups have been identified:

Blood group A - has 'A' antigen on the surface of red blood cells and anti 'B' antibodies in the blood.

Blood group B - has 'B' antigens and anti 'A' antibodies on the surface of red blood cells. This blood group is common in the Asian people.

Blood group AB - is the rarest blood group, which has both antigens on the surface of red blood cells and no antibody in the blood.

Blood group O - the most common blood group, has no red cell antigens and anti 'A' and anti 'B' antibodies in the blood. This blood group is common in the European people.

RH factor - blood is further classified into RH + and RH – and different ethnic groups have different RH factors.

Blood Donation

We can donate 250 to 300 milliliters of blood at a time. After donation, the production of red blood corpuscles increases. Our heart pumps blood at the rate of 4.73 liter / minute in normal condition and 14.2 liter / minute, when we exercise. Vasometer is the part of our brain, which regulates the flow of blood to different parts of the body. The requirement for the blood supply varies from time to time depending upon: we are resting, walking, exercising or running. Blood is to be oxygenated and for this we breathe 50 crore times during our average life span.

Blood Pressure (BP)

BP is the force exerted by the blood against the walls of arteries. Blood pressure depends on the rate and force of heart's contraction. Heart rate and blood pressure are controlled automatically to ensure adequate supply of blood, hence the oxygen to the organs. Adult heartbeats at the rate of 60 - 80 beats / minute at rest and rate can go up to 200 beats / minute at exercise. If BP is too low, not enough blood reaches to the body tissues. If BP is too high, it may damage blood vessels and organs.

Short term BP changes, are induced due to heavy bleeding or change in body posture and this is detected by Baroreceptors, situated in the walls of major arteries. They send signals along sensory nerves to the brain and an automatic response adjusts the heart rate and the volume of blood to be pumped.

Long term control of BP depends upon the action of hormones and kidneys respond to low BP by secreting rennin, which constricts the arteries. This raises the BP.

Systolic pressure - is created when heart contracts and diastolic pressure prevails when heart expands. Blood pressure is measured in millimeters (mm) of mercury (hg). World Health Organization (WHO) standard for assessment of an individual's blood pressure:

Systolic / Diastolic	*Grade*	*Hypertension*
180 / 110 mm hg	3	Severe
160 / 100 mm hg	2	Moderate
149 / 90 mm hg	1	Mild
130 / 85 mm hg	Normal at rest on higher side	
120 / 80 mm hg	Normal at rest on lower side	

Hypertension - is abnormally high blood pressure. It is a common disease and 17 % of population suffers from it. The condition puts extra strain on heart and arteries, which can result in damage to delicate tissues, eyes and kidneys in the long run and ultimately the condition can lead to heart attack, but by adopting the following measures, hypertension can be controlled:

1. Stop smoking
2. Reduce salt and fat in diet
3. Maintain proper body weight
4. Exercise moderately, but regularly.

High BP (blood pressure) is a common disease and symptoms are giddiness, headache, uncomfortableness and some times nothing at all. It is advisable to take water in a copper vessel and reduce the quantity of salt, pickle, papad, ghee and take bath in lukewarm water. Light exercise before breakfast and brisk walk for half an hour in the evening may help to control high BP in a natural way.

Hypotension - is lower than normal blood pressure. If circulation falls below the needed level to the brain, it may cause fainting or sudden getting up may lead to light-headedness. Hypotension can result due to dehydration or salts in the body. Symptoms of hypotension are: tiredness, weakness, fainting, blurred vision, nausea and shock

Cholesterol - is a form of fat, remains in a dissolved state in blood and along with blood circulates in the body. Cholesterol is essential for our body, as it helps in making hormones, which are: 1 Cortisol - guards against infection, 2 Bile acid - helps in absorbing fat from intestines, 3 Vitamin D - helps in building bones. Cholesterol is of five types: 1 Cailomicron, 2 Very low-density lipoprotein, 3 Intermediary density lipoprotein, 4 Low-density lipoprotein and 5 High-density lipoprotein.

Cholesterol level at the time of our birth is 70 mg / deciliter, after one year it increases to 150 mg / deciliter, but does not increase further up to the age of 17 years. The ideal level in an adult is 200 - 239 mg / deciliter and at this level, good high-density lipoprotein should be 50 mg / deciliter. If cholesterol level rises above 250 mg / deciliter, it becomes dangerous for the body, as it sticks to the arteries blocking the blood flow and the heart gets over loaded.

3.6. Human Heart

Heart has 40,000 neurons, which communicate with the brain. Hormones travel in the blood stream, every time the heart beats. It creates pulse waves of pressure and electromagnetic energy, which travel through the body and to the brain. Amazingly, the heart generates a magnetic field 5,000 times more powerful than that of the brain and this can be measured 2 m away from the body.

Heart in a normal condition is: 15 cm long x 10 cm wide and weighs 340 gm. It is situated in the chest, slightly towards the left side. Heart is a muscular organ, made up of special muscle called Myocardium, which is capable of working continuously without rest. Our heart starts working 8 months before our birth and keeps on working till the very end of our life.

Heart as a pump is divided into two halves: 1 Upper half and 2 Lower half:

1. Upper half - has thin walls and has two chambers: 1 Right Atrium - which receives de-oxygenated (Blue) blood from the body and 2 Left Atrium - which receives oxygenated (Red) blood from the lungs.

2. Lower half - has thick walls and has two chambers: 1 Right Ventricle and 2 Left Ventricle. One half pumps blood (Blue) into the lungs to get rid of carbon-di-oxide and absorb oxygen, while the other half pumps blood (Red) into the body.

Thus heart has four chambers and works like two pumps: one to move the blood into the lungs and other to push blood into the body. Pulse is the rate of heart beat / minute, which can vary from 40 to 200 beats / minute depending upon the level of activity being performed.

Heartbeat

Single pumping action of heart is called heartbeat, which normally takes 0.3 second to contract, 0.2 second to expand and takes rest for 0.5 second. Normal adult heartbeat is 60 – 80 beats / minute at rest, children have higher heartbeat and elderly person may have 50 beats / minute. Heart normally beats 55 times / minute during sleep and 72 times / minute, when we are awake. One-way valves in the heart permit flow of blood in one direction only and blood cannot return unless the valve leaks.

A new born baby has resting heartbeat of 120 / minute, the rate continues to slow down, by the age of 12 - 18 years, the resting heartbeat becomes 60 to 80 / minute. After the age of 40 years, artery walls loose elasticity and cause rise in blood pressure. At the age of 60 years, heart muscles become less elastic; heart has to pump harder and is not able to respond to increased efforts. At the age of 85 years, the heart is not able to endure for long periods of activity and soon the person becomes tired.

Three Phase of Heartbeat

1. Diastole - heart relaxes, blood flows into the upper chambers of the heart.
2. Atria systole - upper chambers of the heart contract and push blood into the lower chambers called ventricles.
3. Ventricle systole - lower chambers of the heart contract, the right ventricle chamber pushes blood into the lungs and the left ventricle chamber pushes blood into the body.

Two Blood Circulation Circuits

1. Systemic circuit - is the oxygen rich blood circuit, which carries nutrients and hormones to every cell of the body

through the arteries, where the nutrients and oxygen are absorbed, waste products like carbon-di-oxide is picked up by the blood. Blood returns back to heart through the veins. Our body contains 5 to 6 liters of blood.

2. Pulmonary circuit - carries the blood to lungs, where carbon-di-oxide is liberated, oxygen is picked up and waste products are taken to the liver for processing and final elimination through the kidneys.

Heart Attack (Myocardial infraction)

Heart attack is loss of blood supply to a part of the heart muscle due to blockage in a coronary artery. Sometimes, blood cells called Platelets stick in the narrowed area of an artery. It triggers formation of blood clot, which blocks blood flow through the artery and this leads to heart attack. Aspirin tablet helps in reducing stickiness in the blood and prevents clotting after a heart attack. Symptoms of heart attack develop suddenly and may include:

1. Crushing pain in the center of the chest, spreading to neck and into the arms especially in the left arm or discomfort or distress in one or both arms.
2. Heavy cold sweating, faintness and pale skin.
3. Shortness of breadth.
4. Nausea and vomiting
5. Anxiety and fear of dying.
6. Restlessness.
7. Sensation of pressure, fullness and squeezing.

Precautions against Heart Attack

One lakh Indians die every year due to heart attack and this alarming condition can be controlled through the following measures:

1. Stop smoking.
2. Stop alcoholic drinks.
3. Take regular exercise for 20 / 30 minutes every day.
4. Avoid stressful situations
5. Eat healthier diet, rich in fruits with low fat and low salt. Fatty meals increase the number of tiny fat-globules in the blood stream. They get attached to the red blood cells and form

sludge like matter, which sticks to the inner surface of the arteries. This blocks blood supply to the heart.

Heart Problems

1. Heart's electrical system - is controlled by Senatorial Node situated in the heart's right atrium. When this natural pacemaker becomes defective due to degeneration of cells, a cardiac pacemaker is installed to maintain regular heartbeat.
2. Angina - is chest pain, originating in the heart muscle during physical activity and it gets relieved on rest. The pain is due to inadequate supply of blood to the heart muscle.
3. Pulmonary Oedema - Is the situation, where hearts ability to pump blood is reduced and back up pressure causes accumulation of fluid in the lungs. This condition is life threatening.
4. Cardiac arrest - is sudden failure of heart to pump blood, brain and organs do not get oxygenated blood. This leads to brain damage within 3 minutes and death within 5 minutes, if the pumping action is not restored by emergency action. Cardiac arrest is caused by electrical problem in the heart and is of two types:
   1. Ventricular fibrillation - lower chambers of the heart rapidly contract in an uncoordinated manner, preventing the heart from pumping out blood.
   2. Asystole - is an electrical problem of the heart, where total failure of the heart muscle to contract occurs. This is called cardiac arrest and within seconds the person looses consciousness. His lips, fingers and toes turn blue, pulse and breadth stop and the person collapses.

3.7. Human Organs

1. Glands - are complex organs, which secrete special fluids into the blood stream and the secreted fluids control body functions. Different glands are:
   (1) Pineal gland - is a peanut size knob of gray and white tissue. It is shaped like a pinecone and is buried at the back of the skull on the mid-line of the brain. Like an eye, the gland is sensitive to changes in light passing

through the transparent membrane. Melatonin is produced out of serotonin, which is present in the pineal gland secretion. Serotonin is found in fig trees, under which Lord Buddha sat for meditation. Serotonin is essential for proper brain functioning and lack of it cause a disease called schizophrenia (Hallucinations). The gland controls reproduction system in animals.

(2) Sweat glands - are 108 / sq. cm of skin area. They release salty water, which evaporates and creates coolness in the body.

(3) Sebaceous glands - are 16 / sq. cm of skin area. They produce oil to lubricate skin and hair. The oily substance also makes the skin and hair waterproof.

2. Vocal chords - when we exhale, breadth travels up through windpipe, passes through vocal chords, which are fleshy flexible folds on either side of the voice box. Vocal chords open or close, become tight or loose, become thick or thinner and are stretched and passage of breath causes vibration in the chords, which produce voice. Higher vibrations give rise to shriller voice. When vocal chords contract, they vibrate at a lower frequency, which produces deeper voice.

When chords tighten or loosen, this raises or lowers the pitch. We normally speak at certain distinct pith. The resonating cavities in the body amplify the voice and the cavities are: chest, pharynx- tract between mouth and gullet, nose-sinuses and mouth. Finally, the speech organs in the mouth, like: tongue, lips and teeth shape the voice in a recognizable speech, which is distinct for each person, as such, we are able to recognize a person on the other side of the telephone through his speech.

3. Ears - provides us with two vital senses: Hearing and Sense of balance:

Hearing - we hear through our ears. Ear comprises consists of three portions: 1 Outer ear, 2 Middle ear and 3 Inner ear:

1. Outer ear canal - ends at the eardrum, eardrum vibrates in response to sound waves.
2. Middle ear - contains three tiny bones called malleus, incus and stapes. Stapes is the smallest bone in the

human body. These bones transmit vibrations from eardrum to the membrane of the oval window, which separates middle ear from the inner ear.

3. Inner ear - sensory receptors inside our ears convert sound vibrations into electrical signals, which pass along the auditory nerve to the brain for interpretation.

   Sense of balance organ - is situated in our inner ear. Inner ear contains three fluid filled cochleas, which contain sensory receptors to detect movement. Cochleas enable us to balance the body in space and we maintain an upright posture. Cochleas also enable us to move around without falling over. When we move our head, the fluid inside the cochleas push against the receptor cells and when we move our head quickly and stop suddenly, the fluid continues to move, which gives a false sense of moving, which is called Dizziness. Our ability to interpret sounds and sense of balance get developed during our childhood.

Our voice - has two components: 1 Sound and 2 Intensity:

1. Sound - is vibrations of the molecules in the air. Pitch of the sound higher or lower, is determined by a property known as frequency, which is measured in Hz (Hertz). Hertz is vibrations / second and higher the frequency, higher is the pitch.
2. Intensity of sound - is the loudness of sound, which is measured in dB (decibels) and for every 10 dB increase, we hear double the loudness, like: 70 dB sounds is twice of 60 dB. Normal level of conversation takes place at 60 dB, traffic moves at 80 dB, which is common in Indian cities, but makes some people irritable. Sound at 90 dB makes some people partially deaf to delicate sounds and sound above 120 dB can damage our eardrums. Human ear can detect sounds of frequencies between 20 Hz to 20,000 Hz, but bats and dogs can hear sounds beyond this range.

4. Teeth - during our childhood from 6 months to 3 years, we grow 20 milk teeth, which fall off as we grow old. Then secondary 32 teeth appear from 6 years to 21 years. Our teeth are of four types:

1. Incisor teeth - are sharp like chisel and are in the front of mouth to cut and hold food.
2. Canine teeth - are longer and pointed. We use them to tear food.
3. Premolar teeth - have two prominences (Cups) on the biting surface for grinding food.
4. Molar teeth - are the largest and have four / five cups for chewing.

3.8. Human Systems

1. Allergy system - is an inappropriate immune response to a normally harmless substance called Allergen. The sensitive substance can be any food item / chemical / plant / any animal product, which cause an allergic-reaction in certain individuals. On initial exposure to allergen, the immune system becomes sensitized to it and allergic reaction occurs, which produce a special antibody chemical called Histamine, which acts on the blood vessels to produce allergic symptoms.

   Histamine produced in such cases is so small that it has not been possible so far to detect it in the persons suffering from allergic attacks. Histamine causes an inflammatory response and produces irritation. The proportion of histamine produced in different persons due to reaction to different substances is different in each case; as such different persons suffer from different substances.

2. Breathing system - is an expansion of lungs, which lowers the air pressure inside the lung's cavity; air goes in, which is called inhaling; contraction of lungs increases the air pressure, which induces exhaling and the whole process is called Breathing. Adult lungs take about 500 ml of air in each breath and we breathe 12 to 15 times / minute. When we inhale, air enters through nose normally, gets moistened, gets warmed up and in abnormal condition, we breathe through mouth.

   Foreign particles or excess mucus irritates airway, lungs contract suddenly and the foreign thing gets expelled out through sneeze or cough. Breathing is an automatic process.

When we sleep, breathing continues and is controlled by a collection of nerve cells in the brain, called Respiratory Centre. From respiratory centre, messages travel down to the diaphragms, to the rib muscles, which stimulate them to continue breathing. Nerve cells in arteries and in brain's respiratory center are sensitive to levels of carbon-di-oxide in the blood; a rise in level increases breathing rate, which restores the level back to normal.

3. Nervous systems - we have two systems: Central Nervous System (CNS) and Peripheral Nervous System (PNS):

   CNS - consists of brain and spinal cord.

   PNS - is made up of nerves, which spread through out our body.

   Neuron cells - carry out the working of nervous system and each neuron has long projection known as Nerve fiber-axon, which relays information in the form of electrical signal. When the signal reaches the end of the nerve fiber, it is carried in chemical form to the next neuron and so on. We have 1,300 crore nerve cells and 96,000 km of arteries, veins and capillaries.

   Nervous system has two types of responses:

   Voluntary response - takes place under conscious control, like walking.

   Involuntary response - which is again of two types:

   Automatic response - regulates body's internal functions, like digestion, BP and temperature.

   Reflex response - affects muscles, which are normally under voluntary control, like removal of hand from a hot object, before we become aware of the heat.

4. Waste products - muscles, brain, heart and other organs need energy to function. This energy is derived from glucose and oxygen, which is carried in the blood. Blood circulates around the body in one minute at rest and in 20 seconds during exercise. Red blood cells carry oxygen from the lungs to the tissues, where glucose is burned in a process known as oxidation. In addition, body tissues require fats, proteins, vitamins, minerals and lipids, such as cholesterol, which are carried in the plasma, the fluid part of the blood. As body

cells carry out their functions of growing, reproduction and repair, they release waste products into the blood stream. Waste products are:

Carbon-di-oxide - that is produced from oxidation of glucose. It is eliminated from the blood stream through lungs during exhaling.

Protein wastes - like urea and bilirubin are produced from the breakdown of hemoglobin and are transported to the kidneys for excretion through urine.

Other wastes - are processed in the liver, before being excreted in the faeces.

5. Pain - is nature's unpleasant warning of danger to stop repeated action that caused the pain. Absence of pain is a dangerous condition, as it can lead to severe damage in some persons suffering from leprosy. When tissues get damaged by trauma or infection or problem with blood supply, the pain receptors get stimulated. They send electrical signals, which originate at the point of pain. Signals travel along the nerves, through the spinal chord to brain, where it is perceived as pain or feel discomfort able.

Six Types of Pain

1. Throbbing pain - is caused by increased blood flow.
2. Shooting pain - is caused by pressure or irritation of the nerve at the point, where it emerges from the spinal chord.
3. Colic pain - is caused by intermittent stretching, contraction of intestines.
4. Referred pain - is caused by nerves carrying the sensation of pain, merge with other nerves before reaching the brain, like: hip pain can be felt as knee pain or tooth pain can be felt as ear pain or heart problem can cause pain in the chest, in the neck and in one or both arms.
5. Severe pain - is caused by heart problem, which leads to pale skin, sweating, nausea, vomiting, rapid pulse, dilated pupils and can result in fainting.
6. Prolonged pain - is caused by depression, loss of weight, decreased appetite or disturbed sleep and may last for few weeks or months.

Severity of pain - can be described on a scale from 1 to 10, where 1 stands for slight discomfort and 10 stands for unbearable pain.

Headache - is pain in the head and is of four types:

1. Tension headache - is caused due to stress, bad posture or stiff neck and is made worse by noise and hot environment.
2. Recurrent headache - is caused due to depression, difficulties at work or at home.
3. Migraine headache - is caused due to visual disturbances, nausea or vomiting
4. Cluster headache - is caused due to increase in blood flow as a result of widening of blood vessels in the brain. Increased blood flow induces severe pain around one eye or temple and leads to watering and redness of eyes. Cluster headache is short lived and recurs one to four times over a period of few days.

6. Emotion - is an excited state of mind, caused by happiness, surprise, fear, sadness, disgust or anger. Our face has 42 muscles and we use them to express our emotions. Extreme emotions can cause problems, like sadness can turn into depression, anger can turn into aggressiveness, fear can turn into phobias and pleasure can turn into addiction. Emotions cause change in our body, like anger and fear increase heartbeat and happiness makes us to smile.

Emotional Quotient (EQ) - is an important factor of human life. Quotient tries to measure emotional behavior. Men have two emotional centers in the brain, while women have many emotional centers scattered all over their brain, as such they tend to be more emotional and feel more attached to their children. In a survey, 80 % men reported that work is more important in life, but 80 % women reported that looking after their children and family is more important and they can go to any length to achieve it.

EQ is calculated through objective type questions: 25 questions are asked on each emotional topic and each question has three alternative answers; where right answer is to be tick marked. If the right answer is ticked, then two marks are given. If neutral answer is ticked, one mark is given. If a wrong answer is kicked, zero mark is given, but all the questions are to be answered.

Emotional topics cover: 1. spouse, 2. children, 3. parents, 4. colleagues and 5. friends. Score against each topic is totaled for analysis. If score in a topic is less, suggestions are given to improve the rating and retest is held after two months. If the score is in the middle range, tips are given to improve it further and retest is held after two months. If the score is high, advice is given to maintain it.

7. Aura - is an energy field that surrounds a human body. It is like a magnetic field, which surrounds a magnet. Aura depends upon the life energies, which are at work within and around us. Aura is generated within the physical body. An aura comprises of seven layers, which can extend up to one meter away from the body. Aura's colour keeps on changing according to one's health, thought, mood and emotion. Auras of spiritually evolved persons can extend up to two meter away from their body. It is so strong, that if one merely steps into their field of aura, one feels elevated and improvements have been reported in ailments, especially in mental cases, like: depression, stress and tension.

   Robert Bruce has the ability to see auras. He claims that an aura is visible as colourful rainbow of light emanating from all over the body and is strongest along the spine, which has circles of energy (Chakras). Aura has been photographed through Kirlian photography technique, which photographs the radiation emanating from the body and depending upon the film emulsion, different colour shadings can be obtained. Presently, this technique is popular in diagnosing and in treatment of certain ailments.

3.9 United Nations Organization's three human development indexes

1. Human Development Index (HDI) - is a composite measure of human well-being, development and is based on: literacy level, life expectancy, gender disparities and income. HDI is

a significant indicator in assessing a country's development. HDI ranking for 162 countries (Base year 2000):

HDI Value (Higher side)	*HDI Value (Lower side)*
No.1 Norway - = 0.942 (Top most)	No. 115 India
No.2 Sweden - = 0.941	No. 127 Pakistan
No.3 Canada - = 0.940	No. 129 Nepal
No. 4 USA — = 0.939	No. 130 Bhutan
No. 5 Belgium = 0.939	No. 132 Bangla Desh
No. 6 UK —— = 0.928	No. 158 Burkina Faso = 0.325
No. 7 Australia	No. 159 Mozambique = 0.322
No. 8 Japan	No. 160 Burundi —— = 0.313
No. 81 Sri Lanka	No. 161 Niger ———— = 0.277
No. 87 China	No. 162 Sierra Leone = 0.275 (Bottom most)

2. Technology Achievement Index (TAI) - is based on use of new technology for human development and TAI ranking report as released for 72 countries (Base year 2000):

Highly industrialized	*Lowly industrialized*
No.1 Finland (Leader)	No.5 Korea
No.2 USA	No.63 India
No.3 Sweden	No.72 Nicaragua (at the lowest margin)
No.4 Japan	

3. Human Poverty Index (HPI) - starts from poor to the poorest nation. HPI ranking report for 90 countries (Base 2000):

Poor countries	Poorer countries
No.1 Uruguay (Poor)	No.55 India
No.2 Costa Rica	No.65 Pakistan

No.16 Brazil	No.73 Bangladesh
No.24 China	No.77 Nepal
No.31 Sri Lanka	No.90 Niger (Poorest).

Number of independent countries in the world are 212, most populous country is China (126 crore), most populous city is Tokyo (2.64 crore) - the capital of Japan and Vatican city - the home of Pope in Rome in Italy is the smallest independent country (0.5 sq km).

3.10. Body Mass Index (BMI) - men and women differ in their height, frame size and weight. Height and weight have relationship called BMI, which indicates the state of health. BMI is a number, which is derived by dividing weight (W) in kg with square of height (H) in meters,

Formula: $BMI = W / H^2$

Example: weight = 65 kg, height 1.6 m

$BMI = 65 / 1.6^2 = 65 / 1.6 x1.6 = 65 / 2.56 = 25.39$ (Over weight)

BMI Index	*Remark*
Less than 20	Under weight
20 – 25	Ideal
25 – 30	Over weight (Caution)
30 – 40	Over weight (Take measures to control)
More than 40	Highly over weight (Take action to loose).

Weight table: MEN FRAME SIZE

Height (cm)	*Small* (kg)	*Medium* (kg)	*Large* (kg)
157.6	50.7 – 54.4	53.5 – 57.1	57.1 – 63.9
160	52.1 – 55.8	54.8 – 60.3	58.5 – 65.3
162.5	53.5 – 57.1	56.2 – 61.6	59.8 – 67.1
165	54.8 – 58.5	57.8 – 63.0	61.2 – 68.9
167.5	56.2 – 60.3	59.0 – 64.8	62.6 – 70.7

170	58.0 – 62.1	60.7 – 66.6	64.4 – 73.0
172.5	59.8 – 63.9	62.6 – 68.9	66.6 – 75.2
175	61.6 – 65.7	64.4 – 70.7	68.4 – 77.1
178	63.4 – 68.0	66.2 – 72.5	70.3 – 78.9
180	65.3 – 89.8	68.0 – 74.8	72.1 – 81.1
185.5	68.9 – 73.4	71.6 – 79.3	76.1 – 85.7
188	70.7 – 75.7	73.4 – 81.6	78.4 – 87.9
190.5	72.5 – 77.5	75.7 – 83.9	80.7 – 90.2
193	74.3 – 79.3	78.0 – 86.1	82.5 – 92.5

WOMEN	*Small*	*Medium*	*Large*
147.5	41.7 – 44.4	43.5 – 48.5	47.1 – 53.9
150	42.6 – 45.8	44.4 – 49.9	48.0 – 55.3
152.5	43.5 – 47.1	45.8 – 51.2	49.4 – 56.7

WOMEN	*Small*	*Medium*	*Large*
155	44.9 – 48.5	47.1 – 52.6	50.8 – 58.0
157.5	46.2 – 49.9	48.5 – 53.9	52.1 – 59.4
160	47.6 – 51.2	49.9 – 55.3	53.5 – 60.7
162.5	49.0 – 52.6	51.2 – 57.1	54.9 – 62.6
165	50.3 – 53.0	52.6 – 58.9	56.7 – 64.4
167.5	51.6 – 55.8	54.4 – 61.2	58.5 – 66.2
170	53.5 – 57.6	56.2 – 63.0	60.3 – 68.0
172.5	54.8 – 59.4	58.0 – 64.8	62.1 – 69.8
175	57.1 – 61.6	59.8 – 66.6	63.9 – 71.6
178	58.9 – 63.5	61.6 – 68.4	65.7 – 73.9
180	60.7 – 65.3	63.5 – 70.3	67.5 – 76.2
183	62.6 – 67.1	65.3 – 72.1	69.4 – 78.4

Calorie - is the unit of heat, which raises the temperature of one gram of water from 14.5 to 15.5° C. Food we eat gets converted into heat. If we spend more calories in doing work, we loose weight. If we spend fewer calories in doing work, we gain weight and the extra calories get deposited in the form fat in the body, mostly over the stomach.

Calorie spent table:

Activity	*Calorie spent*
1 Resting	1.3 Calories / minute
2 Brisk walking	5 Calories / minute
3 Cycling	8 Calories / minute
4 Swimming	11 Calories / minute
5 Running	20 Calories / minute

Calories requirement table:

1. Average adult person requires 2 - 3 thousand calories per day
2. Average manual worker requires 3 - 4 thousand calories per day
3. Average athlete person requires 4 - 5 thousand calories per day

3.11. First Aid tips - these are very useful tips, which help in emergency

1. Shock
    1. Lay the patient down on back.
    2. Stop bleeding by pressure.
    3. Relieve pain by supporting the injured part.
    4. Make the patient comfortable by fanning.
    5. Fluid may be given in small quantity, unless unconscious.
2. Electric shock
    1. Remove the patient from source of supply.
    2. See the air passage is clear, if not clear it.
    3. Restore breathing by artificial respiration.

Effects of electric current (milliamperes) on human body:

Current	*Effects*
0.2 - 0.3	Can be felt.
0.4 - 0.7	Pinching.
0.8 - 1.0	Gripping
1.1 - 4.9	Unpleasant stimulation.

5.0 - 15.0	Muscles contract or paralyzed leading to inability of victim to free himself from source of supply, if large number of muscles are stimulated, then sudden violent contraction of muscles create throwing effect and the victim is thrown away from the source of power supply, which may result in injuries.
15.0 - 19.0	Paralysis for the duration of contact with the power source.
20.0 - 25.0	Permanent damage to nerve tissues and blood vessels.
26.0 – 69.0	May be fatal.
70.0 – 90.0	Fatal. Current of 70 milliamperes and above can be produced by a voltage as low as 25 Volts, if passed directly through the chest, which may produce ventricular fibrillation and death.

3. Wound
    1. Stop bleeding and raise the affected part.
    2. Avoid touching the wound with unsterilized materials.
    3. Clean the wound with running water.
    4. Give no stimulant or anything by mouth.
    5. Never apply antiseptic ointment / lotion / iodine / germicide to the wound.
    6. Maintain warmth by covering the body with blanket.
    7. If intestines protrude from the abdominal wound, do not attempt to touch or push them inside, but leave the job to the doctor.
4. Eye injuries
    1. Removal may be attempted, if foreign body is not embedded by washing with water.
    2. If foreign body is embedded in the eyeball, apply pad and loose bandage and consult doctor, but do not apply any oil or ointment.
5. Three degree of burns

    1st Degree burn - affect the outer most first layer of skin, called Epidermis, but blisters do not form and the damaged skin peels off within few days.

    Treatment - put the affected part in cold water or pour water over burn that cannot be immersed. Cold water relieves pain and reduces fluid loss.

2nd Degree burn- destroys the second layer lower skin, called Dermis and damage to both these layers is called 2nd degree burn, which is very painful and blisters get formed and get filled with clear fluid. After three days, pain reduces and the burn wound heals within 14 days.

Treatment - cover the burns with sterilized dressing and move the patient to a doctor.

3rd Degree burn - in this type of burn epidermis, dermis and the underlying fat is destroyed and damage extends up to the muscle tissue. The affected area becomes numb, thickened and discolored and healing is very slow and even skin grafting may be required.

6. Fracture - put the patient on a rigid frame (plywood) / stretcher or support the affected part and transport the patient to a doctor, immediately.
7. Snake bite
    1. Apply constriction band to the proximity of bite to reduce blood supply.
    2. Incise the bite with sharp blade to allow bleeding.
    3. Clean the area with potassium permanganate solution.
    4. Move the patient to a hospital.

3.12. Mystery of Life, aging and Death

Extension of human life - has taken place over the last century, due to advancement in medical science and the evidence is:

Year	*Men*	*Women*
1900	48.3 years	51.1 years
1950	66 years	71.7 years
2000	75.7 years	82.7 years

Search for Extra Terrestrial Intelligence (SETI) - is a program in which efforts are being made to search life in other Sunlike stars in the Milky Way Galaxy. There are many star systems that have planets like our Earth, which can support intelligent life. It is believed that intelligent life forms may have evolved on many star systems in the habitable zones of Milky Way Galaxy. Intelligent beings might be using radio-waves for communication, which can be detected from Earth. Such intelligent civilizations may be about 10 lakh in our Milky Way Galaxy, but so far no contact has been established with them. SETI program is still going on to locate alien-non-earthly-intelligent-beings, who use radio-waves.

Search for life - so far it has been established that Earth is the only planet in the Solar system, which has life forms. It has been found that Apcilon Andromeda Star, which is 50 light-year away, has three Jupiter sized planets, which have gas and water in their atmosphere and life may exist over there. This fact for life is yet to be established.

Strongest Radio Signal (SRS) - has been beamed on 16.11.1974 to M 13 Globular Cluster in the constellation Hercules in an effort to communicate with Extra-terrestrial-life over there. The beamed radio signal message shows the basic data about humanity on Earth. The message will take 25,000 years to reach there and if there is a reply, it will take another 25,000 years for their message to reach back to us.

Aging - researches have found the processes, which take place in the cells that bring about aging and two theories have emerged in this respect:

1. Entropic theory of aging - wearing out naturally.
2. Telomeric theory of aging - death by design, where substances within the body attack, destroy the cells to bring on aging, which eventual lead to death, but experiments have proved that substances like melatonin, antioxidants, free radicals and somatrophin have increased the life span of test animals.

Death - doctors and scientists do not agree on exactly what constitutes death, however two terms are quite oftenly used:

1. Brain dead (Comatose) - brain stops functioning, but rest of the body continues to function for years.
2. Clinically dead - heart or lungs stop functioning, but brain continues to function and there had been cases, when the persons have been resuscitated with no permanent ill effects.
3. Bible's description of death - states that death is a state of total unconsciousness, devoid of awareness, knowledge and

perception. If this description of death is accepted, then there had been cases, when persons having been declared dead, have returned back to their consciousness after some time. When revived back to life, they narrated their experiences. In such cases, it is said that they were not really dead, but were in an unconscious state, their vital organs like heart and lungs may have temporarily ceased functioning, but brain activity had not ceased.

Scientific explanation of death - scientists have found that human nervous system and brain operate through electrical impulses. Brain requires blood and oxygen to function. When breathing or blood supply is impaired, the brain malfunctions and if this state is prolonged enough, the brain eventually ceases all activity. Researchers have concluded that unusual sensations, like seeing lights or hearing of sounds, as reported by the revived persons after having been declared clinically dead, is attributed to malfunction of brain and the nervous system.

Out of body experience - Raymond Moody has written a book in which he revealed his study of more than 100 cases of out of body experiences of persons, who have been declared clinically dead and later they revived. This happened when their spirits returned back to their physical bodies. They narrated their experiences, which they had experienced during their so called state of clinical death.

After life experience - revived people, who had been declared clinical dead, have stated that their spirit experienced a passage through a tunnel into a place of light, where they felt uplifted with life energy, which fills that realm of existence. In this realm, they met a spirit-person, who is often recognized as a close relative or a friend, who had passed away earlier. Tunnel towards the light experience is believed to be the transference of a person's spirit-body from the physical realm of Earth to the next realm of higher existence, which is called after life experience. Human spirit body resonates most readily to the frequency of the spirit realm and this transfer takes place, as soon as, it has been released from the confines of the physical body.

Prime of life experience - revived people, who had been declared clinical dead, have stated that the infirmities of their physical bodies no longer existed, as their physical bodies had been left behind. They further stated that their spirit-bodies do not age, like their physical-bodies had done earlier. Thus unimpeded by aging of their physical bodies, their spirit-bodies appeared to be in prime of life; just like that they had been 28 years old. Spirit-bodies seem to be made up of etheric-energy based material, as opposed to physical bodies, which are composed of dense-electron based material

My own experience - my father Bua Dutt Shukal retired as State Engineer (PWD). He suffered a paralysis attack in 1949. We were staying at Narsingh Garh near Bhopal. Father slipped from up stairs, fell on the ground and for ten minutes was lying in an unconscious state with no heart beat, no pulse and no breadth. We did not know as to what to do, except weeping? We shifted him on a cot and mother sprinkled some water on his face. This revived him. When we asked, he stated that he had passed through a tunnel, at the end of tunnel there was light and a person was sitting over there, who said that this man had been brought to him wrongly and send him back. In the reverse order, he again passed through the tunnel and is surprised to see as to why we fellows are weeping?

4

Intelligence

Civilization is based on higher level of human intelligence.

Intelligence is the mental ability, with which we interpret information, understand the things around us, take logical decisions and learn new skills. Our intelligence peaks at the age of seven years, then keeps on improving up to the age of 10 years and after this age practically remains constant through out our life. However, as we grow old, the power of understanding keeps on increasing.

Intelligence in different life forms:

1. Fish life forms - are the least intelligent, as for food bigger fish eat smaller fish, but there is an exception in the case of dolphin fish, which is very intelligent.
2. Grazing life forms - are intelligent, as for food they depend on their sense of smell. They do not eat any poisonous vegetation and have eyes at the sides, which give them wide-angle vision to spot their predators.
3. Carnivorous life forms - are very intelligent, as for food they survive by killing other animals. They have binocular eyes in front to correctly judge the distance to catch their prey. Dogs have a very highly developed sense of smell, which helps them in detecting the things.
4. Insect life forms - are more intelligent, as for food they work in companionship, live in communities, have the ability to communicate with others and lead a social life. They have six legs and have the ability to sense an inclement weather by instinct.

5. Bird life forms - are most intelligent, as they have an ability to search their food from a distance, have an instinct to build nests as per their requirements and some species can migrate over long distances in search of favourable weather and food.
6. Human life form - is extra ordinarily intelligent. We have the ability to cook food, make tools and use them, while no other animal can do this, except mole, which uses stone to break hard food items and beaver, which builds dams. All animals have body, heart and brain, but in addition, we have mind, which enables us to learn from experience, gain knowledge and transfer the same to the next generation. Human beings use intelligence in working, while other life forms use their instinct.

Spinal cord and brain weight ratio - has a bearing on intelligence:

Animal	*Spinal cord*	*Brain weight*	*Remark*
Cat	1 unit	4 units	Less intelligent
Monkey	1 unit	18 units	More intelligent
Man	1 unit	50 units	Most intelligent

Intelligence Quotient (IQ)

IQ is an indicator of intelligence and is based upon oral and written tests, which have been developed for different age group children. Alfred Binate in Paris developed the system about 100 years ago and since then it is used widely. In IQ test, mental age is determined by asking a child first lower age group questions, and then progressively, higher age group questions are asked to determine his mental age in years. Example:

Child's actual age 10 years, he is able to answer correctly the questions of 13 age group children, so 13 years is the mental age. IQ = Mental age x 100 / Actual age

IQ = 13 x 100 / 10 = 130

Interpretation of IQ result:

Q = 130 and above- Most intelligent.

IQ = 130 – 120 - Very intelligent.

IQ = 120 –90 - Average intelligent.

IQ = 90 – 70 - Below average intelligent.

IQ = 70 and below - Mentally retarded, child requires medical attention.

IQ score can be improved by exercising the brain to work at a higher level of performance by solving puzzles, crosswords and playing chess.

4.1 Human brain - during our evolution cycle, forehead became longer, this increased the volume and the number of folds of the brain increased to fit inside enlarged skull. Brain is the most complex part of human body, as it regulates consciousness, intelligence, creativity, communication, experience, emotion, monitors body functions, movements, regulates the automatic functions of breathing, blinking, heartbeat to complex activities involving thought process and learning. Brain weight is 1.372 kg in men and 1.265 kg in women.

Brain consists of 10 million million neurons, which work like a computer and in a split second, establishes thousands of inter-connections, that is why nature has taken great care to ensure that brain remains safe. It is immersed in a liquid, which acts like a shock-absorber. It is encased inside several protective layers, covering around the brain to the dome shaped skull with a padding of hair and a blood supply with built in pressure regulator.

We have two brains:

1. Main brain - is known as Cerebrum, which is most complex, most intricate part of human body, which controls every function of the body.
2. Small brain - is known as Cerebellum, which controls the action of muscles and lies underneath the cerebral portion of the main brain. Cerebellum has two hemispheres, which are buried underneath the brain stem. They control heart, lungs and digestive system.

Reflex Action

Reflex action is the function of the small brain, in which the main brain is not involved. This saves time for instant action to be taken to save the body from an imminent danger and this happens in three ways:

1. Instant closure of eyes - saves the eyes from an imminent danger.
2. Instant raising of hand - saves one from an imminent attack.
3. Instant removal of hand - saves the hand from damage from a hot spot.

Brain hemispheres - human brain is divided into two hemispheres, which are mirror image of each other. The two hemisphres are:

1. Right hemisphere - controls the movements and sensations on the left side of the body. In some persons, the right hemisphere is dominant and the person becomes left-handed. In addition, the right hemisphere controls cultural activities, emotions, recognition of faces and music.
2. Left hemisphere - controls the movements and sensations on the right side of the body. In most of the people, left hemisphere remains dominant, as such, mostly the people are right handed. In addition, the left hemisphere controls reading, writing, arithmetic, reasoning and language. Normally, left hemisphere is larger than the right hemisphere, as such 90 % people prefer to use right hand in writing.

Right and left hemispheres share information through nerves that join them. We use our senses of hearing, seeing, smelling, tasting and touching all together to collect information about the outside world, but at the same time, we also detect pain, pressure, temperature, position and movement of our body. All these sensations are changed into electrical signals, which are carried to the brain for perception.

Brain's Composition and Function

Brain is composed of two types of matter: Gray matter - that processes nerve impulses and White matter - that transmits the impulses. Brain is the hub of our nervous system and consists of 10,000 crore nerve cells, called Neurons. Each neuron cell is connected to around 10,000 other neuron cells and thus the number of connections run up to 1,000 trillion (Trillion = 1 followed by 18 zeros). Neurons transmit information in the form of electrical signals and communicate with other neurons at their junction points, where chemicals help to bridge the gap.

Nerve impulse is an electrical activity that passes from one end of a nerve cell to the other nerve cell. Each impulse is same in size, but frequency varies with the information, like frequency modulated radio waves and a fatty substance called Myelin quickly insulates the neurons that need to transmit electrical signals.

Brain Processes the Information

Brain receives information from five senses: 1 Ear, 2 Eyes, 3 Nose, 4 Tongue and 5 Touch sensors, which are distributed through out the body. Information as collected from the senses, is combined to help us to react, remember, think, plan and pass instructions to other body parts to take suitable action. Normally, we use only 6 % of our brain's capacity; Einstein used 10% of his capacity. We do not know yet how to use the remaining 94 % of our brain's capacity?

Information in the brain is stored subconsciously. We do not become aware of it, as how it happens, but only one hemisphere of the brain works at a time, while the other hemisphere remains switched off. This makes us impossible to think of two things at a time, but we are capable of thinking on many topics one after another.

Brain Acts as Control Center

Our brain is a remarkable control center, where many activities happen simultaneously, like: thinking, breathing, heartbeat, ideas, ambition, and dreams, feeling of love, happiness, sadness and based on all these factors, suitable remedial action is taken to control the situation. It is our brain, which enables us to remember, as to who we are; where we live; what we do; etc.

Brain's Wiring Up

As we develop in mother's womb, neurons in our brain grow and wiring up starts even before we take birth and even continues after birth:

Before birth - 6 to 8 weeks after conception, different operating systems get installed in the brain in different locations. Brain gets coded with what we would like or dislike; what our behavior would be. Brain activity generates electrical impulses, which controls the heart beating.

After birth -

3 Weeks after birth - our eyes get wired up with the brain, as we look around.

6 Weeks after birth - our facial muscles get wired up with the brain, as we learn to express ourselves with smiles.

9 Months after birth - our leg muscles get wired up with the brain, as we learn to crawl.

1 Year after birth - our sense of balance gets wired up, as we learn to walk.

2 Years after birth - wired up connections get inter-connected to form loops. Brain of male and female child gets wired up in different ways due to production of different hormones:
Baby girl - prefers to watch the faces of persons.
Baby boy - prefers to watch every thing around him.

10 Years after birth - wiring gets completed, intelligence peaks, understanding power starts increasing and circuits in the brain start getting pruned to get rid of connections that have not been used, as such, after this age, it becomes difficult to master new skills or learn a new language.

12 Years after birth - our brain becomes unique by itself. We develop our own individuality, based on what we have experienced as a child, what skills we have learnt in home or in school.
Boys - become naughty and tend to do better in spatial skills.
Girls - become sober and tend to do better in language skills, They become more alkative.

Brain's automatic system - enables us to react in an emergency and in response, heartbeat rises to supply more blood to the body parts, breathing increases quickly to increase oxygen supply, sweating increases to cool the body and instantly, we either fight with the attacker or run away from the danger.

Brain stroke - is the blockage or breakage of a blood vessel, which interrupts the supply of blood to an area of the brain, the brain cells in the affected area get damaged within few minutes and cannot regenerate themselves, as other body cells do, as such, brain stroke can impair speech, vision, movement or memory depending upon the part of brain, which has been damaged.

Brain's electrical impulses - are measured in the form of graph for interpretation. When we sleep - 70 % of brain's electrical impulses get stopped in males, but in females - 10 % impulses get stopped, as such, females keep on receiving information from the environment, analyze it, as such, pregnant women have to be careful, as what to do, what not to do, what to see, what not to see, what to listen and what not to listen, as these activities influence the baby in the womb.

Example: Abhimanyu - the child hero of Mahabharata War, listened to the technique of penetrating into the complex barricade in war, while he was in a fetus state in his mother's womb, but when the technique of coming out from the barricade was told, his mother slept, as such, after penetrating the barricade, he failed to come out, which resulted in his death.

Brain's capacity - our brain normally uses 8 % of its capacity, but when it confronts with a serious problem, it switches to a pattern of frustration and emotion. Intense emotion leads to weeping, while the brain should switch to logic and work mode. Few people have learnt the technique to switch to logic and work mode, as such, they can handle the situation calmly. Most of us have not learnt the mode of switching the mind to a state of intense concentration and meditation may help in this respect.

4.2. Mind

Every living creature has brain to interpret information as received from the sense organs, but in addition to brain, we have mind, which makes us different from the other animals. Mind enables us to learn from experience; enables us to share information with others; enables us to plan for the future. It is the mind, where ideas originate, which gets converted into action. It is mind, which has made us one of the most intelligent creatures on Earth and has enabled us to dominate over all other species.

Mind's existence is entirely independent of the physical brain. Mind is the seat of conscious thought, attention and opinion, which gives us the feeling of right or wrong. Our mind works at two levels: 1 Conscious level and 2 Subconscious levels, as described below:

Mind at conscious level - makes us aware of the surroundings, gives us the moral sense of right or wrong in respect of our behaviour, provides us creativity and logic.

Mind at subconscious level - influences our actions and habits, like: smoking, drinking and creates phobias.

Mind's control - mind plays a dominating part over our body's behavior. Body obeys the commands of mind, like: If one thinks that he has temperature, other people confirm it, the concerned person gets convinced that he has temperature and the body develops temperature without any medical reason. If one feels that he is suffering from a particular disease, other people confirm it, the concerned person develops the symptoms of that disease without any medical reason. These experiments have been performed secretly with out any previous knowledge or plan to the concerned person.

Yogis in India - have demonstrated their control over their mind. They have developed the ability to control their involuntary functions, like: If they command that the heart to stop beating, the heart does stop for a while. If they command that breathing to stop, breathing does stop for few minutes without any medical reason. If they command that the body temperature to rise, the temperature does rise without any reason. These experiments prove that mind is very powerful and body simply obeys its command.

People with weak mind show signs of restlessness and when faced with a problem, they have no control over their actions and thoughts. People with strong mind have signs of calmness under adverse circumstances, they exhibit normal behaviour.

Mental state - brain waves determine the state of one's thinking, which in turn govern their actions. Science has discovered that in some people these waves create peak performance for learning, thinking, studying, while they listen to music. Waves have a frequency range from 0.5 to 40 Hz, neuroscientists have investigated that these waves with special equipments, like: Electro Encephalo Graph (EEG), Positron Emission Tomography (PET), Single Photon Emission Computerized Tomography (SPECT), Magnetic Resonance Imaging (MRI) and Super-conducting Quantum Interference Device (SQUID). It has been observed that the different levels of mental functioning are consistently linked to specifically defined patterns of activity and events, which change the brain's electrical activity. Vast networks of neurons power our brain and they discharge waves of electrical energy at different frequencies and patterns. These brainwave activities take place between four frequency ranges and each range has a type, which has a particular mental state:

Frequency	*Type*	*Mental State*
13 to 40 Hz	Beta	High Beta - brain wave frequencies make us attentive, conscious; we are awake, attentive, highly alert; mind is sharp and focused. Neurons fire in great numbers and in rapid succession to achieve high performance, but bar the flashes of intuition, which may create anxiety and panic. Mid Beta - brain wave frequencies make us super focused, hyper alert, mental attentive abilities increase and we feel physically relaxed. This is the best state to understand something and tackle problems. Low Beta - brain wave frequencies make us focused, mental abilities, cognition and IQ increase.
7 to 13 Hz	Alpha	We feel relaxed, awareness expands and accelerated learning occurs and creative energy increases. New ideas and solution to problems flash and fears vanish. A sense of peace and well being is

		experienced. Left brain activity of logic, which acts as a filter to the subconscious mind, drops its guard to allow more intuitive, emotional and creative depths of the mind to increase their influence.
4 to 7 Hz	Theta	We fall into a state of deeper relaxation, where mind slows almost to the point of sleep. This state brings heightened receptivity and surges of inspiration. This is the state of deep meditation, where we experience a sensation of floating and the mind expands beyond the boundaries of our body and enters the energy fields that circulate around our physical self.
0.5 to 4 Hz	Delta	The slowest of all brain waves frequencies, here the brain waves are long, deep and are associated with deep dreamless sleep and leads to harmonious relaxation, where both sides of the brain work in synchronization. This state accelerates physical healing.

4.3. Human Traits

1. Anxiety - is a normal useful state, which helps us to recognize; cope with stressful situation. If anxiety is severe, it stops us from leading a normal life; may lead to panic attacks; may create phobias; sometimes anxiety may lead to worry about health, money, family or work. These situations may lead to unnecessary headache, trembling or nausea may develop.

2. Aptitude - is one's ability, suitability and fitness for a job or business. It depends upon one's interest, liking, education level, skill, information available on a subject and decide the profession in which one will be successful.
3. Aspiration - is the sum total of an individual's aptitude, attitude, intellect, interest, friend circle, social environment and information as obtained from others or through newspapers or magazines. Aspiration is measured through Ratter's Aspiration Test and test result depends upon the level of interaction one had with his parents, teachers, counsellors and peers in society. Aspiration decides how much progress one will attain in his profession.

   Reading good newspapers, magazines, observing knowledgeable TV programs, listening to news, reviews with an analytical mind, can improve ones aspiration level. Person with higher aspiration level does better in life. He rises higher in his professional career. It is nature's law that one gets, what he had aspired for?
4. Attitude - is one's way of thinking, his behavior in response to some thing. It is an inborn trait in response to the arising situations and his approach in tackling them. Attitude decides how quickly one will rise in his professional career.
5. Seven types of criticism:
   (1) Simple criticism - accept it, as a disguised compliment, that one has been successful in drawing another's attention.
   (2) Unnecessary criticism - is that, one has aroused jealousy in others.
   (3) Unjust criticism - is like a rain, one must use umbrella to ward it off.
   (4) Unbiased criticism - is helpful; welcome it as it shows that no one is perfect.
   (5) Constructive criticism - improves one's thinking and ways of working.
   (6) Foolish criticism - is to be ignored, for peace of mind.
   (7) Healthy criticism - record it for follow up action.
   (8) Self criticism - is to be indulged in first, before others find the fault.

6. Danger - can make us frightened or angry, both these states trigger a part of brain, called Amygdala, which triggers hypothalamus - the region of brain, which controls body temperature, thirst, hunger and the induced state enables one to react instantly.
7. Fear - may make our hairs to stand on end, makes the heart beat faster and all this is done to get the body ready to either attack or run away from the fear causing situation.
8. Two types of gratitude - gratitude is a cultivated trait and is a manner in which one remains grateful to others and the gratitude may be either positive or negative:

   Positive gratitude - Jesus healed ten lepers in a day, only one thanked him, so this leper exhibited positive gratitude. He had the tendency to create heaven out of hell. If fate hands him an orange, he will enjoy the juice and will be thankful to the unknown person, who gave the orange. When we do well to others, others may be grateful to us, but do not expect it. We must try to create an atmosphere of happiness for all to enjoy.

   Negative gratitude - the nine lepers, who did not thank Jesus, exhibited negative gratitude. These are the people, who have the tendency to create hell out of heaven. They will never be grateful to others and ultimately, they will loose good friends.
9. Pleasure - triggers areas in our brain known as Pleasure Centers, which release a chemical called Dopamine. Nicotine derived through smoking or alcohol taken, triggers a feeling of pleasure due to release of dopamine, but with increased usage, the feeling of pleasure subsides and to derive the same amount of pleasure, a craving to smoke more or take more alcohol arises. This state leads to addiction, which is difficult to cure later on.
10. Desire - breads craving; craving leads to action, which may be either good or bad. Good action leads to enjoyable experience. Bad action leads to sorrow and suffering in life.
11. Panic - is feeling of terror that strikes suddenly. It may last for several minutes or may lead to mis-interpretation of body symptoms, like: sudden increase of heartbeat or onset of

dizziness or fear that one is about to die. Panic worsens the situation.

12. Phobia - is an extraordinary fear or scare about snakes, lizards, heights or flying. Phobia results from past traumatic experiences, which one had suffered during childhood or having been chased by a dog.

13. Two types of thoughts:

    Positive thoughts - people with positive thoughts consider their problems as opportunities. They seek solutions to solve them, as there is no person in the world who has not faced problems. Their thinking is that most of the problems require some efforts to solve them; some problems may require more efforts; while few problems may require calculated risk to be taken. People with positive thoughts fill their mind with thoughts of peace, courage, health, hope and self-confidence.

    Negative thoughts - people with negative thoughts fill their mind with gloom; depression, worry, irritation. These traits can lead to failure in life. Negative thoughts can be changed to positive thoughts to a certain extent by training and exposure to people with positive thoughts. General Eisenhower said that never waste time with people, who have negative thoughts, but face the situation with people, who have positive thoughts and win the war.

4.4. Our Abilities

1. We normally think @ 400 to 500 words / minute
2. We normally write @ 20 to 30 words / minute
3. We normally type @ 50 to 60 words / minute
4. We normally speak @ 100 to 150 words / minute. The time difference between thinking and speaking, is utilized in choosing right language; analyzing the response from others; establishing eye contact; generating hand movements to emphasize what we are speaking.
5. We normally read - different things at different rates. Rate depends upon interest and grasping to be obtained in the

subject, as reading at a higher rate has no meaning, if the subject cannot be grasped.

Reading Rates

Reading @ 200 words / minute - is considered to be below average.

Reading @ 250 to 300 words / minute - is considered to be average.

Reading @ 350 to 400 words / minute - is considered to be above average.

Reading @ 450 to 500 words / minute - is considered to be excellent.

Reading Habits

Ability to read the text in a time period depends upon the habit, for which one is habitual in assimilating the information in a better way. Three reading habits are:

1. Block reading - we read text in blocks, each block is the number of words, we see at a time. If we increase the number of words in each block, the speed of reading will increase. This can be done by holding the text a little distance away.
2. Fixation time reading - when we read a word, it requires time to be analyzed, perceived by the brain. Fixation time is about 0.25 seconds and this time can be reduced with practice.
3. Pointer reading – pointer can be a finger, pen, pencil or a pointed thing, which is made to run along the line, we are reading. Our eyes follow the tip of the pointer, which helps in reading. If the speed of pointer is increased, speed of reading will increase automatically. This method is very helpful in childhood, but with practice the method can be applied in the case of adults to increase speed of reading.

4.5. Sixteen ability tests - we have different abilities for different things, which can be measured

1. Arithmetic ability test - measures numerical ability and is based on the principle of filling up of blanks:

1. If 2 men pack 120 boxes in 3 days, 3 men will pack 360 boxes in .... days. (Answer- 6 days)
2. Series: 2, 4, 7, 11, ... (Answer- 16)
3. Water flows down hill due to .....(A- density, B- gravity, C- attracted by sea. (Answer- B)

2. Logic ability test - measures the reasoning power:
Write + for similar number and 0 for dissimilar number and write the answer:
A = 576 83 576 83 .... (Answer- +)
B = 703 821 703 921 .... (Answer- 0)
C = 315 927 4 315 927 4 .... (Answer- +)

3. Perception ability test - measures the perceptional ability and is based on the principle of logic:
Count letter 'k' in the series and write the answer in the bracket:
dmkwksitqkbsbtzbtlkpxf (......) (Answer- 4)

4. Vocabulary ability test - measures vocabulary:
Peripatetic means———————— (Answer- walking from place to place.)
Salamander is a———————— (Answer- lizard like reptile.)
Tribulation is the opposite of———————— (Answer- tranquility.)

5. Comparison ability test - measures the comparison ability:
Write + for similar and 0 for dissimilar words in the bracket:
A = Little able-bodied, Forester & co. — Little able-bodied, Forester & co. (.....) (Answer- +)
B = John F. Grayson — John F. Gragson (.....) (Answer- 0)
C = Lieutenant George Johnson — Lieutenant George Johnsen (.....) (Answer- 0)

6. Substitution ability test - measures the substitution power:
1 2 3 4 5 6 7 8 9
F C K A E Y B H D
Substitute- E H F Y ———— 5 8 .... (Answer- 1, 6)
D A C B ———— .... (Answer- 9, 4, 2, 7)

7. Reading comprehension ability test - is conducted to see how well one grasps the contents of a piece of text.
8. Scholastic Aptitude Test (SAT) - is a composite test, which measures the scholastic achievements for admission in prestigious colleges in the United States of America. US College Board has released the following statistical findings for different religious communities:
   National Average Score in SAT = 1020
   Unitarian Universal Association = 1209 (Highest)
   Jews .... = 1161
   Quakers .... = 1153
   Hindus .... = 1110 (Fourth).
   Students from the above religious communities are favored for admissions in USA colleges and they achieve better academic standards in comparion to others.
9. Five types of spatial ability tests:
   1. Tracing spatial ability test - measures the ability for speed and accuracy:

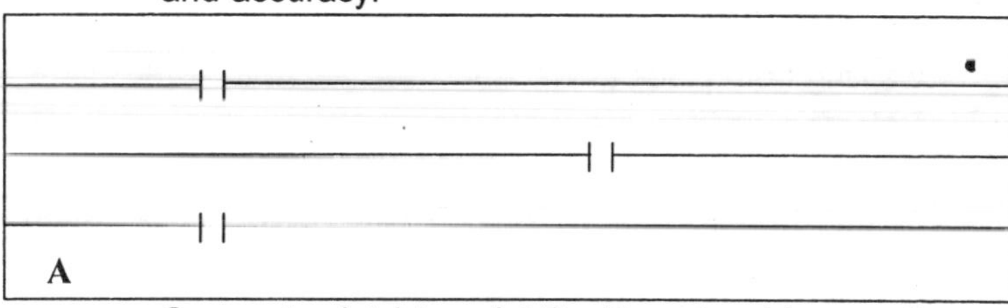

Connect point A to point B without touching any line.

   2. Location spatial ability test - measures the judgment ability for the distance between pairs of points:

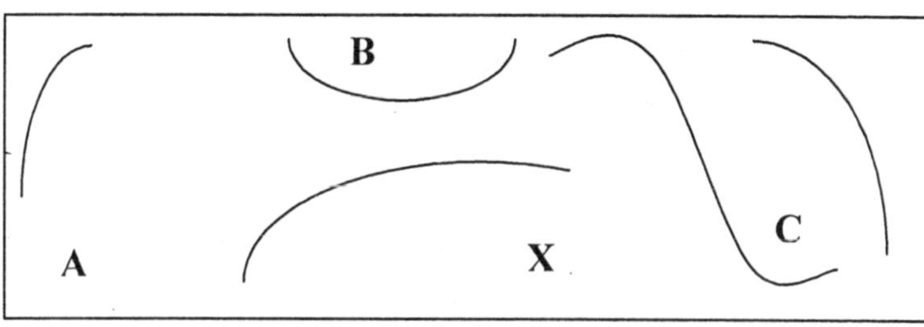

Shortest distance between points .... (Answer- AB)
Longest distance between points .... (Answer- AC)

3. Pursuit spatial ability test - measures the eyesight ability in a winding path by using eyesight only and not by tracing with a pencil:

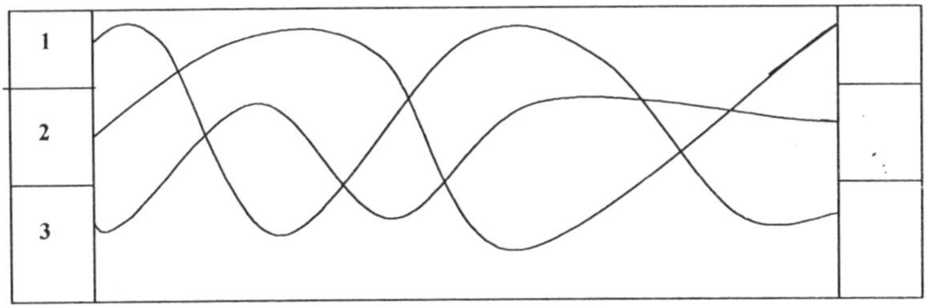

4. Relation spatial ability test - measures the distinguishing ability between different irregular objects to form a bigger object, like: Forming the whole picture from cut pieces of a picture puzzle.
5. Perception spatial ability test - measures the speed with which differences or similarities could be perceived, like: The lower leg of L is towards- , , . . (Ans R, L. R, L)

10. Two concept ability tests - measures the powers of understanding for the basic principles involved in mechanical devices for their working and write the answer in the bracket:
    1. Wheel turning concept, which wheel will turn faster A or B (...........) (Answer: Equal)

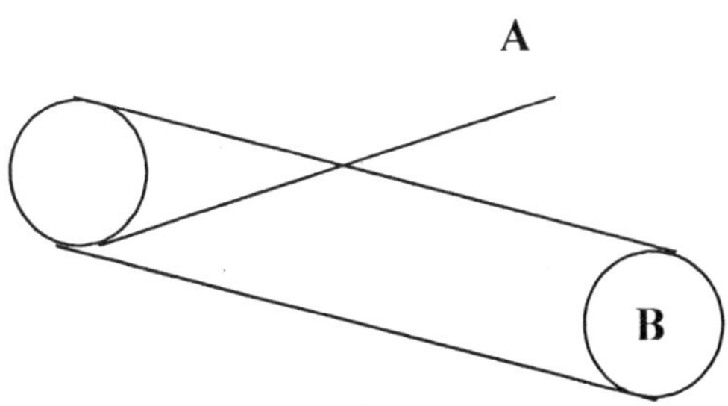

2. Nail pulling concept, which hammer will pull the nail easily A or B (.........) (Ans: B)

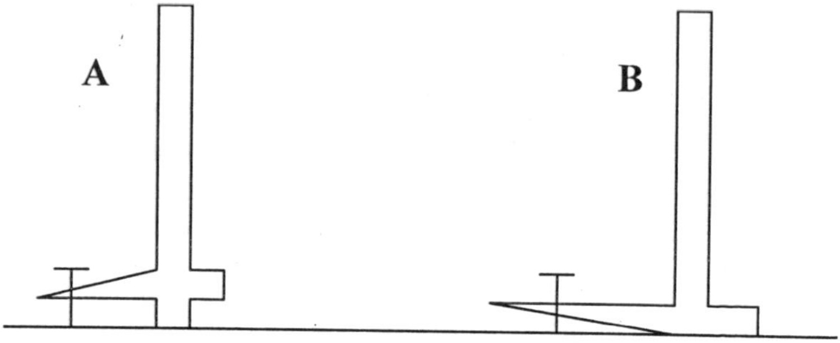

11. Motor ability tests:
    1. Dotting motor ability test - measures the speed and precision with which hand can move, to put dots at the central places in a series of small circles:

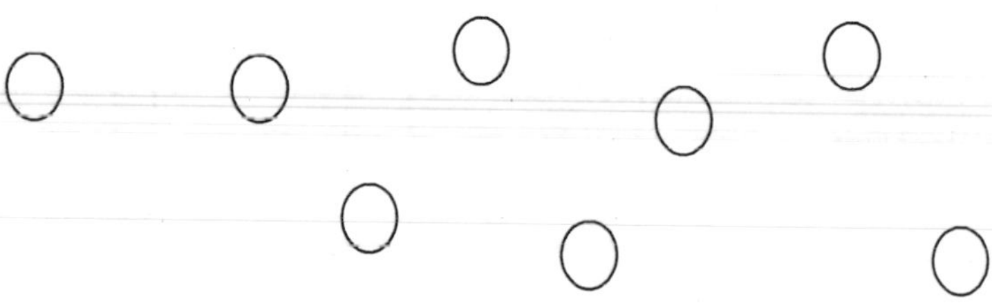

2. Tape motor ability test - measures the speed of action, the individual is capable of, but no precision is involved and the individual is asked to connect the circles in a series with a straight line, as illustrated below:

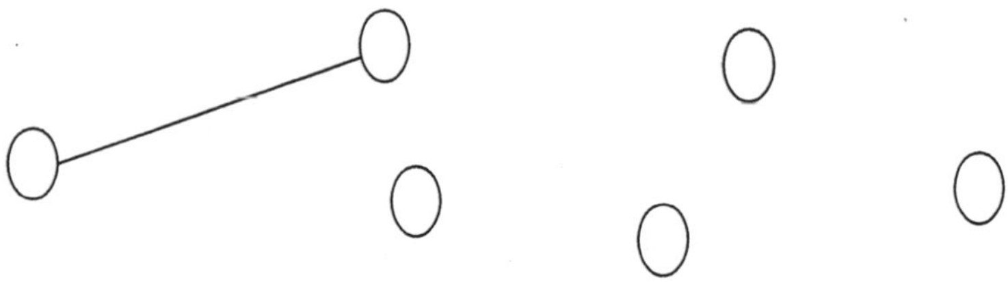

12. Dexterity ability test:
    1. Finger dexterity ability test - measures the quickness with which assembly of small parts can be done on a bench, like: Picking small nails and inserting them in holes or screwing small nuts on bolts within a fixed time period.
    2. Hand dexterity ability test - measures the co-ordination between hand and wrist movement, like: Small blocks are required to be turned over and replaced in their original position within a fixed time period.
    3. Arm dexterity ability test - measures the movement of arm and fingers in picking up small blocks, like: Carry the blocks, turn them over and place them again in some order within in a fixed time period.
13. Reaction ability test:
    1. Time reaction ability test - measures the response in milli-seconds with which a pedal can be pressed on seeing a red light or an obstruction. Quick reaction time is essential in avoiding an accident and the response is measured in milli-seconds.
    2. Complex reaction ability test - measures the accuracy of response under different stimuli, arising in quick succession and the number of errors committed is counted.
14. Social ability test - is very important for working in a team and is measured through questions and answers:
    How one move in the society?
    What level of emotional maturity one has?
    What is the state of stability of one's mind?
    What level of sincerity one has in doing his work?

Answers against the above questions are obtained by asking a person to respond by ticking either yes or no against the following sentences within a time period of 5 minutes:

1. Do you feel uncomfortable in a social gathering yes / no?
2. Do you feel miserable in life yes / no?
3. Do you feel embraced, when talking to a large group yes / no?

4 . Do you object, when some one pushes ahead in the queue yes / no?
5. Do you advise when expenses of a junior are unduly high yes / no?
6. Do you object, when your junior is talking too much yes / no?
7. Do you control misbehavior in the friend circle yes / no?
8. Do you deal, with the family problem yes / no?
9. Do you guide your junior yes / no?

SCORE	*REMARK*
9 - 8 yes	very social
7 - 6 yes	social
5 - 4 yes	not so social
3 - 2 - 1 yes	improve social behavior

15. Endurance ability test:
    1. High-speed endurance ability test - measures the limit of a person by asking him too many questions in quick succession in a fixed time period of 5 minutes, here younger persons score more and older persons score less.
    2. Power endurance ability test - measures the limit of an individual by asking him few typical questions, which are to be answered in ample time, here younger persons score less and older persons score more.

16. Career choosing test - write 1 for does not know, 2 for not liking and 3 for liking, on the dotted line space:
    1. Profession choosing test:
       Architect = ..., Barber = ..., Machinist = ..., Typist =...,
       Doctor = ...,Engineer = ..., Advocate = ...
       Higher score indicates one's interest in a particular profession.
    2. School subject choosing test:
       Algebra = ..., Biology = ..., History = ..., Physics = ...,
       Chemistry = ..., Arithmetic = ..., higher score.
       Higher score indicates one's interest in a particular subject, which requires to be confirmed from the previous years mark sheets.

3. Team spirit test - choose either from the sentence:
    1. Meet people = ... / Read a book = ...
    2. Play in a team of baseball / football / hockey = ... / Play solitaire with playing cards, lido, gems or games for single person = ... Higher score indicates team spirit in doing a work.
4. Complete the sentence test: All my life, I have been ———————————————————— Indicates - one's thinking, aspiration, attitude and aptitude in life.
5. Career choosing table - in conformity with above score, one can choose the career:

	Interest in	*Choose career in*
1.	Science (PCM)	Engineering (Mech., Elect., Chem., Electronics)
2.	Social studies	Hotel, Airlines, Management.
3.	Political science	Journalism, Administration, Library science.
4.	Acting, music, singing	Film and Entertainment industry.
5.	Life sciences	Medical and pharmaceutical industry.
6.	Computer science	Software and hardware engineering.
7.	Leadership qualities	Marketing, sales and business.
8.	Mathematics	Accounts and finance.
9.	Studies	Higher studies and teaching.

4.6. Memory

Memory is our brain's filing system containing every thing we learn in life. Memory is also the ability to recall facts, when required. Memory is long lasting, fades with time, but comes back from a clue, like: sight of some thing or listening to a particular sound or sensing a peculiar smell.

Three types of memory:

1. Action memory - we learn through action, like: tying a shoelace for the first time, learning swimming for the first time, riding a cycle for the first time, playing tennis and badminton.

2. Factual memory - things get stored, like in a computer and recalled when required, while certain things are always remembered, while others, if not used get erased with time.
3. Personal memory - is the accumulation of past experiences, like falling when trying to walk or falling while cycling or using knife and getting injured. These experiences help us in doing the things in the right way and guide us in future action.

   Seven kinds of memory:

   1. Sensory memory - tells us what is going around us and stops us walking into closed doors or stops tripping over an obstacle.
   2. Early memory - we learn maximum during our childhood, but these memories are laid down in a form that our mind either cannot understand or cannot find, like: burning finger in a fire.
   3. Immediate memory - works for a short time, when we see some thing, hear some thing or experience some thing.

Immediate memory test:

A photograph is shown for a minute and immediately afterwards, a person is asked to write down, what he has seen in the photograph or a person is asked to write down the numberplate details of a passing vehicle or a person is asked to memorize in one minute, the following numbers and immediately afterwards, the person is asked to write them down on the next page what he has seen, without referring to the previous page:

A = 396 829, next page A = (................)

(Answer- 396 829)

B = 483 909 3, next page B = (..................)

(Answer- 483 909 3)

C = 207 683 95, next page C = (...........)

(Answer- 207 683 95)

Immediate memory is like holding facts for a while, but acts, like a leaky bucket.

4. Short term memory - we store most of the things in our brain for a short time, like we remember phone number for a period long enough to make the call, but soon we forget it.

Short Term Memory Test

An interesting story or an incident with some numerical figure is given to study and a person is asked to write down after few days, what he had studied previously.

It has been seen that normally a person remembers 20 % of what he studied yesterday; remembers 17 % of what he had studied one week back; after a fortnight remembers 15 % of what he had studied one fortnight back; after one month remembers 14 % of what he had studied one month back. Our brain is able of storing unlimited information, but what is not used often gets slowly eliminated from memory. We have to revise the things to obtain a good memory. Short-term memory is like storing facts for a while, if not used, get lost.

5. Working memory - is short-term memory in action, but repeated use of phone number, puts the information in the long-term memory. We use working memory to do things and instantly, we retrieve many bits of information to accomplish a task. Working memory is the key to human intelligence, which enables us to solve problems in a logical manner. We must remember that knowledge gained by cramming is always shallow, unreliable, uncertain and produces confusion.
6. Long term memory - facts such as names, events and places have to be remembered consciously and retrieved, when required. Short-term memory gets converted into long-term memory through following steps:
    1. Discuss - the matter studied with colleagues, teachers and link the matter with daily life activities. In this manner, difficult things can be remembered.
    2. Regularly - remain in touch with the matter studied through notes and textbooks. In this manner, the subject matter will trickle down into the long-term memory.
    3. Revision - memory of a lecture begins to fade after 10 minutes, so revise the matter for 10 minutes after one-hour, again revise the lecture for 5 minutes after one day, again revise the lecture for 3 minutes after one week, again revise the lecture for 2 minutes after one

month. After this last revision, the lecture goes into long-term memory and only top up will be required before an annual examination.

We must not expect miracles in the field of long-term memory, as it is an inborn ability; however familiarity with the processes involved in memorizing the things, helps in scoring higher marks in the examination. Long-term memory is like writing the facts in a diary and referring them when required.

7. Life long memory - things, like riding a bike enable us to ride a bicycle for all time to come, once we have acquired the skill.

Memory Storage

Takes place in a portion of the brain, called Hippocampus. Our senses pick up information; convey the information to the Cortex and then to the different areas surrounding the hippocampus. In this manner, the storage of short-term memory take place and there is no separate storage for long-term memory, which exists all over the cortex. The massive memory section in the cortex is believed to contain enough potential to receive ten new items of information every second of our life.

Sense of Perception

Our brain is split into two hemispheres: 1 Right hemisphere and 2 Left hemispheres, one side hemisphere is usually in-charge of a particular skill, like: left side hemisphere deals with language and with a split second delay, the information gets transferred to the other hemisphere, thus one hemisphere gets information twice, ones directly and later with a split second delay from the other hemisphere and this gives the sense of perception.

Brain Neurons

Our brain consists of neuron cells, which are so small that 250 of them can be accommodated on a pinhead. Our brain is made up of 100 billion neurons; as we grow old, these neurons get wired up to each other and they communicate through thousands of inter-connections. When certain connections are established and strengthened, they form the memory.

Mnemonic Word

Is designed to memorize the facts in a sequence, like: Vibgyor (Violet, Indigo, Blue, Green, Yellow, Orange Red) - gives the sequence of colours present in the rainbow, Mvem-jsunp (Mercury - nearest to Sun, Venus, Earth, Mars – Jupiter, Saturn, Uranus, Neptune and Pluto - farthest from the Sun) - gives the sequence of planets present in the Solar System. Mnemonic word acts like a picture, to recall the things in a sequence. Picture improves memory for facts, like: associating a picture with a word or counting in a particular sequence or memorizing facts in a form of poem.

Twenty two tips on memorizing:

1. Write down the points and glance them quickly before speaking.
2. Absent-mindedness is caused by trying to do many things at a time.
3. Confidence builds with the ability that when things are required, they will be remembered.
4. Pay attentions to the details of a matter, as it improves memory.
5. Discuss the points, which are required to be remembered.
6. Listing the items help in memorizing them.
7. Understanding the points help in remembering them.
8. Organizing the things help in remembering them.
9. Association of the difficult things helps in memorizing them.
10. Sequencing the events help in memorizing them.
11. Revising the subject help in memorizing it.
12. Interest in the subject matter helps in memorizing the details.
13. Keen observations help in recalling the details.
14. Listening to a speech intently help in memorizing the said things.
15. Sound sleeps improve memory.
16. Alcohol, drugs, smoking, lack of sleep, fatigue, stress and worry adversely affect memory. Yoga is an exercise of the brain, which improves memory.
17. Remaining mentally active, like: solving crossword puzzles, learning new stills, improve the memory.
18. Scent of lily, mint and eucalyptus aid in concentration. This improves memory.

19. Enjoying the company of good friends and family improve memory.
20. Laughter relaxes the mind and relaxed mind improves memory.
21. Eating fish and almonds improve memory, as they contain polyunsaturated fats that brain cells need to function.
22. Brain needs amino acids, which are present in egg yolk, fresh milk, cheese and in Soya beans.

4.7. Higher Levels of Mental Consciousness

Nature is reshaping the human brain for higher levels of mental consciousness, as 7,000 years ago, when Rigveda was composed; red, yellow and black colours were recognized as three separate shades. Aristotle spoke of tri-coloured rainbow. This concludes that men at that time were able to perceive three colours only and sense of seven coloured rainbow is a comparatively recent acquisition of mankind. Evidence suggests that sense of music developed about 5,000 years ago and sense of fragrance developed even much later. These additions to higher levels mental consciousness are the evidences that human brain is still in the process of evolution.

Science has advanced by leaps and bounds, but still it is in infancy to know as to how the human consciousness works. As it is our brain, that provides us the consciousness, which in turn develops into perception and thought? Brain provides us the interface with the external world. It is the most precious possession of mankind.

Our civilization is carrying the entire humanity towards a better future; TV, Radio and Internet Services are the agents of this transformation, which signifies the enhancement in human intelligence. Our perception depends upon the information, as conveyed by the five human senses, but it has been observed that some individual's exhibit rudimentary faculties of perception of a higher order, which requires further research.

5

Materialistic Aspect

5.0. Astrology

Astrology is science; is not superstition; guidance from it can be taken.

Astrology is Empirical Science

Rules have been framed based on statistics and observations. Albert Einstein, the American scientist had said that astrology is an illuminating body of knowledge, which has taught him many things. Astrological horoscope is cast based upon: 1. Time of birth (When baby cries for the first time), 2. Date of birth and 3. Place of birth. Astrology is a higher science, 30 lakh palm-leaves in India carry the history of people, who are born in different parts of the world. This indicates that planets do influence, as to when an individual will take birth, whom he is going to marry, how many children he is going to have, what job he will be doing. All this information had been written hundreds of years before an individual take birth.

Scientific View

iron is a component of human blood; Earth's magnetic field affects it. Dr Percy Seymour stated that when baby is in mother's womb, Earth's magnetic field affects the development of baby and the wiring up of the nervous system with the brain. Earth's magnetic field fluctuates with the different locations of Sun and planets in the zodiac, which had prevailed during the pregnancy stage of the baby. These magnetic field fluctuations become part of baby's early knowledge and influence the behaviour in later life, when the same planetary positions occur again in life. However on ones birth day, some of the planets do come again in the same positions, which they had occupied during baby's pregnancy. This produces a natural feeling of happiness, as the magnetic field has already been experienced in mother's womb.

Birth of Astrology

Long before astrology became a subject of study, it was observed that some animals and plants used to vanish from a landscape for a period, only to re-appear, when certain patterns of stars and planets again appear in the sky. This experience lead the individuals to identify those patterns of stars and planets as auspicious or in auspicious. In 1989, Canadian province of Quebec lost power for days and pictures from space, just before the power failure showed that the power lines were glowing. This coincided with the flare-up of Sun and the flare-up was caused by certain planetary alignments in the sky.

Five Astrological Traditions

1. Western astrology, 2. Indian astrology called Jyotish in Hindi, 3 Chinese astrology, 4. Persian and Arabic astrology and 5. Tibetan astrology. These traditions share same astronomical data.

Three divisions of Indian Astrology

1. Vedic astrology - is supreme knowledge (Paravidya). It originated when Lord Shiva narrated it to his wife Parvati. Vedic astrology is based on Vedas, which are 6,000 years old. It believes that one takes birth as per his previous life's traits (Sanskars). He takes birth on a particular date, time and place; based on these datas, his horoscope is cast, which is information in a coded form and indicate his tendencies.
2. Ravana's astrology - the legendary ruler of Lanka, had written Red book (Lal Kitab), which is popular in North India. It is a treatise on astrology, astro-palmistry and is based on position of Sun, but does not believe in planet-periods (Dasas), transit

movement of planets (Gochar) and gives prime importance to Jupiter (Guru).

3. Horoscopic astrology and its four subdivisions:
   1. Natal astrology - is the study of an individuals chart to gain information on events and happenings in his life.
   2. Kartarchic astrology - determines the most auspicious moment to begin an enterprise or start a work.
   3. Horary astrology - is used to answer a specific question, by studying the chart of that moment, when the question is asked.
   4. Mundane astrology - is the application of astrology to world events including weather, earthquake, and fate of an empire or religion.

5.1. Vedic Astrology

It is known as Jyotish, which means light. It deals with influence of planets on human affairs. It is believed that Lord Brahma revealed it to mankind for the first time. It is based upon Brihat Parashara Hora Shastra written by Maharishi Parashara. Sun is considered to be the king of all planets. It requires deep study to correctly interpret the planetary positions and the predictions carry a probability of 60 % and rest depends upon ones efforts put in the right direction, to achieve the desired result, however guidance can be taken on major issues.

Horoscope - is coded information, which reveals the behaviour and life pattern of an individual. His horoscope is as exclusive to him, as his fingerprints or DNA code is. The permutation and combination of 9 Planets, 12 Rashis, 12 Houses and 27 Nakshatras give a total of 53, 74, 77,120 horoscopes. As such, it is difficult to get two horoscopes with the same configuration of planets. Casting of a horoscope involves lot of arithmetical work, which best can be done through good computer software.

Two Systems of Casting a Horoscope

1. South Indian System - the horoscope is cast based upon Krishnamurti system (Padhdhati). Horoscope is made in the form of a rectangular-path, which contains 12 houses. 1st Aries sign (Mesha Rashi) is always at the top left corner of

the rectangular-path and the number of signs increase in clockwise direction and ascendant (Lagna) varies as per the time of birth of an individual.

2. North Indian System - the horoscope is cast in the form of a rectangle with crossed lines to have twelve houses and ascendant (Lagna) is always the first house, which is at the top center of the horoscope. Signs (Rashis) are written in figures, which increase in anti-clockwise direction. Planets are indicated with alphabets in a short form. In olden days, Ujjain in Madhya Pradesh India was the center of astronomical observations and position of planets used to be calculated with respect to this city. Now a days ephemeris (Panchangs) are published with respect to Indian Standard Time (IST).

Nomenclature of life span:

1. Alp Ayu - less than 32 years.
2. Madhy Ayu - less than 64 years.
3. Purn Ayu - more than 96 years.
4. Shata Ayu - more than 100 years.
5. Dev Ayu - more than 120 years.

Significance of twelve houses:

1st House - is called Lagan, which is always at 12 o'clock position, concerns with head, neck, pelvis, age, logic, body structure and soul

2nd House - counting in the anti-clockwise direction concerns with right eye, shoulders, reproductive organs, speech, face, nose, family, inherited wealth, personality and love.

3rd House - concerns with ear, arm, ovary, testicles, leg, throat, valour, brothers, sisters and servants.

4th House - concerns with right cheek, knee, heart (Right lobe and valves), stomach, spleen, liver, property, mother, vehicle and peace.

5th House - concerns with education, children, voice, earning and management.

6th House - concerns with right jaw, chest, and calf of leg, body swelling, VD, TB, cancer, enemy, illness and tension.

7th House - concerns with wife, marriage, health, mouth, lips, naval region, groin, feet and profession.

8th House - concerns with left jaw, chest, anus, piles, VD, urinary track, age, life, death and voyage.

9th House - concerns with left cheek, heart, knee, luck, religion and pilgrimage.

10th House - concerns with left side body, nostrils, thigh, business, career, profession, father and service.

11th House - concerns with left ear, arm, ovary, testicles, earning, property and vehicle.

12th House - concerns with left side eye, shoulder, sexual organs, injury, tension, expenditure, loss, habits and foreign relations.

Vinshottri Dasha (Periods) - planets as situated in the horoscope, have a general influence on the native, which lasts through out the life, but at certain times particular planets predominate for certain periods. This period is known as period of planet (Dasha) and is calculated on the basis of Nakshatra, in which Moon is placed at the time of birth.

Signs (Rashis) - sign is 30° part of the zodiac path in the sky, which is 15° wide, zodiac path makes a circle of 360°, each zodiac division is called sign and twelve signs (Rashis) are: 1. Aries (Mesha), 2. Taurus (Vrishabh), 3. Gemini (Mithun), 4. Cancer (Karka), 5. Leo (Simha), 6. Virgo (Kanya), 7. Libra (Tula), 8. Scorpio (Vrischik), 9. Sagittarius (Dhanu), 10. Capricorn (Makar), 11. Acquarius (Kumbh) and 12. Pisces (Meen), which are written in the horoscope in figures starting from 1 to 12.

Time period of planets - Earth is moving round the Sun in 12 months and rotates on its own axis in 24 hours, but when Earth's speed is added to Sun, Earth becomes stationary for the purpose of astrological calculation. Thus Sun is made to move in different signs (Rashis). This makes arithmetical part of astrology easy to interpret. Sun and planets take different time to move from one sign to the next sign (Rashi) and the time periods are:

S/N	*Planet*	*Time*
1.	Sun (Surya)	30 days
2.	Moon (Chandra)	2.25 days
3.	Mars (Mangal)	45 days
4.	Mercury (Budh)	30 days
5.	Jupiter (Guru)	12 months

6.	Venus (Shukar)	27 days
7.	Saturn (Shani)	30 months
8.	Dragon's head (Rahu)	18 months
9.	Dragon's tail (Ketu)	18 months

Five limbs of Indian ephemeris (Panchang) - the day starts with Sunrise and lasts up to the next day's Sunrise and week starts on Sunday (Not on Monday, as happens in Western system). Hindu festivals are celebrated based on lunar days, lunar months and five limbs (Angas) of Panchang are:

1. Week day (Var) - is named after the Lord (Swamy) of the first period of one hour (Hora), which is present at the time of Sunrise. Order of Hora Lords (Swamies): 1 Sun (Surya), 2 Venus (Shukra), 3 Mercury (Budh), 4 Moon (Chandra), 5 Saturn (Shani), 6 Jupiter (Guru) and 7 Mars (Mangal). In Vikram calendar week starts on Sunday (Ravivar), because the fist Hora at the time of Snrise is of Sun (Ravi / Surya).

   Example: On 1st January 2004, the 1st Hora was of Jupiter (Guru) and the day was called Thursday (Guruvar) and counting in the order of Hora Lords (Swamies), as given above the 24th Hora was of Sun (Surya) and the next 25th Hora (Time of Sunrise) was of Venus (Shukar), as such, the next day was called Friday (Shukarvar). In Hindu system, the day changes at the time of Sunrise.
2. Lunar day (Tithi) - gives the stages of waning and waxing of Moon. It is anticlockwise angular distance between Sun and Moon, as measured from Earth along the ecliptic in which Sun, Moon and Planets seem to move. It is 360° divided into 30 parts of 12° each. The time spent by the Moon in each of these parts is called one lunar day (Tithi). When Moon is between Earth and Sun (All the three in one line), it is Dark Moon (Amavasiya) and lunar day (Tithi) is written as 30. When Earth is between Sun and Moon (All the three in one line), it is Full Moon (Purnima) and lunar day (Tithi) is written as 15. Tithi begins at varying times of the day and variation can take place from 19 to 26 hours.

Lunar fortnight (Paksha) - consists of 15 lunar days (Tithis). The decreasing phase of Moon from full Moon to new Moon is called dark fortnight (Krishna Paksha). When Moon is at 90°, it is 8th Tithi of dark fortnight (Krishna Paksha). Similarly increasing phase of Moon from new Moon to full Moon is called bright fortnight (Shukal Paksha). When Moon is between 84° to 96°, it is 8th Tithi of bight fortnight (Shukal Paksha).

Lunar month (Masa) - each Masa has two fortnights (Pakshas). It consists of 30 days. Each fortnight (Paksha) has 15 lunar days (Tithis). Each lunar day (Tithi) is of 12°. Season (Ritu) is of two lunar months. Each six monthly period (Ayanam) is of three seasons (Ritus). Year consists of two six monthly periods (Ayanams).

Lunar day lord (Tithi Swamy) - Tithis have Lords (Swamies), indicated in bracket: 1st Tithi is called Pratipada (Agni), 2nd Dwitiya (Brahma), 3rd Tratiya (Gori), 4th Chaturthi (Ganesh), 5th Panchmi (Sheshnag), 6th Shashti (Kartikya), 7th Saptmi (Surya), 8th Ashtami (Shiv), 9th Naumi (Durga), 10th Dashmi (Kali), 11th Akadashi (Vishvadeva), 12th Dwadashi (Vishnu), 13th Trayodashi (Kamdeva), 14th Chaturdashi (Shiva), 15th Purnima (Moon) and 30th Amavashiya (Piter - the ancestors).

Tithi for the day - Moon located at the time of Sunrise, is the Tithi for the day, but sometimes due to relative motion of Earth and Moon, Moon seems to travel faster and this leads to loss of one lunar day (Tithi), which means that the fortnight will have 14 days; on the other hand, sometimes Moon travel is slower and then the lunar day (Tithi) is repeated, which means that the fortnight will have 16 days. Moon takes 29.53059 days to go once round the Earth.

Lunar day and week day (Tithi and Var) table - lunar day (Tithi) is very important and in combination with week day, forms an auspicious or inauspicious day for the start of new work:

Tithis	*Auspicious*	*Inauspicious*
1, 6, 11	Friday	Sunday, Tuesday
2, 7, 12	Wednesday	Monday, Thursday

3, 8, 13	Tuesday	Wednesday
4, 9, 14	Saturday	Friday
5,10,15	Thursday	Saturday

3. Half lunar day (Karan) - it is the time period for the angular distance between Sun and Moon to increase in steps of 6°. There are 11 types of Karans, 7 Karans are of repeating (Char) nature, they get repeated many times in a month; remaining 4 Karans are of stationary (Esthir) nature, they come once in a month. Karan present at the time of Sunrise, the same is written for the day. When Moon goes 6° ahead of Sun, one Karan passes. Four fixed Karans are: 1 Kimstughna, 2 Shakuni, 3 Chatushpad and 4 Nagava; seven repeating Karnas are: 1 Bava, 2 Balava, 3 Kanlava, 4 Taitula, 5 Garaja, 6 Vaija and 7 Vishti (Bhadra) - in this Karan start of auspicious thing is avoided. First half of the first Tithi is always Kimstughna
4. Yog - is the angular distance along the ecliptic measured from Aeries (Mesha) sign (Rashi) is the longitude, when longitudes of Sun and Moon are added, they give a value from 0° to 360°, this is divided into 27 parts, which means 1 / 60 of a degree. These parts are called Yogs. Yogs are 27; the Yoga active at the time of Sunrise is the Yog for the day. Yogs are of two types:

   1st Type Yog - is obtained by dividing the position of Sun and Moon in the Zodiac by 12. These Yogs are 27.

   2nd Type Yog - is the combination of week day (Var) and constellation (Nakshatra). These combinations are 28; 14 are auspicious; remaining 14 are inauspicious. The 28 combinations are subdivided into four groups:

   1. Sarvasidhiyog - work gets completed amicably.
   2. Ananddadiyog - execution of work gives pleasure.
   3. Dwipuskeryog - two works get completed, provided Tithi is 2 or 7 or 12.
   4. Tripushkeryog - three works get completed, provided Tithi is 2 or 7 or 12.
   5. Constellation (Nakshatra) - is a group of star in which Moon is aligned at the time of Sunrise. This is the

Constellation (Nakshatra) for the day. Constellations (Nakshatras) act like milestones in the sky and form the Zodiac circle of 360°. Constellations (Nakshatras) are 27, which divide the Zodiac into 27 divisions of 13.2° each. Constellations (Nakshatras) are used in match making for marriage and for putting on new clothes. Each Constellation (Nakshatra) is subdivided into four steps (Charans), which is considered in naming a new born baby. Constellations (Nakshatras) have their own behaviour (Savbhav) and form four groups:

1 Mool (m) - if a child is born in this group, special worship (Puja) is to be performed for peace in family.
2 Dhruv (dh) - obstacles in the execution of new work may arise.
3 Punchak (p) - not considered to be auspicious for start of new work.
4 Darun (da) - difficulties arise from the very beginning of the new work.

Constellation (Nakshatra) Table

Table is used to find an auspicious day for the start of new work. Legend: m - Mool, dh - Dhruv, da - Darun, p – Panchak; Sarvasidhiyoga - every thing goes well, Ananddadiyoga - work gives pleasure, Dwipuskeryoga - two works get completed and Tripushkeryoga - three works get completed; Su - Sunday, M - Monday, Tu - Tuesday, W - Wednesday, Th - Thursday, F - Friday and Sa - Saturday:

5.2. Astrological Tables

1. Earning capacity (Paya) table - is based upon Moon's position in the horoscope; the 1st house in North Indian style of horoscope is always at 12 o'clock position, which is called ascendant (Lagna); house numbers increase in anti-clockwise direction; position of the Moon in the house of gives a number, which signifies the earning capacity and well being of a native:

S/N	Nakshatra	Savbhav	Sarvarsidhi	Anandadi	Dwipushker	Tripushker
1.	Asvani	m.	Su, Tu, Th, F.	Su, Tu, Th, Sa.		
2.	Bharni					
3.	Kritika		Tu, W.	M, W, F, Sa.	Su, Tu, Sa.	
4.	Rohini	dh.	M, W, Sa.	Su, M, Tu, W, F, Sa.		
5.	Mragshira		M, W.	Su, M, W, F.	Su, Tu, Sa.	
6.	Adra	da.				
7.	Puranvasu		Th, F.	Su, Tu, Th, Sa.	Su, Tu, Sa.	
8.	Pushiya		Su, M, Th.	Su, M, Tu, W, Th, Sa.		
9.	Ashlaisha	m, da.	Tu.	M, Tu, T, Sa.		
10.	Mgha	m.				
11.	Purvaphaguni		Su, M, Tu, W, F.			
12.	Utraphaguni	dh.	Su.	Su, M, W, Th, F.		Su, Tu, Sa.
13.	Hast		Su, W.	Su, Tu, W, F.		
14.	Chitra		Su, Tu, Sa.			
15.	Swati		Sa.	M, Tu, Th, Sa.		
16.	Vishakha		M, Tu, W, Th, F, Sa.	Su, Tu, Sa.		
17.	Anuradha		M, W, Th, F.	M, W, Th, Sa.		
18.	Jayashta	m, da.				
19.	Mula	m, da.	Su.	Su, Tu, W, F.		

S/N	*Nakshatra*	*Savbhav*	*Sarvarsidhi*	*Anandadi*	*Dwipushker*	*Tripushker*
20.	Purvashada		Su, Tu, W, Th, F, Sa.			
21.	Utrashada	dh.	Su.	Su, Tu, Th, F.		Su, Tu, Sa.
22.	Shravana		M, F, Sa.	M, W, Th, Sa.		
23.	Dhanishta	p	Su, M, W, Th, F, Sa.	Su, Tu, Sa.		
24.	Shatbhisha	p	M, W, F, Sa.			
25.	Purvabhadrapa	p				
26.	Utrabhadrapa	p, dh.	Su, Tu.	Su, Tu, Th, F.		Su, Tu, Sa.
27.	Ravti	p, m.	Th, F.	Su, M, Tu, Th, F, Sa.		

House Nos.	*Paya*	*Earning capacity*
1, 6, 11	Golden	Above average
2, 5, 9	Silver	Very good
3, 7, 10	Copper	Good
4, 8, 12	Iron	Average

2. Significance table - Moon remains in a sign (Rashi) for 2.25 days; then moves into the next sign (Rashi); counting in the anti-clockwise direction from the position of the Moon in the native's horoscope to the current location of the Moon in the sign (Rashi), gives a number, which has significance in respect of the coming events:

Number	*Significance*
1, 3, 5	Gives money
2, 4	Gives desired results
7, 10, 11	Gives extreme pleasure
8, 9	Gives disappointment
6, 12	Gives unhappiness

3. Auspicious / inauspicious time (Choghadiya) table - indicates the auspicious time for the start of a work. It is based on the day of the week, time during the day / night. Legend: Ud (Uddaig) - start of work gives trouble, Ch (Chal) - start of work neither good nor bad, La (Labh) - start of work profitable, Am (Amrit) - start of work is as good as elixir, Ka (Kal) - start of work not beneficial, better postpone the start of work, Sh (Shubh) - start of work most beneficial, Ro (Rog) - start of work not auspicious, better shift the start of work.

Daytime	*Sun*	*Mon*	*Tue*	*Wed*	*Thu*	*Fri*	*Sat*
0600 - 0730	Ud	Am	Ro	La	Sh	Ch	Ka
0730 - 0900	Ch	Ka	Ud	Am	Ro	La	Sh
0900 - 1030	La	Sh	Ch	Ka	Ud	Am	Ro
1030 - 1200	Am	Ro	La	Sh	Ch	Ka	Ud
1200 - 1330	Ka	Ud	Am	Ro	L	Sh	Ch
1330 - 1500	Sh	Ch	Ka	Ud	m	Ro	La

1500 - 1630	Ro	La	Sh	Ch	Ka	Ud	Am
1630 - 1800	Ud	Am	Ro	La	Sh	Ch	Ka
Nighttime							
1800 - 1930	Sh	Ch	Ka	Ud	Am	Ro	La
1930 - 2100	Am	Ro	La	Sh	Ch	Ka	Ud
2100 - 2230	Ch	Ka	Ud	Am	Ro	La	Sh
2230 - 2400	Ro	La	Sh	Ch	Ka	Ud	Am
2400 - 0130	Ka	Ud	Am	Ro	La	Sh	Ch
0130 - 0300	La	Sh	Ch	Ka	Ud	Am	Ro
0300 - 0430	Ud	Am	Ro	La	Sh	Ch	Ka
0430 - 0600	Sh	Ch	Ka	Ud	Am	Ro	La

4. Match making (Melapak) - is an astrological guide to check the compatibility between would be husband and wife. The position of Mars (Mangal) planet plays an important part in matrimonial relations. If Mars (Mangal0 is located in 1st, 4th, 7th, 8th and 12th house in a horoscope; the concerned person is said to be Manglik. His / her horoscope ought to be matched with another Manglik person, otherwise disharmony or early death of a partner or bad health is suspected.

   Match making (Melapak) is very popular in Hindu society, as such; divorce cases are less in the society, when compared with other communities. Match making (Melapak) is based on matching of eight attributes (Gunas) of boy and girl. If attributes of boy and girl are matching, then each attribute (Guna) is allotted points from 1 to 8, which are added, if attribute totals more than 18 points, the marriage is likely to succeed.

Eight attributes (Gunas)

1. Varna - is egoism between the couple; if compatibility exists between the couple; then one point is allotted, which means that husband will treat wife with respect and wife will treat the husband with affection.
2. Vashya - is intensity of mutual attraction and affection; if compatibility exists between the couple; then two points are allotted, which means that they are made for each other.

3. Tara - is harmony and well being; if compatibility exists between the couple; then three points are allotted, which means that they will be living in good harmony and will look after each other.
4. Yoni - is the biological satisfaction and dispute; if compatibility exists between the couple; then four points are allotted, which means that they will have biological satisfaction and there will be no dispute between them.
5. Graha - is intellectual outlook and spiritual thinking; if compatibility exists between the couple; then five points are allotted, which means that their intellectual outlook and spiritual thinking will be the same and they are likely to lead a good harmonious life.
6. Gana - is temperamental characteristic; if compatibility exists between the couple; then six points are allotted, which means that they will have good temperamental adjustment and will lead a happy life.
7. Bhakut - is growth of family, well-being and welfare; if compatibility exists between the couple; then seven points are allotted, which means that they will have children, have good relations with other members in the family and will look after their family well i.e. they will help each other.
8. Nadi - is outward physical health and internal constitutional (metabolic) health; if compatibility exists between the couple; then eight points are allotted, which means that they will have good physical and constitutional health. If there is Nadi defect (Dosha) between the couple; then match is not recommended for marriage, as early death of a person is suspected. This is the single most important Guna.

Match making (Melapak) Score Interpretation

All the allotted points against each attribute (Guna) are added together and recommendation for the score range is:

Score	*Recommendation*
0 – 17	Match not acceptable
18 – 21	Match acceptable (average)
22 – 27	Match good

28 – 31	Match very good
32 – 36	Match theoretically good, but not conducive to long-term relationship, as it ends up making the couple similar to each other and better reject the offer.

5. Hindu Marriage Code

Hindus believe that marriage is predetermined in the heaven and on Earth it is solemnized. Both husband and wife have to follow the code, which is a life long agreement. Hindu marriage has a much deeper meaning, which gets solemnized by taking seven rounds around a sacred fire. This marriage is known as seven steps (Saptpadi) system.

Girl takes Seven Promises (Vachans) from Boy

1. You will perform religious duties, like: pilgrimage (Tirth), fasts (Varat), completion of fast ceremony (Udhapan), sacrifices as offered in a sacred fire (Yagiya), donation (Dan); all these religious duties you will perform along with me and with my consent; if you promise, I will come to sit on your left side. Boy agrees.
2. You will perform holy works (Karyas), like: worship (Puja), offering food to the ancestors (Shradh), spend money (Kharch); all these religious duties you will perform along with me and with my consent; if you promise, I will come to sit on your left side. Boy agrees.
3. You will be responsible to provide protection to the family (Raksha), provide boarding and lodging facilities to the family (Bharan Poshan), look after cattle (Pashudhan); all these duties you will perform along with me and with my consent; if you promise, I will come to sit on your left side. Boy agrees
4. You will be arrange for money (Dhan), expenditure (Vayav), property (Jayadad); all these duties you will perform along with me and with my consent; if you promise, I will come to sit on your left side. Boy agrees.
5. When you construct - temple (Devalaya), garden (Bag), water well (Kuup), pond (Trag), rectangular water pit (Bavri), worship of site (Bhumi Pujan); all these duties you will

perform along with me and with my consent; if you promise, I will come to sit on your left side. Boy agrees.

6. Wether you work in local town or go outside to earn money (Dhan Uparjan) or do business; all these duties you will perform along with me and with my consent; if you promise, I will come to sit on your left side. Boy agrees.
7. You will not allow emotion and money (Maya) to be showered on another girl or try to touch or embrace her with bad intentions; if you promise, I will come to sit on your left side. Boy agrees.

Boy takes Five Promises (Vachans) from Girl

1. When I am in the house, you will engage yourself in entertainment and enjoyment (Amond Pramod). Girl agrees.
2. When I am in the house, you will have bath, apply oil to your body (Upatan), set your hair, wear ornaments (Sharangar), go for social engagements (Samajik Dharm), join in the gatherings, go to temple (Mandir), go to see the deity (Darshan), go to other's house for a visit. Girl agrees.
3. When I am on tour out of town, refrain from all the above activities. Girl agrees.
4. Adopt the customs of my family, pay respect to my parents, brothers, sisters and to other family members, be loyal to me. Girl agrees.
5. Family life (Grahasta-ashram) depends upon your co-operation, be obedient to me; if you promise to do all the things, please do come to sit on my left side. Girl occupies the left side of the boy and the marriage gets solemnized.
6. Auspicious times for doing things - Moon radiates electro-magnetic energy towards Earth. This influences the growth of metabolism and mind of the living beings, as mentioned below:
   1. Waning Moon fortnight (Krishna Paksha) - good for house cleaning house, removing negative emotions and bad habits.
   2. New Moon - good for meditation, prayer, religious rites, but no new work to be under taken.

3. Bright fortnight (Shukal Paksha) - good for love, wealth, new projects, business and friendship.
4. Full Moon (Purnima) - good for organizing cleaning.

7. Saturn's (Shani's) seven and half year period (Saadhe Sati) – the period starts, when Saturn comes one house before the house in which Moon is located in the horoscope. Saturn remains in this house for a period of 2.5 years and then it moves to the house, where Moon itself is located. Here, Saturn remains for a period of 2.5 years. Lastly, Saturn moves one house next to the Moon's location in the horoscope. Here again it remains for a period of 2.5 years. Thus planet Saturn (Shani) influences the native for a period of: 2.5 yr + 2.5 yr + 2.5 yr = 7.5 years. This period normally repeats three times in an individual's life. The effects are:

   1st Time during childhood - Saturn creates problems in education and relations with parents, but is good for earning.

   2nd Time during adulthood - Saturn creates problems in work areas, in finances and in relations with family, but leads to less expenditure.

   3rd Time during old age - Saturn affects a person's health.

8. Saturn's (Shani's) two and half year period (Dhaiya) - when Saturn comes in the fourth house and again in the eigth house from the location of Moon in one's horoscope. Saturn in each case remains for a period of 2.5 years. During this period in each case, it is called two and half year period (Dhaiya). The effects are:

   Fourth house two and half year period (Dhaiya) - good for valour.

   Eighth house two and half year period (Dhaiya) - good for family life.

   If Saturn (Shani) is well placed in a native's horoscope, it will lead the native to a higher standard of life. If not, then it may cause hardship in life.

9. Diseases - planets do play a vital role in pre-determining one's disposition to a particular disease, which may occur during the lifetime of a native. Human body is divided into 12 parts, each part is ruled by a particular planet and Zodiac sign, like: 4th house represents heart. India has the dubious

role of having the largest number of heart patients in the world and 6th house is for all types of diseases.

10. Serpent time configuration (Kalsarp Yog) - if all the seven planets are located between Dragon's head (Rahu) and Dragon's tail (Ketu), it is called serpent time configuration (Kalsarp Yog). This can lead to deterioration of health, wealth, longevity, imprisonment, serious accident, divorce, marital discard, destruction of business and downfall of the person in politics.

5.3. Astrology under test - Mugal Emperor Shahjahn wanted to test the reliability of astrological predictions. He called astrologer Pati Ram to his Red Fort in Delhi. Shahjahn said that see Pati Ram, there are four gates in the Red Fort to go outside with army to inspect Delhi. Pati Ram give me your prediction that through which gate, I will go out tomorrow? If your prediction is wrong, you will be beheaded. Pati Ram was trembling with fear for his imminent death. Pati Ram prayed; cast the horoscope (Prashna-kundali) for that time. He wrote his prediction on a piece of paper; in the presence of all present; placed the paper in a box; locked the box and handed over the key to Shahjahn. Pati Ram requested that the box may please be opened after completion of inspection tour.

Shahjahn sealed the box; put the box under a guard's custody; ordered that 5th gate be made by breaking the fort-wall. From this newly constructed gate, Shahjahan along with his army, went out to inspect Delhi. On return from his tour, Shahjahn broke the seal; opened the box and was surprised to read the prediction. Pati Ram had written that a new 5th gate will be made; Shahjahn with his army will go out through this new gate. Shahjahn was pleased; Pati Ram was handsomely awarded; the place where Pati Ram stayed was renamed as: Kucha Pati Ram. This name still continues and the place is situated in Chandi Chok area of Delhi.

5.4. Other methods of predictions - since the dawn of civilization, mankind is eager to know the future and for this has invented many methods, some of which are:

1. Face reading - is a tricky affair, but some people do have the ability to study the faces and give predictions. Presently,

this method is used as a confirmatory corollary to the predictions as obtained from astrology.

2. Thumb print reading - is a cumbersome method. It involves taking thumbprint impression and matching them with the available thumbprint data to obtain the predictions. The system is popular in South India. Thumbprints are divided into 108 categories; each category is subdivided into 55 types; each type is further subdivided, till the thumbprint matches to the nearest available thumbprint impression and predictions are read from scriptures. If the thumbprint matching is correct; predictions obtained are quite reliable.
3. Palmistry - as civilizations advanced, they found that a relationship exists between palm- lines and fate of a person and from this corollary palmistry developed, where predictions can be obtained in a fairly reliable manner. It is the most readily available method for predictions, but interpretations of hand-lines is difficult, as such, it is not much practiced.
4. Taoism (Path way) - is prevalent in China. Tao is a natural force, which makes the universe act, as it does. Tao creates everything, unity of all existence. Taoism has two opposing forces: 1 Yin and 2 Yang:
    1. Yin- is heavy, dark, moist, earthy and feminine, like: Moon.
    2. Yang- is airy, light, dry, hot and masculine, like: Sun.

   These opposing forces are in everything, locked into an eternal struggle, but neither can destroy the other. All life is made possible by Chi, which is the life breadth and energy of universe. Taoism developed 10,000 years ago. It believes in meditation and has Priests, Monks and Nuns and has 1440 books. Taoists believe that certain things in life, like: family and inherited wealth is fixed, but other things are in the hands of an individual and depend upon his efforts.
5. Feng Shui - originated in China about 5,000 years ago. It is not based on any religion, mysticism or superstition. It is purely mathematical in nature. Feng Shui has four aspects: 1. Building, 2. Environment, 3. People and 4. Time. Feng

Shui believes in five elements: 1. Earth, 2. Wood, 3. Metal, 4. Fire and 5. Water (Similar to Indian belief in the five elements: 1. Earth, 2. Sky, 3. Air, 4. Fire and 5. Water)

Feng Shui believes in fate. Fate has three parts: 1. Past fate - with which one is born and cannot be changed, 2. Present fate - which one builds and depends upon him, which he builds in the present life, 3. Future fate - one gets out of Earth, from the environment, which he gets in house, factory, office, shop and this fate can be modified.

Yin and Yang - are the two opposite forces of the Feng Shui System, which are to be balanced in the house and in the landscape through the productive circle: 1. Wood, 2. Fire, 3. Earth, 4. Metal and 5. Water.

Chi - is soul, which is invisible; cannot be touched; cannot be seen; cannot be herd. Chi is of two types: 1. Live Chi - it brings luck and is pleasurable and 2. Dead Chi - brings sorrow and bad luck. Chi flows in and around the building. Feng Shui works on the basis that the world is alive with these forces.They shape the land and life on it, while fortunetellers give guidance, but they can not fix the fortune.

6. Bhrigu Sanhita - is an astrological classic, which was written by Maharishi Bhrigu during Vedic period. Sanhita prescribes a method to predict past, present and future. Bhrigu along with Lord Ganesha compiled five lakh horoscopes called Kundlies. These horoscopes were based upon the planetary positions of nine planets; each horoscope has a prediction. These half a million horoscopes (Five lakh) were stored at Nalanda University.

It is unfortunate that when Mugal and European nations invaded India, three lakh Bhrigu Sanhita horoscopes (Kundalies) were taken away to foreign countries for study and remaining two lakh Kundalies got scattered in various parts of India, like: at Hoshiarpur in Punjab and at Kankroli in Rajasthan. Most surprisingly, these horoscopes give the date, day and time, when the native will come to hear his past, present and future life events. It also prescribes remedial measures to rectify the bad effects of planets.

5.5. Calendars

1. Gregorian Calendar (2005)- Julius Ceaser of Rome in Italy, introduced Julian Calendar, which was based on the knowledge that Earth takes 365.25 days to go once round the Sun in one year. In Julian calendar, the first month was March and last month was February, but the calendar was fast by 11.25 minutes every year, so by 1500 AD, the error mounted to 11 days and to correct this error 13th Pope Gregory of Rome ordered that 15th October 1582 to follow 4th October 1582. New calendar moved the beginning of New Year from 25th March to 1st January.

   In New Julian calendar, the year is taken to be 365.2425 days, but still the year had an error of 26 seconds, which is accounted for, if after 3200 year, February has 28 days. Pope declared that February not to have 29 days unless the centuary is divisible by 400 and after this rectification, the new Julian calendar was renamed as Gregorian calendar.

   In 1775, Government of United Kingdom adopted Gregorian calendar; introduced it in all their colonies and looking at the scientific base of the calendar; other countries adopted it for their official work and fixed their local calendar dates with respect to it. Gregorian Calendar year has 365 days in a normal year and 366 days in a leap year (Accurate 1 year = 365.242196 days = 365 days, 5 hours, 48 minutes and 48 seconds), day and date change at midnight. Originally, the calendar was started to commemorate the birth of Jesus Christ, but later it was found that Jesus Christ was born in 4 BC (Before Christ). He was crucified in 29 AD (Anno Domini - in the year of our Lord) at the young age of 33 years.

2. Samvat (Hindu Calendar) - many Samvats are in use in India and some of them are: 1 Shri Krishna Samavat (5029), 2 Gautam Samvat (2578), 3 Mahaveer Samvat (2530), 4 Shri Shankaracharya Samvat (2283), 5 Kalchuri Samvat (1755), 6 Vallabhi Samvat (1683), 7 Fasli Samvat (1414), 8 Bangla Samvat (1411), 9 Islami Hijari (1425) and 10 Harsh Samvat (1394).

3. Vikram Samvat (2061) - astrologer King Vikramaditya of Ujjain in Madhya Pradesh in India, whose kingdom stretched

from Multan in Pakistan to Takshila in Bihar, started Vikram Samavat on his victory over Shaka Kings. This is world's oldest calendar still in use and has Tithi system, which is measurement of Moon's position in degrees with respect to Earth and Sun.

Samvat is based on lunar months (Not Solar months), each lunar month has two Pakshas (Fortnights) called: Krishna Paksha (Dark half) and Shukal Paksha (Bright half). Lunar month begins on 1st Tithi of Krishna Paksha, which comes after Purnima (Full Moon day). Each Paksha has 15 Tithis. Krishna Paksha ends on Amavasiya (Dark Moon day) and is written as 30. Shukal Paksha starts on 1st Tithi of Shukal Paksha and ends on Purnima, which is written as 15.

Vikram Samvat has 12 lunar months and 1 year = 354 days + 9 hours. Gregorian year has 12 Solar months and 1 year = 365 days + 5 hours + 48 minutes + 48 seconds, as such, lunar calendar is less by 11 days. In Vikram Samvat, day starts at Sunrise and lasts up to the Sunrise of the next day (Day does not change at midnight).

Moon's variable motion around the Earth; Earth's variable motion around the Sun; both these relative motions, sometimes cause that two successive days have same Tithi; in this case, latter Tithi is called Adhik (Extra) Tith; sometimes one Tithi may never touch Sunrise, as such, no day is labeled by that Tithi and the Tithi is called Kshaya Tithi (Lost Tithi). This arrangement of Tithis has been adopted to keep a permanent relationship with the lunar months.

Two travels of Sun (Ayan) :

1. Sun's travel towards South (Dakshinayan) - Sun travels from Kark Rashi to end of Dhanu Rashi for the period of 178 days. This period is not considered auspicious for many things.
2. Sun's travel towards North (Uttaryayan) - Sun travels from Makar Rashi to end of Mithun Rashi for the period of 187 days. This period is considered to be more auspicious for many things, even for death. The difference between 187 and 178 of 9 days is due to inclination of Earth's Axis (23.5°).

Vikram Samvat lunar months (Masas) - lunar month starts after Purnima; Chaitra is the 1st month of the year; month names are based on constellations (Nakshatra), where Moon is aligned at the start of the month; Vikram Samvat - 2061, started on 7th March 2004. Table gives the constellation (Nakshatra,) Number of month, Number of days in a month and corresponding season in India:

Nakshatra	*No.*	*Month*	*Days*	*Season*
Chitra	1st	Chaitra	30	Vasantha (New Year)
Vishakha	2nd	Vaisakha	31	Grishma
Jaishta	3rd	Jyaistha	31	Grishma
Purvashada	4th	Asahdha	31	Varsha
Shravana	5th	Shravana	31	Varsha
Purvabhaderpada	6th	Bhadrapad	31	Sarat
Ashvini	7th	Asvina	30	Sarat
Kartika	8th	Kartika	30	Hemanta
Margshirsh	9th	Margshirsh	30	Hemanta
Pushya	10th	Pausa	30	Sisira
Magha	11th	Magha	30	Sisira
Uttraphaguni	12th	Phalguna	30	Vasantha

5 years = 1 Yug, 12 Yugas = 1 Chakra.

Vikram Samvat year can be changed into Gregorian calendar year by subtracting 57 before 1st January and 56 for the later dates.

Starting of lunar month (Masa) - in Mukhya Mana System, the month begins with a new Moon. This system is followed in South India. In Gauna Mana System, the month begins with a full Moon. This system is followed in North India.

Extra month (Adhik Masa) - if Sun does not transit into the next Rashi, but simply keeps moving within a Rashi in a lunar month, then that month is named Adhika Masa. In other words, when Sun does not transit after two fortnights or Sankranti (Movement of Sun from one Rashi into the next Rashi) does not take place, then the period is called Adhik Masa, which comes after 23 months, 16 days and 10 hours. This arrangement keeps a permanent relationship with Gregorian calendar and with the seasons in India.

If a lunar month elapses without solar transit; the next transit is into Mesha Rashi; then the month without transit is labeled Adhika Chaitra; the next month is labeled according to transit as usual and this month is called Shuddha (Clear) Masa name.

Loss of month (Kshaya Masa) - if Sun transits two Rashis within a lunar month, then the month is labeled as Kshaya Masa. If Sun transits into Mesha Rashi and Vrishabha Rashi in a lunar month, then it is called Chaitra Vaishakha Kshaya. There will be no separate months labeled Chaitra and Vaishakha. Kshaya Masa occurs between 19 and 141 years, the last was in 1983 from 15th January through 12th February and was Pausha Magha Kshaya and 13th February onwards was Ahika Phalguna.

Sun is observed to travel along an ecliptic, which is divided into 12 parts called Rashis and the first Rashi is Mesha Rashi. The day on which the Sun transits into each Rashi before Sunset, it is taken to be the first day of the month, in case, the Sun transits into a Rashi after Sunset, but before the next Sunrise, then the next day is the first day of the month.

4. Rashtriya Shaka (National calendar) - Old Shaka calendar was used for 200 years, but had deficiencies, as such, Kushana dynasty King Kanishka (120 - 160 AD) modified the Old Shaka calendar; Modified Shaka calendar was used in the kingdom for official purpose and payments used to be made based on it, but still the prevalent Shaka calendar had deficiencies, as such, after independence in 1947, Government of India appointed a committee to review the prevalent Shaka calendar. The Shaka calendar was reviewed on scientific lines; was renamed as Rashtriya Shaka (National Calendar). Dates in Rashtriya Shaka can be converted into Gregorian calendar dates by adding 78 for a date before 31st December and 79 for a date after 31st

December. Rashtriya Shaka calendar dates have a permanent relationship with Gregorian calendar dates. Rashtriya Shaka begins on 22nd March and on 21st March in a Shaka leap year and the leap year calculation is:

1st case: Shaka + 78, if divisible by 4 with no remainder.

2nd case: Shaka + 78, if a multiple of 100 and sum divisible with 400 with no remainder.

In both the above cases - Shaka will be a leap year, example: 1926 + 78 = 2004, divisible by 4 with no remainder, Rashtria Shaka began on 21st March 2004.

5. Chinese Calendar - is lunar based; varies between 12 or 13 months of 29 or 30 days in a year; months are numbered, not named; 13th month is inserted every three or four years; Chinese New Year begins on different date each year; each year is named after an animal, like: Sheep Year began on 1st February 2003, Monkey Year began on 22nd January 2004. Animal names follow a cycle of 12 years, like: 1 Rat, 2 Ox, 3 Tiger, 4 Rabbit, 5 Dragon, 6 Snake, 7 Horse, 8 Sheep, 9 Monkey, 10 Rooster, 11 Dog and 12 Pig. Persons born in a particular animal year have the characteristics of that animal.

6. Time

In 1675 AD, Royal Observatory was established on a hill in the middle of Greenwich in London [United Kingdom] with the intention to use astronomy to establish standard time. Since 1833 AD, it is a practice that a bright red ball climbs the observatory's turret at 12:58 hrs and drops at 13:00 hrs to allow ships on the Thames River to set their time.

Greenwich Mean Time (GMT)

In 1884 AD, International Conference designated Greenwich as the Prime Meridian 0° longitude, which was drawn on the ground in the North to South direction. All the countries of the world accepted the Prime Meridian and GMT (Greenwich Mean Time) became universal standard time. Presently, world clocks are electronically synchronized to GMT.

Indian Standard Time (IST)

IST was adopted on 01.01.1906 for 82° 30' E for Mirzapur, Uttar Pradesh. IST is five and half-hour in advance of GMT. During 2nd World War to utilize day light, IST was advanced by one hour from 01.09.1942 to 15.10.1945.

Universal Time (UT)

UT is sometimes referred to as GMT. UT is always expressed in terms of 24 hour clock, like 2:42 pm or 14:42 is written as 1442; 9:17 pm or 21:17 is written as 2117 and sometimes 'Z' is appended to indicate UT as 0935 Z.

Universal Time Co-ordinated (UTC)

UTC is the base of world wide system of civil time; time is kept by time laboratories around the world, is determined by using highly precise atomic clocks; UTC is accurate to nano-second (Billionth of a second). UTC second is defined in terms of an atomic transition of the element Cesium under specific conditions. UTC is not related to any astronomical phenomena.

Universal Time International (UTI)

UTI is the specific time, which is a measure of the rotational angle of the Earth as observed astronomically. It gets affected due to very small variation in the rotation of the Earth, which can differ slightly from the civil time on the Greenwich meridian. UTI is the time determined by the rotation of the Earth, over which there is no control, where as UTC is a human invention. As per International Agreement, UTC is not permitted to differ from UTI by more than 0.9 second. When the difference between UTC and UTI approach this limit, one second change called Leap Second is introduced into UTC and this occurs on an average about once every year or to one and a half year, depending upon circustances.

Astronomical data

International Date Line - is fixed at 180° W or 180° E, here day and date take birth.

Sidereal (Star) day - is 23 hours 56 minutes 04 seconds and Earth rotates 360°

Solar day - is 24 hours.

Sidereal year - is when Mesha Rashi (Aries) crosses 366 times, while Sun crosses 365.25 times, as it appears to make a journey along the elliptic path and can be explained in the following manner:

If we observe a star rising in the East, just before sunrise:

1st day - star at the horizon.

1st day - Sun rises 15 minutes later.

2nd day - star rises 4 minutes earlier.

2nd day - Sun rises 4 minutes earlier, but 15 minutes after the rise of the star.

Earth revolves - round the Sun in 365.242196 days (One year).

Moon revolves - round the Earth in 29.53059 days.

Equinox

Equinox equal day and night, spring equinox falls on 21st March and autumn equinox falls on 23rd September each year and on both occasions Earth goes nearest to the Sun and on Equinox days, the Sunrise 06:15 hrs and Sunset 18:15 hrs in Delhi.

Solstice

Solstice the point at which Sun is farthest from the equator and appears to pause before receding, summer solstice in the Northern Hemisphere falls on 21st June and the day is longest (Sunrise 05:27 hrs and Sunset 19:18 hrs), winter solstice in the Northern Hemisphere falls on 21st December and the day is shortest (Sunrise 07:15 hrs and Sunset 17:24 hrs)

Sun and Mesha Rashi (Aries) - pass over the Prime Meridian (0° longitude) at the same time on 21st March each year at Greenwich in London at 12 AM, GMT (Greenwich Mean Time)

Earth's Rotation

Earth's rotation is from West to East, so we see Sun and stars rising in the East, but the rotation is slowing down @ 0.02 seconds / cen

Earth's Axis

Earth's axis of rotation is tilted by 23° 30' on the plane of revolution round the Sun and axis always points to the Pole Star in the Northern hemisphere.

Latitude

Latitude 0° is Equator, which divides the Earth into two hemispheres and Tropic of Cancer is 23.5° North and Tropic of Capricorn is at 23.5° South.

North Pole

North Pole of the Earth is currently aligned with the fixed star Polaris, but this was not the case 3,000 years ago and by the year 14,000 AD the North Pole star will be Vega and not the star Polaris, as at present.

5.6. Numerology

Numerology is simple. It is easy to apply in daily life activities. It is used in supplementing the predictions as obtained from astrology. Prime numbers of numerology are 1 to 9. These have relationship with the nine planets: 1. Sun, 2. Moon, 3. Mars, 4. Mercury, 5. Jupiter, 6. Venus, 7. Saturn and the two shadow planets 8. Dragons head (Rahu) and 9. Dragons tail (Ketu). Prime numbers also have relationship with 9 colors (7 colours in rainbow, VIBGYOR - 1. Violet, 2. Indigo, 3. Blue, 4. Green, 5. Yellow, 6. Orange and 7. Red) and two invisible colours 8. Ultraviolet and 9. Infrared.

1. Alphabet based numerology - as civilizations advanced, it was realized that a relationship exists between alphabets and numbers and value numbers are allotted to each alphabet, as given below:

   A-1, B- 2, C- 3, D- 4, E- 5, F- 6, G- 7, H- 8, I- 9,
   J- 1, K- 2, L- 3, M- 4, N- 5, O- 6, P- 7, Q- 8, R- 9,
   S- 1, T- 2, U- 3, V- 4, W- 5, X- 6, Y- 7, Z- 8

   Value numbers are given to the alphabets of a person's name; all the value numbers are added to obtain a derived-number; if the derived number is in two digits; these digits are again added to obtain a prime number from 1 to 9. Based on prime number, harmony between persons can be found, from the following table:

Alphabet based harmony table and examples:

Prime No.	*Harmony*	*Disharmony*	*Equality*
1	1, 4, 8.	2, 6, 7.	3, 5, 9.
2	2, 7, 9.	1, 5, 8.	3, 4, 6.
3	3, 5, 6.	4, 7.	1, 2, 8, 9.
4	1, 4, 8.	3, 5.	2, 6, 7, 9.
5	3, 5, 9.	2, 4, 7.	1, 6, 8.
6	3, 6, 7, 9.	1, 8.	2, 4, 5.
7	2, 6, 7.	1, 3, 5, 9.	4, 8.
8	1, 4, 8.	2, 6, 7.	3, 5, 9.
9	2, 3, 6, 9.	7.	1, 4, 5, 8.

Examples:

O M P R A K A S H
6 4 7 9 1 2 1 1 8 = 39 (Derived No) = 12 (Derived No) = 3 (Prime No)

P R E M L A T A
7 9 5 4 3 1 2 1 = 32 (Derived No) = 5 (Prime No)

A R U N
1 9 3 5 = 18 (Derived No) = 9 (Prime No)

T A R U N
2 1 9 3 5 = 20 (Derived No) = 2 (Prime No)

S U N I L
1 3 5 9 3 = 21 (Derived No) = 3 (Prime No)

M A H I P A L
4 1 8 9 7 1 3 = 33 (Derived No) = 6 (Prime No)

S H Y A M K U M A R I
1 8 7 1 4 2 3 4 1 9 9 = 49 (Derived No) = 13 (Derived No) = 4 (Prime No)

Om Prakash (Prime No 3) will have harmony with Prem Lata (5), Sunil (3) and with Mahipal (6) and disharmony with Shyam Kumari (4) and equality with Arun (9) and Tarun (2).

2. Number based numerology

Characteristic numbers are allotted to each alphabet of a person's name:

A-1, B- 2, C- 3, D- 4, E- 5, F-5, G- 3, H- 5, I- 1,
J- 1, K-2, L- 3, M- 4, N- 5, O- 7, P- 8, Q- 1, R- 2,

S- 3, T- 4, U- 6, V- 6, W- 6, X- 5, Y- 1, Z- 7

All the allotted numbers are added together to derive a number, if the derived number has two digits, then these digits are further added to obtain a single digit prime number (P No) from 1 to 9. Friendship between persons can be found from the following table:

Number based friendship table and examples:

P No	*More friendly*	*Friend*	*Equal*	*Difference of opinion*	*Argument*	*Affinity*
1	2, 7	5	3, 4, 9	6	8	1
2	5	3, 6, 8	1, 4	7, 9	-	2
3	2, 7	8	1, 4, 9	-	5, 6	3
4	2, 7	5	3, 9	1, 6	8	4
5	1, 4	3	2, 6, 7	8, 9	-	5
6	-	3	1, 2, 4, 5, 7, 8	9	-	6
7	5	3, 6, 8	1, 4	2, 9	-	7
8	-	3	2, 5, 6, 7, 9		-	1, 4
9	-	8	1, 2, 3, 4, 7		6	5

Examples:

O M P R A K A S H
7 4 8 2 1 2 1 3 5 = 33 (Derived No) = 6 (Prime No)

A R U N
1 2 6 5 = 14 (Derived No) = 5 (Prime No)

T A R U N
4 1 2 6 5 = 18 (Derived No) = 9 (Prime No)

P U R N I M A
8 6 2 5 1 4 1 = 27 (Derived No) = 9 (Prime No)

A S H U
1 3 5 6 = 15 (derived No) = 6 (Prime No)

Om Prakash (Prime No 6) will have equal behavior with Arun (5), different opinion with Tarun (9) and Purnima (9) and affinity with Ashu (6).

Tarun (Prime No 9) will have affinity with Purnima (9), different of opinion with Ashu (6) and argument with Arun (5).

Number based characteristics of cities and states:

Bombay (2+7+4+2+1+1=17=8), 8 stands for peace, but Mumbai (4+6+4+2+1+1=18=9), 9 stands for strife.

Calcutta (3+1+3+3+6+4+4+1=25=7), 7 stands for peace and harmony, but Kolkata (2+7+3+2+1+4+1=20=2), 2 stands for problem.

Delhi (4+5+3+5+1=18=9), 9 stands for strife, New Delhi (5+5+6+9=25=7), 7 stands for peace and harmony.

Jaipur (1+1+1+8+6+2=19=10=1), 1 stands for peace, but under threat.

Kota (2+7+4+1=14=5), 5 stands for peace.

London (3+7+5+4+7+5= 31 = 4), 4 stands for strife.

Madras (4+1+4+2+1+3=15-6), 6 stands for love and harmony, but Chennai (3+5+5+5+5+1+1=25=7), 7 stands for peace and harmony.

New York (5+5+6+1+7+2+2=28=10=1), 1 stands for peace, but under threat.

Tokyo (4+7+2+1+7=21=3), 3 stands for loss to property.

Gujarat (3+6+1+1+2+1+4=18=9), 9 stands for strife.

Kashmir (2+1+3+5+4+1+2=18=9), 9 stands for strife.

Planet based characteristics of countries:

Plant Mercury (Budh) - governs USA. The country is composed of multi-nationals, settlers from outside the land, who have come to seek their opportunities.

Planet Saturn (Shani) - governs India. The country stands for peace, spiritualism, foreigner's rule, loss of wealth through plunder and classical music.

Planet Mars (Manga) - governs England and Germany. These countries stand for warfare, aggression, disease, death and devastation.

3. Lucky Number Based Numerology

Lucky number is derived from birth date of a person (Gregorian calendar date). All the digits in birth date, birth month and birth year are added; sum is reduced to a single digit from 1 to 9; this single digit number is called Lucky Number (L / N).

Example: Om Prakash - birth date 27.09.1932 = 33 = 6 Lucky Number

Prem Lata - birth date 08.11.1936 = 29 = 11 = 2 Lucky Number

Purnima - birth date 24.05.1961 = 28 = 10 = 1 Lucky Number

Arun - 23.07.1968 = 36 = 9 Lucky Number

Tarun - birth date 30.10.1971 = 22 = 4 Lucky Number

Lucky Number (L/N) based marriage table: Lucky numbers (L/N) have been categorized into four groups: A, B, C and D and marriage recommendation is:

L/N	*Category*	*Recommendation*
1, 2, 4, 7	A	Give preference to marry in category A and second preference in category B and L / N 2 is likely to have late marriage.
3, 6, 9	B	Prefer to marry in category B and second preference in category A.
5	C	Better marry in category C only and not in A, B, D category, as L / N 5 has a chance for remarriage.
8	D	Better marry in category D and not in A, B, C category, as L / N 8 has a chance for remarriage, as such, exercise due caution in first marriage itself.

Lucky Number (L/N) based husband desire table:

L / N	-	*Desire*
1	-	to get respect, honor and authority to prevail
2	-	demand love and are emotional
3	-	highly conscious of self respect
4	-	demand importance, obedience and like to command
5	-	truth to be told and will listen to everyone, except wife

6 - neat and tidy surrounding
7 - to be looked after well
8 - do not ignore them, as they are short tempered
9 - look after them, as they soon loose temper

Lucky Number (L/N) based wife desire table:

L/N - *Desire*

1 - to be treated as an individual
2 - love to be expressed and are emotional
3 - intelligence be recognized and have ego
4 - talkative and react very fast
5 - cooperation
6 - beauty and glamour be recognized
7 - intuitive and have problem in delivery
8 - allergy against corruption
9 - anguish personality

Lucky Number (L/N) based children desire table

Children learn maximum up to the age of 6 years, can learn any language easily up to the age of 7 years and after this age extra efforts are required to learn a new language. Children expect involvement of their parents in their work and cultural activities.

L / N - *Desire*

1 - respect and no violence in front of them
2 - truth be spoken and one parent to look after them as per the matching lucky number
3 - intelligent, like good food and self respect
4 - always in hurry and prepare well for exam
5 - to listen to business talk and may win lottery
6 - to see paintings, are handsome and romantic
7 - speak truth and have health problem below stomach
8 - serious and no one to tell lies in front of them and are accident prone
9 - quarrelsome, impressive and parents must not fight in their presence

Lucky Number (L/N) based behaviour table:

L / N	-	*Behavior*
1	-	give order, but cannot tolerate insult
2	-	very sensitive, but are not dangerous
3	-	self respectful, cooperative, but get annoyed with bad food
4	-	consult, give importance, but get annoyed unexpectedly
5	-	give importance to outsiders, but have good judgement
6	-	maintain neat and clean surroundings, but can not tolerate disorderliness
7	-	truth to be told, but get angry on hearing lies
8	-	speak truth, but soon get caught on telling lies
9	-	adventurous, but are quarrelsome

Lucky Number (L/N) based interest table:

L / N	-	*Interest*
1	-	expends much more, then required
2	-	expends much more, then required
3	-	interested in eating
4	-	trustworthy and good friends
5	-	friendship good
6	-	enjoy music
7	-	good friends
8	-	multi friends and experimenting
9	-	body building and fast driving

Lucky Number (L/N) based purchase table:

L / N	-	*Nature*
1	-	purchase expensive items
2	-	are double minded in purchasing
3	-	make a list for purchasing
4	-	purchase unnecessarily on the advise of others
5	-	purchase as per choice
6	-	purchase costly fashion items

7 - purchase as per list
8 - go for product research, before purchasing
9 - purchase costly items

Lucky Number (L/N) based career selection table:

L / N - *Career selection*

1 - electronics, academic, administration, modeling, metal work
2 - engineering, teaching, planning, leaves home, birth place and even country
3 - hotel, diary, teaching, restaurant
4 - chemical, electrical, medical, managing, computer, but not teaching
5 - commerce, mathematics, foreign trade, business
6 - printing, fashion designing, creative work, painting, computer, painting, music, has 6th sense to interpret things
7 - doctor, intuitive work, talented work
8 - advocate, lecturer, manufacturing, research work
9 - government service, leadership, management, adventurous sports

Five Step Prediction Chart:

Answer can be obtained on any question, in the form of YES or NO and the answer can be further qualified through a supplementary question and in five steps:

Step 1- Close the eyes, think about the question and randomly put a pointer (Pencil or pen, but do not spoil the paper) in the following Number Chart:

1	11	22	28	29
6	2	12	23	30
15	7	3	13	24
19	16	8	4	14
25	20	17	9	5
27	26	21	18	10

Number chart

Example: Let the number located is 21.

Step 2- Use the initial alphabet of the concerned person's name and note the corresponding number against the alphabet from the following Alphabet Chart:

A – 4, B – 6, C – 26, D – 18, E – 12, F – 4, G – 21, H – 28, I – 11,

J – 11, K – 16, L – 12, M – 19, N – 11, O – 9, P – 12, Q – 8, R – 12,

S – 4, T – 6, U – 9, V – 9, W – 13, X – 13, Y – 2, Z - 3

Alphabet chart

Example: Concerned person is Om Prakash and against the initial alphabet 'O' the corresponding number is 9.

Step 3- Question can be asked on any weekday and each weekday has a corresponding number, which can be found from the following Day Chart:

Sunday – 140, Monday – 97, Tuesday – 82, Wednesday – 216, Thursday – 109, Friday – 113, Saturday - 100

Day chart

Example: Let the question was asked on Monday and the corresponding number against Monday is 97

Step 4- Addition- add the numbers as obtained from Step 1- 21 (Number Chart), Step 2- 9 (Alphabet Chart), Step 3- 97 (Day Chart), Addition = 21 + 9 + 97 = 127, divide 127 / 30 and the remainder is 7.

Step 5- Look for the remainder 7 in the prediction table, in which line it is located and against the line the prediction is given in the form of YES or NO.

Example: Remainder 7 is located in the First line, where against YES- distant future is written and the prediction can be further qualified by asking a supplementary question through the same five step procedure. If the question is for some one else, then other person's initial alphabet of the name has to be taken into account and not the user's initial name alphabet.

Prediction table:

First line: 1, 2, 3, 4, 7, 9, 11, 13, 14 – YES- distant future
Second line: 10, 16, 17, 18, 20, 21, 24, 26, 27 – YES- within a year
Third line: 5, 6, 8, 12, 15, 19, 22, 23, 25, 28, 29, 30 – NO

5.7. Prophesies of Three Divine Persons

1. Shri Ram Chandra Ji Maharaj's (1899 – 1983) prophesy:

He was born at Shahjahanpur in Uttar Pradesh in India. He had the divine gift of Inner-sight (Anter-Drashti) to foresee the future events and his prophecies:

1. Great inundation (Maha Pralaya) - will occur in a very distant future. Pole Star will move away from its present position by few degrees. Pole Star will heat up and will radiate large quantities of energy, which will destroy all forms of life on Earth.
2. London (UK) - is situated on a volcano. Volcano will become active and the great city will be destroyed in a distant future.
3. Gulf Stream - will change its course. Life in UK and in Eastern parts of Europe will become very harsh in a distant future.
4. United States of America - will loose its super power status, wealth and will become a poor country. (It is unimaginable today, but it seems that the process has started)
5. India - will attain scientific progress in future and world will look upon it for leadership.
6. Bangladesh - will be submerged under seawater with the rising level of sea in the distant future.
7. Bihar State in India - will suffer great damage due to volcanic activities in the distant future.
8. Indian Southern Peninsula - will become an island in the distant future.
9. Spiritual based civilization - will arise in India. All countries will have to adopted spiritualism for their survival, but before this happens, world will experience great destruction.

2. Nastradamas' (1503 AD - 1566 AD) prophesy

He was born at Santraimi in France. During his childhood, he was known as Michel De Nastredami. He was a French national of Jewish origin, but was compelled to accept Roman Catholicism. He was a doctor and had super-sensory vision of clairvoyance.

He wrote a book named Centuries, which contained 1,000 prophecies in four line stanzas. At the age of 52 years, declared that the reach of his prophecies extends up to 3797 AD. His 700 prophecies have proved to be correct in the last 400 years and the remaining 300 prophecies may become true in the next 1792 years.

Nastradami at the age of 12 years recognized the future Pope of Rome, who was then a very young junior father Felipaireti. Nastradami touched his feet several times, but the accompanying senior fathers joked and laughed at the ignorance of the child, but few decades later, the same father became Pope. Every one was surprised and they all remembered Nastradami.

Nastradamas wrote a letter to his son, that it is very risky to make prophecies concerning the influential people. This makes them angry and they will take revenge against him. So he started writing his prophecies in a concealed poetical form. For making the prophecy, he used to keep a bowl of water on a copper-tripod; used to look into tripod to look into the future events. Based on his visions, he wrote the prophecies in the first edition of Centuries book in 1555 AD in France.

His Historically Important Prophecies

1. He prophesied that in 1727 AD, Iran would loose large tracts of land. It happened, when Afghanistan and Turkey reached an unscrupulous agreement. Iran lost Georgia and Armenia.
2. He prophesied that in the year 1889, Luis Pasture will take birth. He will establish a medical research institute, which will revolutionize the whole medical science and mankind, will be greatly benefited. It happened and Pasture Institute of Medical Research is functioning in France.
3. He prophesied that in the first 20 years of 20th century, Great War will take place, in which almost all the countries of the world will take part; millions of people will be killed. It happened in 1st World War.

4. He prophesied that the fall of British Empire will start from 1942. When he prophesied, at that time Britain did not even exist. Britain came into existence in 1603, when England and Scotland got merged together. It happened during 2nd World War.
5. He prophesied that in 1939 World War II would break out. Hister would take birth in Germany. He will start the war and Atom Bombs would be dropped on Hiroshima and Nagasaki in Japan. He was the first person to have used the word Atom bomb, while this name was unknown at that time in the scientific community.

   Japan and Germany would suffer the greatest damage and 1, 39, 00,000 persons will be killed. It happened; 1st Atom Bomb was dropped on Hiroshima in Japan on 6th August 1945 and 2nd Atom Bomb was dropped on Nagasaki in Japan on 8th August in 1945. The name of the person, who started the war, was Hitler, not Hister as he prophesied. It is most surprising that British War Office issued a list of 1,39,00,000 casualties after 2nd World War, which tallied with his prophesy.
6. He prophesied that Pope Pius VI would meet a tragic death in captivity near Rhone River. In 1781 Pope Pius VI banned the book Centuries, which contained this prophecy. It happened in 1799, when France under Napoleon took over the papal dominion. Pope Pius VI was taken prisoner; he died in 1799, when he was being taken to a French jail.
7. He prophesied that Russian revolution will start in November 1917 and will last for 73 years, but communism will not disappear. It happened; Russian communist revolution started in November 1917; it lasted for 73 years upto 1990. In 1991, Russia abandoned the communist ideology, but China remains wedded to the ideology with militant devotion.
8. He prophesied that Napoleon would take birth in France. He at the age of 25 years, will conquer many countries of the world, but will meet his tragic death. It happened.
9. He prophesied that in the year 1921, a saint would take birth in India, who will obtain independence for the country from

white people dominance, but will be killed in 1948. It happened. It is surprising that at the time of his prophecy, India was not even under British rule.

10. He prophesied that in the year 1936, King Edward of United Kingdom would marry a divorced American woman against public opinion. It happened. King Edward married Mrs. Wallis Simpson of America. King was dethroned on 10th December 1936.
11. He prophesied that Japan would become a super financial power in the world, but will be extremely weak in political and military fields. It has happened.
12. He prophesied that after 1970, China would become a super-power, whole world would be afraid of this country. China would use biological weapons. Today China is a super-power, but use of biological weapons is awaited.
13. He prophesied that 3rd World War would take place from 2007 to 2012. USA would have confrontation with Iran and North Korea. Nuclear weapons would be used and this would happen, when two super-powers would join hands to destroy a third super-power.

    Chinese ambition would trigger 3rd World War. They would launch a nuclear war on a country known by the name of sea (India is known by the name of Indian Ocean). The war will last for five years. Israel would show solidarity with India against her neighbours. Libya would be wiped out. It is awaited.
14. He prophesied that India would emerge as a super-power in 7th month of 1999. A powerful leader with faith would emerge on Thursday in South India. He would bring glory to the country and the golden era will last for 57 years.
15. He prophesied that:
    "In the year of the new century and nine months,
    from the sky will come a great King of Terror,
    The sky will burn at forty-five degrees,
    Fire approaches the great new city,
    in the city of York there will be a great collapse,
    two twin brothers torn apart by chaos,
    while the fortress falls the great leader will succumb,
    Third big war will begin when the big city is burning".

He said this would be bigger than the previous two wars. It happened on 11th September 2001. The twin towers of world trade center collapsed in New York in USA, when two hijacked passenger airliners hit them. September is the 9th month of the new century and New York is situated on 41° latitude.

3. Jenny Dickson - an American Lady's Prophesy

1. Blue eyed American President will be shot in 1960. When blue-eyed Kennedy became president of America, security authorities were concerned. The authorities had taken adequate precautions to prevent it, but it happened. Kennedy was shot, when he was going in a motorcade.
2. Mahatma Gandhi- will be killed in India. It happened in 1948.

5.8. Interpretation of Rudraksha and occult words

Rudraksha - is the dried fruit of a Rudraksha tree, which is found in the Himalayan region of Nepal, Bhutan, Sikkim and Assam. Rudrakshas are of 38 types. Rudrakshas are available in 21 faces, different faces of Rudraksha represent different powers, yield different results and different faces represent:

1. Face (Rare and highly priced) - power and wealth. Indira Gandhi used to wear rosary of 108 one-faced Rudrakshas
2. Faced - increases power of concentration
3. Faced - increases wealth, knowledge and luck
4. Faced - increases wealth and gives good health
5. Faced (Common) - success in all walks of life and good health
6. Faced - used in attaining special powers (Sidhis), success in business and distinction in education.
    1. Tantra - encapsulates soul, body and mind mechanism
    2. Yantra - vehicle that carries the Tantra and is made up of numbers or symbols or Mantras or the combination of all
    3. Mantra - is the sound vibration of 'Aum', which is believed to travel at the speed of light

5.9. Vaastu (Dwelling)

Vaastu Shilpa means science of house building. Vishwakarma Vaastu Shastra says that Lord Brahma got the knowledge from Lord Shiva. Present day Vaastu owes its origin to 125 Verses contained in Brihat Sanhita of Varahamihira. Vaastu is 5,500 years old. It is exhaustively scripted in Atharva Veda. Vaastu is based on universal energy known as Prana, which has four elements: 1 Space, 2 Fires, 3 Air and 4 Water. Vaastu recognizes eight directions and for determination of directions, the compass has to be kept in the central part of the house or plot.

House Vaastu

1. Plot - be rectangular or square, sloping towards North, East or Northeast, open space be on all four sides of the house, space be higher in South or West and lower in North or East. Rainwater outlet is in Northeast or North.

2. Rooms:

Bathroom and toilet - be in Northwest or West or South of the house. Bathroom is located on East or North side, if attached to bedroom then is located in North or East of bedroom. If bathroom is outside, it be located in Northeast, but do not build lavatories in Northeast or Center or Southwest or West direction.

Bed room - is in North or Southeast or Southwest of the house and sleep with head towards South and this ensures long life, but do not sleep with head in the North. If feasible during the journey, sleep with head towards the West.

Children's room - is in North or Northwest or Southeast, but not in South or Southwest of the house.

Guest room - is in Northwest or Northeast of the house.

Living room - is in North or Northeast or East of the house or is in the centre of the house and is free from any kind of obstructions, like: beam, pillar, fixture, toilet, staircase and lift.

Store room - is in Northwest corner and this leads to abundant supply of essential commodities and use dark blue or dark green colour, but do not use light colour and keep a holy picture on Eastern wall. Do not sleep in the storeroom at night and do not take out grains from the storeroom during night.

Study room - is to face North or East and use yellow or white or pink colour, but do not use a dark colour and put bookshelf in North or East and bathroom can be there in the study room, but do not have a toilet.

3. Main entrance - is in North or Northeast or East of the house.
4. First floor - is on the Southwest, but do not build a store over there.
5. Kitchen - is in Northwest or Southeast or East of the house.
6. Paintings and statues - depicting war scenes, especially of Mahabharata and Ramayana not to be placed in the house and scenes depicting sorrow, struggle, calamities, tragedy and violence including of wild beasts not to be placed in the house.
7. Trees - Mango, Banana, Jamun trees be planted slightly away from the house, but Peepal tree be planted at a distance in West direction and Imli in Southwest direction. It is auspicious to have Annar, Ashoka, Chandani, Champa, Chameli, Gulab, Nariyal and Keshar around the house.

City Vaastu

1. City situated south of a river - develops faster than the city north of a river.

   City situated east of a river - develops faster than the city west of a river.
2. Residential areas - in South, West and Southwest are more prosperous, as such, more construction to take place in these areas.
3. Rich and influential people - stay more in South, West part of the city than the people staying in the East or North of the city, like: Delhi's South and West parts of DLF and Dwarka developed faster than the Northwest part of Rohini, which is older.
4. Waterfronts - like: river, streams, ponds in North, East or Northeast, the city becomes prosperous. Waterfront in the East- administrative establishments come up, waterfronts in the Northeast- people are happy and spiritual, but Mumbai

has waterfront in the South- even rich people do not enjoy happiness.

5. Mountains, hills and plateau - on the South, West or Southwest of the city, the city becomes more prosperous, like Manaser in Haryana is becoming more prosperous.
6. Commercial establishments - like banks, shopping malls in the North, West or Northwest the city progresses financially.
7. Multi-story buildings - hotels be constructed in the South, West or Southwest and cinemas in the Northwest.
8. Stadium - be in the center of the city, like Kota has it.

5.10. Kidnapping and its Discussion in a Seminar

At Kota on the evening of 11th March 2005, a schoolboy of an engineer was kidnapped from a playing ground for ransom. Soon after kidnapping, telephone call was made to the boy's house that if they want to see their boy alive, they must pay ransom of Rs 10 lakh. The telephone call was getting repeated after every few hours. The parents pleaded that they cannot arrange for such a large amount in a short time. The caller immediately said that the recently made house be sold and ransom be paid.

Telephone calls for ransom were being made from different STD booths situated in different parts of Kota. Police, CID and Flying Squads were frantically searching all round the city to locate the boy, but all was in vain.

A two-day seminar on astrology was being held in an auditorium of a marriage hall in Kota. In the afternoon of 13th March 2005, the father of the kidnapped boy came in the seminar and requested the astrologer on the dais, to foretell what will happen to his son. The astrologer cast the horoscope for the time the question was asked. It was announced, that the boy is somewhere in Kota; the life of boy is in great danger; boy will never return to his house. The prediction cast a gloom in the auditorium.

On 14th March 2005, newspapers reported that the police have apprehended two kidnappers, when they were coming out from a STD booth, after making the call to the boy's house for ransom. It was unfortunate, that soon after kidnapping, the boy was killed, as the kidnappers had no place to keep the boy. The dead body was recovered from an abandoned house.

5.11 Astrological Age Cycles:

Astrological Age is a time period, which causes major changes in the life of inhabitants on Earth. The age occurs due to a phenomenon known as precession of the equinoxes. One complete period of this precession is called Great Sidereal Year, which is of duration 25,800 to 25,920 years. This period is divided into 12 astrological ages of 30° each, which are of duration 2,150 to 2,160 years. The entrance into an astrological age is not sudden, but is a gradual process by which one age initiates its influence in a slowly increasing order, before the previous age declines completely. Astrological Age Cycle is due to the very slow wobbling of the Earth's axis of rotation, which results in the Sun passing through different constellations (Nakshatras) every two thousand years. Each astrological age is characterized by a star sign, in which the Sun is moving. Astrological Age Cycles:

1. Leo and Aquarius Sign Age

Leo (Singh) and Aquarius (Kumbh) Sign Age - prevailed from 10,000 BC to 8,000 BC. Sun returned to its strength, which symbolized end of ice age. Humanity started to flourish, which gave rise to artistic creativity. This is evident from the vast number of cave paintings done during this age.

2. Cancer and Capricorn Sign Age

Cancer (Kark) and Capricorn (Makar) Sign Age - prevailed from 8,000 BC to 6,000 BC. Moon returned to its strength, which encouraged building of houses and dwellings. Mankind moved outside the caves and figures of mothers with big bosoms got carved out, which is evident from the vast number of statues carved out during this age.

3. Gemini and Sagittarius Sign Age

Gemini (Mithun) and Sagittarious (Dhanu) Sign Age - prevailed from 6,000 BC to 4,000 BC. Gemini is a good communicator, which helped in developing the languages. Libraries came up in different parts of the world. Sagittarius made the religions to take their roots. Lord Rama of India became the religious symbol of this age.

4. Taurus and Scorpio Sign Age

Taurus (Vrashabh) and Scorpio (Varashchik) Sign Age - prevailed from 4,000 BC to 2,000 BC. Taurus gave rise to civilizations. Mankind built long lasting buildings. Scorpio encouraged carving of bulls, which was common in this age. Religious rituals developed for death. Egyptians put efforts to preserve there dead bodies (Mummification).

5. Aries and Libra Sign Age

Aries (Mesh) and Libra (Tula) Sign Age - prevailed from 2,000 BC to 1 BC. The age symbolized the escape of Israelis from Egypt. Moses and Abraham started propagating Christianity and said that eventually every thing would end on a day of judgment. Libra is a sign of justice and law courts started coming up into their full swing. Aries helped in building great empires.

6. Pisces and Virgo Sign Age

Pisces (Meen) and Virgo (Kanya) Sign Age - started from 1 BC. The age will continue up to 2,600 AD. Pisces symbolizes the beginning and spread of religious awareness. Christianity came up in almost all the countries and today has the largest number of followers in the world (Fish is the symbol of Christ and is called fisher of men). Next most important figure in Christianity is Virgin Mary, which symbolizes the Virgo sign and stands for service to others. Hindu Religion climbed to higher levels due to efforts of Adi Guru Shankaracharya and Pisces (Kanya Rashi) gave rise to worship of Mother Goddess in her different forms.

7. Aquarius and Leo Sign Age

Aquarius (Kumbh) and Leo (Singh) Sign Age - will start from 2,600 AD and will last up to 4,600 AD. Jesus Christ had predicted the coming Age of Aquarius and Leo Sign Age. Jesus Christ had said that a man will meet you carrying an earthen pitcher of water; follow him into the house, where he goes. In this age, science and electronics will become most important and prominent in every field of human activity; respect for religious authority and traditional institutions will decline; this age will be warmer and wetter thanthe present age and signs for warmer climate are visible due to global warming.

6

Language

Quality of language shows our personality, it is the key to success in life.

Mankind - has developed many languages for communication. Language comprises of words and symbols, which represent objects, actions, qualities, ideas, while animals communicate in less complex ways. Language learning is a normal human trait, which enables us to communicate with others. Many languages share many common properties. Every language has a grammar, which sets the rules to manipulate the word. Language is a series of images, which have become more and more abbreviated with time. This has enabled handling of smaller conceptual components, which ultimately lead to formation of words and with the help of grammar, words get arranged into sentences.

Sign language - is a manual communication, which combines movements of hands, arms, body, facial expressions and is not based on spoken language and hundreds of sign languages are in common use around the world.

Speech - is the manner and style with which we speak and express our ideas, emotions, emphasize certain points, use hand movements and facial expressions. Speech establishes a link with other people. The art of speech can be learnt from good speakers and practiced in society. Meaningful communication requires command over the spoken language.

Voice - is used for oral communication and success in life depends upon it. Voice is produced when breath is exhaled; as it travels up through the windpipe, it meets the vocal cords, which are fleshy flexible folds, situated on either side of the voice box. Cords can open or close; become tight or loose; thin or thick depending upon instructions from brain. As the breath forces through glottis (Space between the cords); the cords start vibrating producing a distinct voice, with which we are born. Our voice is unique to ourselves, as are our fingerprints and on account of this uniqueness; others can recognize us on telephone.

Four ingredients of human voice

1. Tone - Is imparted to voice as breath travels up through the body cavities, like: chest, pharynx (Track between mouth and gullet), nose and sinuses. Breath's passage through these cavities sets resonance and a peculiar tone is imparted to our voice, which is individualistic in character, which can be described as nasal, metallic or plumy.
2. Pitch - of voice is determined by the length and thickness of our vocal cords. As the cords are stretched, they vibrate with a higher frequency; our voice becomes shriller. On the other hand, as the cords become loose; they vibrate with a lower frequency; our voice becomes deeper. When we speak, our voice operates comfortably at a certain pitch, which distinguishes us from other people.
3. Clarity - is imparted to the voice by our tongue, lips, palate, teeth and jaw. If for any reason, these organs cannot function properly, this may lead to mumbling.
4. Volume - of the voice is proportional to the pressure of breath on the vocal cords; pressure can be increased by breathing out with more force and at the same time, contracting glottis; greater the pressure, stronger are the vibrations; louder is the sound and vice versa.

6.1. Brain - in most of us, the left side of the brain controls the right side of the body; left side of the brain deals with language and this becomes evident, when we hear two different words being played simultaneously over our headphones, but we are able to repeat the word, which we had heard in the right ear.

Two areas of brain:

1. Broca area - controls speaking of words.
2. Wernicke area - controls understanding of words.

Babies have the potential to speak any language. They at first listen to the people talking to them from the time they are born, as such, they are learning a particular language from the very beginning. Babies from the age of six months; begin to concentrate on the language; learn single words by the age of nine months; learn to form a whole sentence around the age of three years; learn about 60,000 different words by the age of 18 years.

6.2. Time scale of language development

20, 00,000 years ago - during the time of Homo habilis, formation of languages started.

1, 00,000 years ago - languages started to develop. It seems that all languages arose from a common language spoken by our ancestors, who were known as Homo erectus in Africa. They used simple sketches in describing the hunting scenes, which are found in ancient crude cave paintings.

40,000 years ago - our modern ancestors known as Homo sapiens started using improved languages. They described the hunting scenes in words, phrases and in good paintings.

Script

Mr. Sami in Arabia developed the first script for the spoken language. Sami Script has 22 alphabets; from Sami Script Russian, Greek and Latin language scripts developed. From Sami script Brahmi script developed, which has 46 alphabets for writing the spoken Sanskrit language. This happened during 500 BC, when Sikandar invaded India.

In the early stages of Hindu culture (Sanskriti) development, there were only three categories of people: 1 Cultured people (Manav), 2 Divine people (Devta) and 3 Non-cultured people (Danav). King Indira Devta and Vaivasvat Manu were from Devta category, which helped in developing Hindu civilization. This proves that Brahmi script was developed much before start of Hindu civilization.

Five language families:

World's languages have been grouped into families, which have common ancestral linkage and language families are:

1. Indo-European language family
2. Afro-Asiatic language family
3. Astro-Nesian language family
4. Sino-Tibetan language family

   And basically the above four language family's names refer to the geographical regions.
5. Constructed language family - is the Esperanto language, which is a compilation of 200 different languages, which are spoken in different parts in Europe. By the end of 19th centaury, a new language out of these European languages developed, which is called Esperanto and a million people, speak it. The language is easy to speak, easy to use and easy to learn for the people familiar with European languages.

Sanskrit language - is believed to be the oldest language of mankind. The word Sanskrit was derived from Sanskriti, which means Hindu culture. Hindu Devta's created hymns (Mantras), which used to be transmitted orally from generation to generation through the spoken Sanskrit language. This tradition of reciting hymns in Sanskrit language still continues.

Hindu Tettiriya Sanhita says that Devta's experienced difficulty in writing hymns (Mantras). Indira Devta developed Devnagri script for the spoken Sanskrit language and hymns were scripted for the first time in this script. There is a mythological saying in Hindu Religion that Lord Ganesh was the originator of the script for the spoken Sanskrit language and Ved Vyas dictated Mahabharata epic to Lord Ganesh, who had scripted it.

Hindi language - Sanskrit language was difficult to pronounce, as such, the language was purified and a new simple language got developed, which is called Prakrit; later Prakrit was further simplified into Hindi language, which consists of 12 dialects:

1 Avadhi, 2 Bhojpuri, 3 Brijbhasha, 4 Chattisgarhi, 5 Dundari, 6 Hadoti, 7 Kanauji, 8 Khariboli, 9 Magadhi, 10 Marwari, 11 Mathili and 12 Rajasthani. Hindi language enjoys the status of being the national language of India.

English language - 5,000 years ago, Indo-European family language was spoken in European countries and in South Russia; out of this language, Germanic language developed, which later split into West Germanic and East Germanic. West Germanic slowly changed into High Germanic and Low Germanic. Later, High Germanic changed into German language. Low Germanic changed into Dutch language; from Dutch language Old English language developed, which was spoken in Britain in 449 AD.

From 1150 AD to 1500 AD, many changes took place in Old English language and during this period the language was known as Middle English; from Middle English, Modern English emerged and the process of development of this language is still going on. About 100 crore people speak English through out the world, but in different countries the people speak English with different ascent, like: in India - people speak English with Hindi ascent and the language is known as Hinglish, in Philippine - the language is known as Inglog, in Japan - the language is known as Japlish and in Africa - the language is known as Acjhosa.

English language's fast development started from 1400 AD, when it began adopting words from different languages of the world. Even from Hindi language more than 700 words have been picked up and still the British Government concedes that English spellings have margin for further improvement. Americans have changed the spelling of many words and have put the pronunciation of words in a more logical manner. This language is known as American-English, which has become even more popular through out the world. However, a slightly different version of English is developing in the European Union, which is called Euro-English. Euro-English will become the official language of the Union in a phased manner:

1st Year - in place of 'C', 'S' will be used; in place of 'C', 'K' will be used, like: 'Civil' will become 'Sivil' and 'Cat' will be spelt as 'Kat'.

2nd Year - in place of 'Ph', 'F' will be used, like: 'Photograph' will become 'Fotograph'.

3rd Year - in place of 'E', silent 'E' will be dropped, like: Language' will be spelt as 'Languag'.

4th Year- 'Th' will be replaced to 'Z' and 'W' will change to 'V', like: 'Fifth' will become 'Fifz' and 'Will' will become 'Vil'.

5th Year- in 'Ou', 'O' will be dropped, like: 'Trouble' will become 'Trubl'. In a phased manner, these changes will be incorporated in computer software's.

English language got a further boost, as many non-English-speaking countries of the world have adopted it for their overseas trade, commerce and scientific research. Speaking English with correct pronunciation has become an art. Every one has to learn the pronunciation from TV and Radio news bulletins.English is the fastest growing language of the world and has 40, 00,000 nouns, the highest amongst all the languages of the world.

Seventeen Main Languages

There are 7,300 languages in the world, but there are seventeen main languages, which are spoken by 446 crore people out of 600 crore world's population i.e. 74.3 % people speak the 17 main languages. The first alphabet of all these languages start with 'A' in some form or the other and 'M' is used in calling for mother. Over the last 100 years, nearly 400 languages of the world have gone extinct. Seventeen main languages are:

S/No.	*Language*	*Spoken by*	*Language characteristic*
1	Chinese (Sino-Tibetan)	110 crore	400 Alphabets, written from top to bottom. Modern Chinese language is being increasingly written in English alphabets.
2	English (Indo-European)	100 crore	26 Alphabets, written from left to right. Modern English language developed after 1500 AD and has the distinction to have developed the first dictionary of the world before any other

			language could do. American English is popular in Canada and Philippines; British English is popular in Australia, New Zealand and South Africa. European Union has announced that English will become an official language for the whole of Europe in a phased manner and English will be known as Euro-English. These measures will still make English more popular and almost all the world leaders use English to express themselves in the world forums. English occupies a commanding position in the world and today, postal article with English address can be posted anywhere in the world to reach its destination. English is the fastest growing language of the world and is adding more than 1,000 words per year to its vocabulary. English is the official language of 56 United Nations Member Countries. English enjoys the status of associate language in India.
3	Hindi (Indo-European)	40 crore	Phonetic script, what ever is written, same is spoken. First alphabet 'Ka' is pronounced from deep throat and pronouncements of successive alphabets keep on traveling up to lips and last alphabet 'Ma' is pronounced by

			joining both the lips. Hindi is the national language of India and is spoken by 40% of population.
4	Spanish (Indo-European)	33.5 crore	Official language of 13 member countries of the United Nations. Spanish is spoken in Spain and in Latin America
5	Russian (Indo-European)	30.0 crore	Spoken in Russia.
6	Bengali (Indo-European)	20.0 crore	Spoken in West Bengal, Bangla Desh and in Eastern parts of India
7	Portuguese (Indo-European)	17.5 crore	Spoken in Portugal and its colonies
8	Japanese (Sino-Tibetan)	13.0 crore	Spoken in Japan
9	French (Indo-European)	12.5 crore	Spoken in France and in North Africa
10	German (Indo-European)	12.0 crore	Spoken in Germany and Europe
11	Bhasha Indonesian (Austro-Nesian)	12.0 crore	Spoken in Indonesia
12	Arabic (Afro-Asiatic)	12.0 crore	Alphabets are compounded and written from right to left and spoken in West Asian countries
13	Korean (Sino-Tibetan)	7.5 crore	Spoken in North and South Korea
14	Vietnamese (Sino-Tibetan)	7.0 crore	Spoken in Vietnam
15	Marathi (Indo-European)	6.5 crore	Spoken in Maharashtra in India
16	Tamil (Indo-European)	6.5 crore	Spoken in Tamilnadu and in Sri Lanka and has the oldest surviving grammar for any language, which was written in 200 BC byTolkappiyar.

17	Turkish (Indo-European)	6.0 crore	Spoken in Turkey

Total 446 crore - people speak the above 17 main languages.

Indian languages

There are 325 languages and 1,652 dialects, which are spoken in India. Northeast India with 0.5 % of world population use 100 languages. The official languages of India are: 1. Assamese, 2. Bengali, 3. Gujarati, 4. Hindi, 5. Kanada, 6. Kashmiri, 7. Malyalam, 8. Marathi, 9. Oriya, 10. Punjabi, 11. Sanskrit, 12. Sindhi, 13. Tamil, 14. Telugu and 15. Urdu. English is the associate language, which is spoken through out the country. All official correspondence takes place in English, even the original constitution of independent India is written in this language. India has the distinction of having the largest number of English speaking people in the world.

Education in India

India has the distinction of having developed the first number value placement system, which is currently used throught the world. Indian mathematician Aryvaabhatta introduced zero in the system and in due course of time, other countries adopted this system.

700 BC: World's first university was established at Takshila in India and more than 10,000 students from all over the world used to study 60 different subjects.

400 BC: Nalanda University was established in Bihar in India.

100 BC: Decimal system of numbering was developed in India for the first time and later it spread to other parts of the world.

2006 AD: India has 311 Universities, 16,000 colleges and every year 3, 00,000 students graduate from these institutes.

6.3. Autograph - reveals ones character in the following manner

1. Slanting forward to the right - friendliness and affection.
2. Slanting backward to the left - feelings not shown on the surface.
3. Going in all directions - mind and heart in conflict.

4. Formations large - interest in people.
5. Formations very small - concentration on facts and details.
6. Capital 'I' very large - self esteem and desire to lead.
7. Capital 'I' very small - lack of self-assertiveness.
8. 'I's dot as a spot - lack of concentration on details.
9. 'I' dot as a circle - artistic taste.
10. 'I's dot away and high - imagination and enthusiasm.
11. Artistic styles - versatility in ideas and taste.
12. Runs up hill - optimistic and trusting nature.
13. Runs down hill - skeptical attitude and caution.
14. Runs up and down - variable mood.
15. Done with heavy pressure - vitality and desire for action.
16. Done with light pressure - sensitivity to people and surroundings.
17. Rounded formations - cooperative spirit.
18. Angular formations - critical mind and competitive nature.
19. 'M' and 'N' like 'U' - non-aggressive and pleasure loving.
20. Alphabets connected in words - careful reasoning.
21. Disconnected alphabets in words - intuitive and quick reaction.
22. 'G', 'F' and looped alphabets with straight lines - resourceful and mind discards nonessentials.
23. Large spaces between words and lines - generous spirit.
24. Narrow spaces between words and lines - thrifty and practical.
25. Signature in different size and slanting - outer manners different from inner personality.
26. Signature underlined - self-confidence.

6.4. Reading

Reading is an inborn faculty of a person; however systematic presentation of a subject in a book plays an important part in the reading process. Illustrations in a book help in grasping the subject matter in a better way. Reading different subjects require different strategies, like: biology requires pre-reading before attempting to dissect an animal; geography requires the facts to be coordinated with atlas; history requires visit to historical places; mathematics requires practice in solving problems; science requires performance of experiments; sociology requires under standing of the prevailing social order and newspapers help in it.

Tips for reading

1. Read slowly - at a steady rate.
2. Read silently - with concentration.
3. Read to gain - knowledge.
4. Read to widen - mental horizon.
5. Read to chew and digest - the subject matter.
6. Read to gain - comprehension.
7. Read to deduce the meaning - of words and consult dictionary.
8. Read to motivate - the cognitive faculties.
9. Read to evaluate, infer and critically - examine to comprehend the text.
10. Read to derive - maximum benefit.
11. Read to make - notes for review from time to time.
12. Read to excite - imagination for further reading.

Students reading habit:

30 % Students - read regularly.

30 % Students - read seriously for knowledge.

20 % Students - read merely for certificates and degrees.

15 % Students - read one month before an examination.

5 % Students - read extra books for through knowledge and these students score high marks in the examination.

Reading how to become rich will not help one to use his salary in a better way, but certainly the knowledge will enable him to manage his investments and control his wasteful expenditures. Reading how to swim, one can not learn swimming, but the knowledge gained will enable him to swim in a better way. Reading how to cycle, one can not learn cycling, but it is the practice that will improve his cycling skills. One should form a habit to read; this will improve his professional knowledge, which will lead to advancement in his career. Three R's are: reading, writing and arithmetic.

6.5. Learning

Learning is the process through which we gain knowledge about a subject. We learn a language to express ourselves through the medium of this language. It is easy to learn any language, if it is done before the age of seven years, as by this age, human brain gets wired up for a particular language. Once the wiring is complete, learning a new language is difficult, as a different area of the brain is required for re-wiring.

Learning is putting the things into memory, however learning and remembering are two different processes of memory, which act like two faces of the same coin. We learn through our five senses; practice makes us perfect; chimps learn through exploring; monkeys learn by imitating. However, children do not learn at the same rate. Their predisposition to learning seems to be built into their brain. Different learning rates between children pose a problem to the teacher, who tailors the lessons towards a general trend of progressive learning.

Five Styles of Learning

1. Sight learning - some people have a sight based learning style; they memorize best using their eyes, either reading a written material or seeing an action performed. If one remembers written information more easily, then one should concentrate using printed material. He should create additional texts by writing notes of the read material and lectures. He should review them from time to time.
2. Visual learning - some people have a visual based learning style; if they remember visual information better, then they should use pictures / videos / graphics; experiments have proved that visual learners remember 30 % of what they see, but remember 10 % of what they read in the text form. However visuals are a good aid in the learning process and the interpretation of visuals is as follows:

	Visual	*Interpretation*
1.	Photograph	How thing looks like?
2.	Illustration	What things are there?
3.	Exploded view	How things are assembled?
4.	Map	Where places are situated?

5.	Line diagram	How the flow takes place in a system?
6.	Schematic diagram	How things are organized?
7.	Working diagram	How things work in a system?
8.	Graph	How a thing varies as a function of another?
9.	Pie chart	How much a quantity is present in percentage?
10.	Bar chart	How one quantity compares with another?
11.	Table	How data is related in a chart?
12.	In put / out put (Quantity)	What goes in and what comes out quantity wise?
13.	Balance (Quantity)	How in-put, out-put and wastage take place?
14.	Balance (Energy)	How in-put, work and loss of energy take place?

3. Hearing learning - some people have hearing based learning style; they should concentrate on the sense of hearing. They should try to use audio materials for their studies, such as, tape recording of class lectures. They should transform the written material into sound. Reading the text aloud; studying by talking aloud; computer discs are a great help in this style of learning.
4. Tactile learning - some people have tactile based learning style; they should use movement for studies; they should try to concentrate practice on the sense of touch. This is the method used extensively by the blind persons.
5. Movement learning - some people have movement based learning style; they should make notes of what they hear, they should draw pictures / graphs; they can walk while they revise the subject matter; they can listen to light music during studies. Scientific studies have revealed that movement style learners remember speech better, when it is accompanied by gestures. They should practice to make the things with their own hands or create models or devise games or think of activities that fit in with their learning style.

One should consider, which learning style suits him the most to learn the things and memorize them. Choosing the right learning style depends very much upon ones aptitude with which he is born.

Learning Process

Learning process depends upon one's aptitude, attitude and interest, how he learns or would like to receive information. Learning process starts the moment one goes through a text, but some individuals learn at a faster rate, while others at a slower rate. Rate of learning can be improved upon by discussing the text with colleagues, teachers, fellow students and friends. Sharing experience with learned people enhances ones learning, however preview of the text helps in the learning process. Learned people go for more learning and adopt all possible means to achieve it.

Rigveda on Learning

We learn -
25 % from a teacher,
25 % from self-study,
25 % from discussions with colleagues,
25 % from revision from time to time.
And experimentation leads to mastery on the subject.

6.6. Study

Study is the application of mind to a subject, so as to gain knowledge, understanding, memorizing the facts and investigating the things by observation and research.

Tips for study:

1. Study - when the mind is fresh, as in the morning hours.
2. Study - quality wise, as it pays more than the quantity of hours put in.
3. Study - with concentration, but do not struggle to study with distraction.
4. Study - each subject for fixed time periods daily and stick to the schedule.
5. Study - regularly, as it pays more dividends than to study on a single day, like: study every day for one hour pays more dividends than 8 hours study on a single day.

6. Study - with dictionary at hand and consult it as often as necessary to increase vocabulary.
7. Study - to solve question papers in time and gain skill in answering questions, as how we write is important than what we are writing and practice makes a man perfect.
8. Study - through notes, as it quickly refreshes the mind in a short time.
9. Study - a habit must be formed to study during fixed hours; once study has started, it must be continued for at least 30 minutes (Ideal 45 minutes); relax for 10 minutes by closing the eyes or staring in the night sky or take a small walk on the terrace or take a cup of tea or water to refresh. Rest improves concentration of mind for the next study session.

   Optimum hours of study have a threshold value, which varies from individual to individual and depends upon ones aspiration level. However, one has to remember that continuous study produces boredom, fatigue and reduces level of concentration. One has to find one's optimum level of study hours through experimentation. For studies, one has to sit in a comfortable position, preferably on a chair.
10. Environment for study - plays a significant part. One has to create a cool, quite, clean environment; flower pots giving out pleasant smell increase concentration; light has to fall on the book from the backside from left-hand side; one has to remove disturbances and distractions.
11. Assimilation of information - takes place through ears (listening); through eyes (seeing); through mind (Concentration and attention); through writing (Making notes) and simultaneous use of all these senses, makes assimilation of information easy. The information thus gained, becomes permanent in the memory.

6.7. Examination

Examination is close inspection of some thing. It is a test that the examinee has the necessary level of knowledge in a subject. It is not enough to know the answers to the questions asked in the examination paper, as cases have occurred where students knew the answers, but still they could not score high marks due to lack of writing skill. Writing skill can be improved upon through practice in solving examination papers in the allotted time.

Tips for examination:

1. Read - carefully the instructions given in the examination paper, as under stress many students do not know, as to how many questions are to be attempted; whether choice is given or not, but in a hurry they start answering the questions.
2. Plan time - to answer the required number of questions; allot time for each question to be answered. Normally six questions (carrying equal marks) are required to be answered in three hours time. Thus each question is to be allotted half an hour for answering and answer in legible handwriting.
3. Decide priority - for the questions to be answered; start with the easiest question; this builds up confidence at the very start of the examination.
4. Presentation - to be decided before attempting any question, spend a little time in analyzing the question, know exactly what the examiner wants and answer to the point, as marks are awarded for what is asked. We must not succumb to the temptation of letting the examiner know, as to how much we know about a particular question, as there are points, which the examiner expects to find in the answer and those points must be covered.
5. Examiner - gets upset when he has to go through the pages after pages of illegible manuscript, which annoys him. He gets prejudiced against the examinee.
6. Mistakes - in writing do happen, but do not correct them by overwriting, simply strike them out and rewrite above the line. This particularly applies to numerical, like: if 7 was written and realizing the mistake, it is corrected to 9 by over writing, then the numerical 7 could be read either as 7 or 9, better strike 7 and write 9 clearly.
7. Before entery - into the examination hall, satisfy the natural calls, like: feeling thirsty - take water, feeling hungry - take snacks, feeling pressure - go to bathroom / toilet, as these calls distract the concentration.
8. Arrive at the examination hall - before the scheduled time and feel comfortable.

9. Check - for pen, pencil, rubber, scale, calculator, instrument box before entering the examination hall. This chect creates self-confidence that every eventuality will be met.
10. Practice - to solve last five year's examination papers in the allotted time. This creates the necessary self-confidence before entering the examination hall that the best has been done in preparation for the examination, now God will help, but do not entice Him with sweets (Prasad).
11. Phobia - some persons, when they enter the examination hall start perspiring, feel uneasiness and start worrying unnecessarily. This can be over come through self-confidence that they will do better in the examination.

6.8. Communication

Communication is an art and through this one establishes contact with friends, seniors and colleagues. Communication establishes social contacts and things can be done through them.

Five methods of communication:

1. Quickest method - is to speak directly in person or on telephone.
2. Easiest method - is to lecture the staff in a meeting or in a group.
3. Mass appeal method - is to address large gathering.
4. Convincing method - is to call a person in the office and convince him on the issue.
5. Permanent method - is to write; issue letters or memoranda or reports. This method is slow, but good for record keeping and future reference.

Five Level Interagency Language Roundtable Scale (ILR) - is a set of abilities to communicate in a particular language. The scale has been devised by United States Foreign Service Institute. ILR is an indication of language proficiency:

Level 1 - elementary proficiency, able to order a simple meal, ask for shelter or lodging, ask and give simple directions, make purchases and tell time.

Level 2 - limited working proficiency, able to handle limited work requirements, understand difficulties, able to converse and has speaking vocabulary, but can make grammatical mistakes.

Level 3 - professional working proficiency, able to speak the language, participate in conversation, able to discuss a subject with ease, vocabulary broad enough to express him and has a good control over grammar.

Level 4 - full professional proficiency, able to speak the language fluently and accurately, able to respond appropriately in unfamiliar circumstances and able to interpret from and into the language.

Level 5 - bilingual proficiency, able to speak equivalent to an educated native speaker.

6.9. Leadership

Leadership is the ability and quality to lead people to do certain things. Local language is the best medium for communication, which influences people and encourages them to do, what is desired by the leader. Good leadership can turn the failure into success and projects it as a new goal for the followers. Leaders always take decisions; followers always follow the leaders; followers always obey the directives of their leaders.

Four levels of leadership:

Level 1 - is the independent level, where the leader exercises his own authority and the position is gained by an appointment.

Level 2 - is the permission level, where senior leader's permission is required before making a final decision on an issue and here the leader has constrains.

Level 3 - is the group level, where leaders form a group to arrive at a decision and the leader represents his followers, who are expected to endorse his decisions.

Level 4 - is the field level, where leaders come together to accomplish a specific task and the leaders have their own opinion to accomplish their desired task.

Leaders and followers:

1. Leaders take initiative - followers just follow.
2. Leaders pick up phone to contact - followers wait for the directions.
3. Leaders spend time in planning - followers just wait.
4. Leaders anticipate problem - followers react to the situation.
5. Leaders invest time - followers spend time amongst themselves.

6. Leaders make appointments - followers mark their calendars.
7. Leaders assign priorities - followers simply follow them.

Good leaders know:

1. Basic philosophy of life.
2. Different elements that constitute the society.
3. Political issues that influence the masses.
4. Economic conditions prevailing in the country.
5. Industrial unrest that is prevailing in the area.
6. Activities to be adopted for the betterment of society.
7. Issues to be raised and taken for protest.
8. Responsibility to be assigned to others.
9. Decisions to be taken confidentially.
10. Feeling of happiness to be generated in the masses.
11. Wants and desires of people.
12. Motivations to be used with the followers and with junior level leaders.
13. Concessions to be obtained from the authorities.
14. Handling of turmoil, before it goes out of hand.

6.10. Friendship

Friendship is established through use of good language, but one has to be careful in choosing his friends. As the friends have the ability to make or break him; friends can guide or misguide him; friends can encourage or discourage him; friends can make or spoil him. Friendship depends upon people and people have following characteristics:

1. Ambitious people - provide vision.
2. Business people - increase the earning power.
3. Constructive people - improve behaviour.
4. Efficient people - increases ability.
5. Executive people - enhances the ability to tackle problems.
6. Good people - guide in adversities.
7. Influential people - increase popularity.
8. Intelligent people - enhance prestige.
9. Leading people - help to win many friends.
10. Loving people - encourage encourage to do good things.
11. Nice people - are source of strength.
12. Noble people - guide in doing noble deeds.

13. Pleasant people - remove the worries.
14. Thoughtful people – give more ideas to tackle things.
15. Wise people - waxes like a new moon.
16. Wicked people - their friendship wanes like a full moon.

7

Interview

Interview is an essential part of human life and success in career depends upon it.

Interview is a formal meeting between an interviewee and interviewers to prejudge a candidate's caliber for an intended job or work or to seek information on a particular subject. However interviews fall into two categories: Selection interview and Topic based interview:

Selection Interview

Takes place to seek a job, which is very crucial in one's career. Mock interviews help in building the necessary confidence. College campus interviews take place to seek suitable candidates for particular career in a company. Career counselors impart pre-selection coaching. It has been observed that 5 % of graduating students take advantage of campus interviews, while 95 % go through their first interview and end up in failure. As such, mock interview is an opportunity to practice interview technique and style of responding to the questions being asked in a practical way. Interview session can be video taped for self-study or constructive feedback, which can improve performance. Three stages of selection:

1st Stage Telephonic Interview

This first stage interview is very popular. It takes place with prior appointment on a fixed date and time, to pre-judge an applicant in his oral response and how serious he is about the applied job. Why he is leaving his present job? Interviewer tests his communication skill, his response time to a question and his attitude in life. Candidate is saved botheration of going outside to attend an interview; he saves his time and money as well. In the interview, candidate's presence of mind; quickness in answering the questions is tested through following type questions:

1. What is your previous work experience?
2. What are your short and long term career goals?
3. Where do you see yourself 5 / 10 / 15 years from now?
4. Why do you want to leave your present job?
5. Why you have applied for this job or organization?
6. Are your skills, qualifications and experience suitable for this job?
7. What do you know about the job, you have applied for?
8. Please, tell some thing about yourself?
9. Have you ever faced a problem in your work area?
   (If yes, describe the problem, its implication and solution)

It is better not to ask for a salary, unless and until asked for during the course of interview. It is helpful to keep important papers near the telephone, like: CV / Resume, certificates, paper and pencil to note down the things, if required.

2nd Stage Main Interview

This is a face to face interview, where the board tries to measure an applicant's abilities, interests, personality and endurance for work, which is essential for success in the organization. Accuracy of information divulged in the interview depends upon the confidence the applicant has with the interviewers and the manner in which questions are asked.

Aim of interview:

1. Is the candidate able to do the intended job properly?
2. Is the candidate willing to put in required efforts to make the job a success?
3. Is the candidate manageable?

Starting questions:

Q: Why do you want to work over here?

A: Research the company first and say, company can provide me a stable and happy working environment. This will encourage me to put in my best efforts.

Q: How you view your progress?

A: Each passing year, provides me an opportunity to learn more. This adds to my experience and this helps me to progress, which is satisfactory.

Q: What would you like to be doing five years from now?

A: As a team player, I will grow with my superiors and would like to share their responsibilities.

Q: What are your accomplishments?

A: I feel my biggest achievements are yet ahead of me; however I feel proud of my involvement in .... (Work) or I made a contribution as part of a team and learned a lot in the execution of .... (Work).

Middle questions:

Q: Tell me something about yourself?

A: I am a team player and I accomplished my work in so and so .... (Manner).

Q: How others rated your performance?

A: My boss said that I am the most valuable engineer / manager / supervisor in the company. I have a letter of appreciation from him or from my last boss, which is available with me. If desired, the letter can be produced.

Q: What are your greatest strengths?

A: I take pride in my work. I have the ability to stick to a difficult job to accomplish it, till it is completed in a planned manner, example can be cited. Normally the strengths are: qualifications, experience and contacts in the professional field.

Q: What is your greatest weakness?

A: I could not get an opportunity to work on a particular job (Cite a difficult job), but with my past experience, I was able to complete all my allotted jobs in time or I always give my best to my work, but (so and so) work lacked behind schedule, as others could not complete their part of job in time, but I over came the problem by working extra hours with my colleagues. (In this manner, one's weakness can be projected, as an asset).

Q: What are you looking for in your next job?

A: I want a company, where my talents and experiences can be appreciated. If selected, I would like to contribute my best.

End questions:

Q: Why did you left your last job?

A: Acceptable reasons for leaving the last job can be:

1. My contract was completed and the company could not secure the next contract.
2. The journey to work was unreasonably long.
3. Company did not have the advancement opportunities to grow professionally.
4. Company was not stable and was loosing business.

Q: What kind of salary you are worth?

A: What the company offers to this grade or type of work please let me know. If the candidate gives a figure, the employer can say that the figure is very high and on the other hand, if the employer gives a figure, the candidate can say that the salary is less than expected. Salary is a game of negotiation and salary fixation has four stages:

1. Minimum - is at the start of the grade, which is not to be discussed.
2. Realistic - is the midpoint of the salary range, which is the desirable salary.
3. Dream salary - is the maximum expected, which can be demanded.
4. Salary package - can include conveyance allowance, professional society or club membership, medical and dental insurance, but neither accept nor reject an offer on the spot, but say, I will think over it or if the package is less, say I request you to please, look into the package again.

Q: Do you have any question to ask?

A: When will I get the opportunity to meet the person, to whom I will be reporting or what would be my first assignment in the company or is there is a written job description or an organization chart, where I can fit. Please can I see the chart?

3rd Stage additional Interview

This interview is normally the repetition of the earlier main interview after some time, where in an attempt is made to discover the stability of behavior of the applicant for a senior positions in the organization. Questions relate to:

Q: Why should we hire you?

A: Express suitability for the job.

Q: Can you tell us a little bit about your present job?

A: State the good points of the present job, but do not express any dissatisfaction.

Seven different topic based interviews:

These interviews are generally held with the serving employees in a large organization to exchange views, ideas and seek information on a topic of interest. Interview can have the following names:

1. Problem solving interview - the concerned person is called; problem is discussed in a cordial manner to arrive at an agreed solution.
2. Decision making interview - interviewer studies the subject matter in detail to become familiar with the case or project and calls the concerned persons for final decision in the matter.
3. Disciplinary action interview - is calling the guilty person; making him to realize his mistake; advise him to improve upon his performance in future and if required give warning not to repeat the mistake in future.
4. Counseling interview - is calling the aggrieved person; counseling him to boost his morale for better performance. This is done in the interest of organization.
5. Survey interview - is calling different persons occasionally; to have first hand knowledge of the prevailing conditions in the organization.
6. Service leaving interview - is calling the person, who is about to leave the organization; to find out the hidden problem, which lead to his resignation. This gives an opportunity to discuss the matter in a friendly manner and give him a creditable certificate with a warm handshake.
7. Performance interview - is calling the departmental head for first hand information on the working conditions prevailing in his department; sort out the matter to achieve higher efficiency and out put in the organization.

Three styles of interviews:

1. Behavior / competency style interview - requires description of a project managed from the beginning to the end or concerns a problem, which has been solved with respect to approach and outcome.
2. Preference style interview - requires description of future career or company's prospects or industry's future or the impact the mentors have made.
3. Adhoc style interview - requires description of work of the organization or five years hence where the candidate will be or what he would be doing or what are the salary expectations or how much bonus one gets or description of the previous employer or what one has to say about a person or what one is doing to improve his performance or what are the spare time hobbies and which books one reads.

7.1. Interview Requirements

Before the interview:

If the employer finds the candidate to be suitable through his CV / Resume study; he is called for interview to seek more information from the candidate; as such, the candidate has to prepare before the interview:

1. Find out information as much as possible about the company / organization.
2. Annual report of the company is a good source of information.
3. Visit company's website.
4. Read again company's advertisement, application, CV / Resumes to strength the stated points and seek more information from reference books.
5. Read newspapers / current affair magazines and watch TV news bulletins.
6. Select the dress, which is smart and suiting to the weather conditions.

At the time of interview:

1. Avoid strong perfume / aftershave lotion.
2. Walk in the room with confidence; look directly in the eyes of interviewers; say politely in a friendly manner - good morning / good afternoon / good evening, sir, as the time

demands. If hand is forwarded; shake hand with warmth, as a week handshake is a sign of week personality.

3. Sit when asked to do so; put the arms resting on sides or on the table, but don't cross arms or shift around uncomfortably; avoid pulling ears; scratching nose; fiddling with tie or ring, as these are the signs of nervousness.
4. Body movement and posture is crucial during the first few minutes of the interview. This is known as body language.
5. Psychometric tests may be undertaken to find aptitude, attitude as part of the selection process; these tests are not pass or fail tests; they are merely indicators of personality, as to how well, one will fit in their job. Candidate has to be honest in the tests.

3. After the interview

Sometimes, it is required to write down in short, what has been gone through in the interview to test one's writing skill and memory.

7.2. Five types of CV (Curriculum Vitae):

CV is a well prepared document to sell one's abilities and capabilities against the advertised post. CV contains relevant information in a script form and is normally of five types:

1. Standard CV - is a performance type CV, suitable for seeking a similar job in the same sector, as one is presently working. It is written in two pages, which contain information under the following headings:
    1. Personal - full name, address, telephone number, mobile no., e-mail address, date of birth (Rather than age), marital status (Single / separated / married / divorced), nationality and passport number / driving license. It establishes ones genuineness.
    2. Education and qualifications - education means schooling / college, qualification means professional course / degree (Start with the highest), training courses attended for enhancing skills and membership of professional bodies.
    3. Languages – known, fluency level in written, spoken, business or technical, computer skill include software and operating system.

4. Interests and hobbies - photography, sight seeing, coin / stamps collection, achievement in sports, membership of clubs and organizations.
5. Career summary and experience - starting with the recent job, going backwards, listing job title, name of company and type of work, responsibility, major achievements, list three or four achievements (Deadlines met / cost saving / increased sales).

2. Functional CV - is ideal for change in the direction of one's career or if employment has not been continuous due to unemployment / health / self employment reasons. CV information can be arranged under the headings: 1. Administration, 2. Consulting, 3. Planning, 4. Research, 5. Training or 6. Choose headings for the previous jobs. CV is normally written in two pages.

3. Alternate CV - is used by the people working in creative industries. Who want to demonstrate their capabilities through a CV. All relevant information is included under four or five headings. These people need to have current portfolio of work in hand, which has to be produced at the time of interview.

4. Summary CV - is for senior appointments. CV is for the persons having wide experience, which need not be detailed in the text, but left to be discussed in the interview. CV is normally written in one page and information arranged under headings: 1. Personal, 2. Education and qualifications, 3. Career summaries are written in four to eight lines, but not employer specific.

5. Online CV - is known as an electronic-CV. It follows the rules as set by the computer software. CV is short, sharp and contained in not more than two pages. CV document be transferable across different software's and computers. CV is stored and is e-mailed in ASC II or plain text format. In its presentation, there is no need to use italics / underlines / bold fonts / borders. Online CV on a web site is searched by keywords, so as many as possible keywords are included in the body of the CV as possible.

Online CV format

1. Name and contact block - is put on top of the page, which contains name, e-mail address, telephone / fax number and each part has its own line.
2. Job objective - to include what one is looking for or list the job title.
3. Profile - contains skills in a summary form and contains keywords for search.
4. Work experience - is arranged in reverse chronological order, starting with the last employment first.
5. Education - lists qualifications, training and professional body memberships.
6. Cyber space - has three options: 1 Register with online employment web sites, 2 Register on company web sites - who invites CV from the would-be-candidates and 3 E-mail directly to individual employers against job vacancies.

CV writing

CV is the first interface with an organization. They do not know the person: if CV impresses, it can lead to one's selection for the advertised post. As such, one has to be very careful in writing CV. CV is printed on quality paper; is neatly layed out; has normal margin; font - Times New Roman, font style - Regular, font size 12 pt; do not use italics, as it produces distraction and confusion.

Do's - in CV writing:

1. Do include name, address, e-mail address, telephone number residence / mobile at the top of the page.
2. Do include achievements / contributions made.
3. Do include birth date and marital status.
4. Do include how the organization got benefited from your services.
5. Do include activities as to how large was your team / budget / territory.
6. Do check the CV and again recheck for grammatical, spelling mistakes and better show it to some one, who can again recheck for correctness.

Don'ts - in CV writing:

1. Do not over stretch abilities.
2. Do not use adjectives, like excellent.
3. Do not send photos.
4. Do not indicate any failure.
5. Do not show salary / bonus information.
6. Do not show weight, height, political inclination and state of health.
7. Do not show reasons for leaving previous jobs.
8. Do not show any activity leading to lethargy, like watching TV, spending time at pub / cinema / playing cards.
9. Do not give negative feeling against the previous employer.
10. Do not indicate gaps in the career history.
11. Do not send poor quality photocopies of papers.
12. Do not use large blocks of texts / paragraphs to make the CV difficult to read and comprehend.
13. Do not use front covers / colored papers / fancy bindings.
14. Do not print with dot matrix, as it gives a bad impression.
15. Do not give unnecessary information, which is irrelevant.

7.3. Three formats of Resume Writing

Resume has a long format as compared to CV. It is a text to sell oneself by providing all the relevant information in a consolidated form for selection against the advertised post. Resume writing has three formats:

1. Chronological resume format - is traditional and is made in reverse order i.e. recent job first, followed by second, third and so on. Resume has the following subheads:
   1. Personal - name, address, telephone number and e-mail address is written at the top of each page.
   2. Objective - is written in short, not more than ten to fifteen words (To build a career in software field or interact with customers or to work in a senior position in a financial institution). Sentences are suitably formed.
   3. Summary - gives the recruiter an overview of the resume in five to six lines, high lighting the best in the resume, qualifications and achievements, like: ability to cope with the future fob requirements indicating the number of years experience in the field.

4. Employment history - indicate accomplishments, dates of employment, designation in each job, name of company, responsibilities in each job. State the facts in reverse chronological order; starting with the last job; followed by previous employments; ending with the first job. This can be better written in a tabular form: Date, Designation, Company and Responsibility.
5. Education - includes qualifications, professional degrees / certificates, name of institute / college / school attended.
6. Interests- include extracurricular activities, hobbies, awards and ability to speak and write different languages.

2. Functional resume format - is harder to read and interpret, but it is for job seekers with gaps in their work history. Who are entering the job market after a long break, like: laid off workers, executives seeking career change in industry, old professionals hunting for jobs in industry dominated by younger people. Resume re-arranges job history into skills; date and time into accomplishments; resume has the subheads:
   1. Personal -
   2. Objective -
3. Summary -
4. Skill sets - management skills, technical skills, customer skills, sales and marketing skills and each category to include two to three points, as stated below:
   1. Sales and marketing skills.
   2. Increased previous company's business by over 15%.
   3. Developed new distribution outlets in the Northern Region.
   4. Participated in exhibitions / shows.
   5. Organizational skills.
   6. Designed and developed educational aids for training.
   7. Developed hardware for computer applications.
   8. Communication skills.
   9. Communicated effectively with customers.
   10. Trained and supervised fresh sales trainees.

5. Accomplishments
    1. Managed the accounts of the company.
    2. Hired, trained and supervised staff in sales and marketing.
6. Employment history:
    1. Senior sales officer in ——— (company).
    2. Sales executive in ————— (company).
    3. Marketing manager in ——— (company).
7. Educational qualifications - Graduation, Business administration etc.

3. Combination Resume Format

Combination resume format - is a composite of chronological and functional resumes formats. Resume shows dates in employment history. This resume is used, when functions have been similar in all jobs and gaps in work history are less.

Comments on CV / Resume Writing

Tailor each CV / Resume for each job advertised. The purpose of resumes is to get an interview call against the advertised post. On getting the interview call, the emphasis shifts to do better in the coming interview. Professionalism demands that an impressive CV / Resume be submitted with all the necessary details in a summary form, as:

80 % CV / Resumes - are eliminated within 10 seconds on first scanning.

15 % CV / Resumes - are rejected within 20 seconds on second screening.

5 % CV / Resumes - are studied, candidates are short-listed to be called for interview, as such, CV / Resume writing is very important.

Read the CV / Resume before going for an interview and take a hard copy along for quick reference.

7.4. Screening

Processing of CV / Resume is called screening and marks are allotted against each criteria:

	Response	*Marks*
1.0	Marital status:	
1.1	Single	30
1.2	Married / Widowed	56
1.3	Divorced / Separated	50
2.0	Age group:	
	2.1 18 to 25 years	30
	2.2 26 to 30 years	35
	2.3 31 to 39 years	67
	2.4 40 to 49 years	60
	2.5 50 and above	30
3.0	Leaving the last job:	
	3.1 Better employment	51
	3.2 Job terminated	48
	3.3 Job unsatisfactory	51
	3.4 Service contract completed	50
4.0	Experience:	
	4.1 First appointment	50
	4.2 Experience on job	50
5.0	Qualifications:	
	6.0 Interest (in profession):	50
	7.0 Intelligence:	60
	8.0 Sociability:	70
	9.0 Qualities:	40
	9.1 Emotional stability	45
	9.2 Initiative and drive	50
	9.3 Self confidence	55
	9.4 Leadership	45
	9.5 Sense of responsibility	55

Based on the total number of marks secured; merit list is prepared; candidates are called for interview as per merit list.

7.5. Group Discussion (GD)

GD is an interactive discussion between groups of candidates. Normally discussions center on a given topic. Group-officer notes down the views as expressed by each candidate in respect of their self-confidence, mental alertness, originality of idea, respect for other's views, balance of mind, leadership quality and ability to discuss the issues without loosing temper. GD is an integral part of recruitment and takes place in the last for recruitment at junior management level. GD's are good indicators of managerial ability, teamwork, group interaction and ability in solving the problem.

Three types of GDs

1. Normal GD - a group of 10 to 12 candidates are given a topic of general nature. Topic remains open ended; two to three minutes are given for preparation; each candidate is asked to speak on the subject.
2. Controversial GD - a group of 10 to 12 candidates are given a topic of a controversial nature. Topic is not open ended; each candidate is forced to take a stance for or against the topic to encourage a debate. Discussions enable the recruiter to gauge the candidates.
3. Case study GD - a group of 10 to 12 candidates are given a complex case study. Candidates are asked to discuss the case and recommend a course of action. This tests the analytical power of the candidates; their ability to pin point the problem and discuss the issue; their ability to come up with a feasible solution and in support give points. Case study can involve overturned boat to be set up right again or company's economy to be put back on rails.

GD evaluation:

1. Is a candidate good in getting along with others?
2. Is a candidate good listener?
3. Is a candidate good leader, who can influence others?

4. Does a candidate antagonizes or put off others?
5. Does a candidate exhibit a logical thinking?
6. Does a candidate exhibit analytical ability?
7. Does a candidate understand the topic well?
8. Does a candidate know the boundaries of the subject?
9. Can a candidate substantiate his arguments with examples?

Observation is made on group members with respect to their leadership, judgment, grasping of opportunity in leading the discussion and who concludes at the end.

7.6. Union Public Service Commission (UPSC) Interview

1 Object of interview - is to assess the suitability of a candidate for the intended service. Competent and unbiased interviewers try to assess a candidate's intellectual qualities, social traits, interest in current affairs, mental alertness, critical power of assimilation, clear and logical thinking, balance of judgment, variety and depth of interest in a subject, ability for social cohesion, leadership, intellectual and moral integrity. The technique of interview is not strict cross-examination, but the interview is conducted in a natural conversational style to assess and valuate the candidate for the intended service.

2 Resume writing - at the end of interview, the commission directs the candidate to proceed to an adjoining room and write down in brief what has transpired in the interview? The object of resume is to judge the candidate's ability to express him in writing and capacity to remember the facts. As such, it is important for a candidate to pay attention to the following points:

1. Candidate to write the resume within ten to fifteen minutes; matter restricted to 150 to 200 words; no extra time is given to complete the resume.
2. Candidate need not refer to the greetings, formalities and preliminaries.
3. Candidate to first write down the important topics by recalling the questions put by each member. Then write them down in the chronological order.
4. Candidate to write down the resume in narrative form, not in question and answer form, give the extract and not to repeat in verbatim the conversation, which took place.

5. Candidate is to state the facts, if all the points can not be covered, then most of the points are to be covered, but the resume must not contain anything, which did not transpire at the interview.
6. Candidate not to express any opinion or draw conclusion, but confine himself to reporting the facts accurately.
7. Candidate to refer to the Board as a whole, not as Chairman or Member of the Board independently with regard to the questions asked.

8. Candidate to use simple words, confine himself to short and crisp sentences.

3. Preparation for Interview

1. Dress - candidate be dressed in a light brown Terylene suit with brown shoes and a maroon Terylene tie or have a matching suit of any other colour.
2. Mood - candidate to remain cool, confident, pleasant and cheerful.
3. Entering room - knock at the door; bear a friendly smile; open the door gently a little; ask for permission to enter; wait till a voice from inside calls - please, come in. Open the door fully; enter in the room and gently close the door behind; take few steps forward; come to attention position and say, "Good morning to everybody, sir". Chairman greets the candidate, asks him to take a seat. Candidate to say, "Thank you, sir"; sits on the chair; looks directly into the eyes of the chairman.

4. Conversation in the Interview:

Conversation is based, when I appeared as a candidate in UPSC interview in 1974 for the post of Technical Officer under Ministry of Heavy Industries. At that time, I was working as Scientific Officer Engineer (Mechanical) in Department of Atomic Energy and was posted at Rawatbhata and was attached to Nuclear Training Centre as lecturer:

Chairman - you are a lecturer in the nuclear training centre.

Candidate - yes, sir.

Chairman - a political VIP's son is in your class. You find that the student is not keen on studies, besides he spoils others. VIP admits that he is aware about the poor performance of his son, but requests to tackle his son, so that he can pass in his examination. How would you tackle the situation?

Candidate - sir, I do not have a candidate of this type in my class, however if a case of this nature exists. Then for him the psychologists say that an individual's behaviour is always caused. I would probe those causes and will establish a rapport with the youngster. I shall begin talking to him in a friendly manner and will take genuine interest in him to win his confidence. There after, I will study the youngster as an individual and under stand his problem. I will discover his interest, ambition, aspiration and goal. I will relate his learning to his goal and enable him to realize, that how learning and studies help in achieving the goal. I will psychologically motivate him and will recommend his transfer to a post, where he can fit in datisfactorily.

Board - do you read newspapers?

Candidate - yes sir, I read - Times of India, from my childhood.

Board - are you fond of tea?

Candidate - I do take tea when I feel tired, but not very fond of it.

Board - suppose, just before coming over here, you went to canteen and spilled the tea on your coat. What would you do?

Candidate - I would wash the stains, as my coat is of Terylene and it would dry soon.

Board - suppose, it was a woolen coat?

Candidate - I would appear in the interview without the coat and would apologize.

Board - what is uranium enrichment?

Candidate - In uranium, there is some per centage of U235, which is a fissionable material and increasing per centage of this uranium is called enrichment. The process is highly complicated and is of secret nature.

Board - why to go for enrichment?

Candidate - It reduces the critical size of a reactor.

Board - what was the name of the first nuclear submarine?

Candidate - Nautilus, sir.

Board - what fuel it uses for propulsion?

Candidate - Enriched uranium, sir.

Board - that's all.

Candidate - thank you sir.

Board - please, go in the next room and write down in short what has transpired during the interview.

Candidate – I went there and wrote the resume in 15 minutes.

After one month, I was informed that I had been selected for the advertised post.

7.7. Tips for Interview

1. Bearing - walk erect with confidence, look directly into the eyes of Board Members while answering their questions, be pleasant, be enthusiastic, be interested, be keen, be cheerful and bear a smile occasionally with optimism and energy.
2. Conduct - be attentive, have politeness, observe etiquettes, neither loose temper nor get irritated as Board deliberately tries to provoke a candidate to see his response.
3. Speech - talk slowly, deliberately, neither shout nor mumble, pronounce words clearly and audibly, neither be dull nor monotonous, avoid the phrases, like: you see, I see, I say, I said, I mean etc.
4. Dress - choose it with care, as it should suit the weather conditions, suit be nicely fitting to the body and be well ironed out.
5. Hygiene - be neat, clean, don't sprinkle strong scent on the body and be well groomed.
6. Confidence - have self-confidence, be patient, while talking, neither get emotional nor show any nervousness, even if an awkward question is asked.
7. Body - check unnecessary body movements, like: leg shaking, shoulder movement or hand movement. In the conversation be normal in facial expression and lip movement.
8. Boasting - don't bluff, try to state what you know to be correct, don't guess unless you are asked to do so, shooting lions may lead to trouble as Board has many years of experience to catch extra smart persons. Lastly, don't try to be too clever.

9. Mistake - if Board points it out, quickly admit it and ask for excuse. Never try to cover up the mistake, as Board respects courage and appreciates honesty.
10. Initiative - helps, but watch the reactions of the Board members, be conscious of the limitations, don't over shoot or draw conclusions, be discreet in describing accomplishments, which are to be conveyed subtly and tactfully.
11. Listen - attentively, keep eyes and ears open, study reactions to know when to stop talking, agree rather then disagree to close the controversy.
12. Practice - interview sessions with friends, elders, use a mirror if available, attend coaching classes. These sessions generate the necessary confidence to face the Board.
13. Don'ts - in interview:

    Do not criticize and try to find faults with others, rather stress good points of others.

    Do not try to enter into unproductive arguments.

    Do not try to win a verbal battle, but try to have an enjoyable conversation.

    Do not interrupt the Board, when they are discussing, but be an enthusiastic listener.
14. Awkward questions normally asked in an interview:
    1. Tell me something about yourself, which you have never told to anybody?
    2. Suppose you are asked to invite any three famous persons on dinner, whom you would like to invite and why?
    3. Speak on any topic of your choice for 5 minutes and why you chose that topic?
    4. Tell me something negative about yourself?

7.8. CV / Resume forwarding letter

1. Opening part - state, who you are, why you are writing.
2. Reference part - state advertisement / web site.
3. Interest part - state, I am interested in discussing entry level / mid level job opportunities, as available with you.
4. Objective part - state an over view of qualifications, experience and skills.

5. Emphasis part - state positive things / efforts in choosing the organization.
6. Request part - state where to go from here for further / follow up action.
7. Tailor the covering letter to the requirements of the advertised post.
8. Send application and covering letter without folding them in a large envelop.
9. State leadership skills, cost cutting measures adopted and contributions made to the progress of the company.
10. Do not use phrases, like: this letter is written in response to ..... , please, consider this application for the post or enclosed, please find.
11. Check for spelling mistakes.
12. Use unlined white A 4 size paper.

8

Management

Management manages a company and administers it. Management initiates managerial actions at the helm of affairs. Management is responsible for the output of employees and of products at economical cost. Management runs an organization in a profitable manner and for this, they frame rules; draw plans to achieve the desired results in a stipulated time frame.

Managing - is a process in which, actions are taken to tactfully control the output of others and get the things done in time at minimum of cost consistent with quality through the active participation of others. But the behaviour of employees is unpredictable. Behaviour is to be controlled and guided through the application of managerial skill.

Manager - gets the things done through the efforts of others. He saves his time to attend to other essential things. Every individual is a manager in a general sense, but one, who achieves the results, is the real manager. It is worth noting that hundreds of managers have succeeded without managerial qualification (MBA), but none without a common sense and a practical approach.

Top management - is responsible to provide direction, exerts influence on the character and caliber of executives. They develop the knowledge of executives, change their habits and attitudes. They continuously raise the productivity of the company. They assign a particular responsibility to each individual and then grant them necessary authority to fulfill their targets. Thus delegating is not assigning work to an executive and then leaving him alone, but to direct him, as often as necessary to achieve his target.

8.1. Managerial Functions

1. Policy - be framed and implemented with authority.
2. Organize - the resources in the best possible manner within the constraints.
3. Directing - is assigning the tasks to particular persons for execution and monitoring their performance towards achieving the desired targets in the planned time frame.
4. Controlling - is impelling the persons in the organization to do work in accordance with the plan, depending upon the organizational structure and supervision.
5. Balance - is maintained between the differing views of the subordinates, but never to loose temper in meetings, what ever may be the provocation.
6. Information - is obtained in time and evaluated for quick action to suppress uprising of discontentment amongst the subordinates.
7. Decision - must be based on all the available facts and once the decision is taken, it has to be implemented with firmness, however bitter it may be.
8. Judgment - be given after obtaining all the required data on the controversial issue by using the assigned discriminatory powers.
9. Order - be given in simple language, which can be understood by all the implementing agencies and follow up action be taken to monitor the progress.
10. Plan work - based on resources and manpower.
11. Cultivate - team spirit and motivate employees for maximum output.
12. Keep – the manpower busy in constructive work.
13. Remove - bottlenecks in the execution of work.

8.2. Managerial policy - is an action plan for production, marketing, customer satisfaction, industrial relations, health, safety, financial and credit terms for running an organization in a profitable manner. Policy is based upon:

1. Objective - of the company.
2. Means - to achieve the objective.
3. Purpose - of the company.
4. Nature - of the company.
5. Responsibility - of the company.
6. Appraisal - method to check the caliber of employees.
7. Draw - plans for education, training and development of employees.

8.3. Managerial Principles

1. Lower levels of management do - what higher levels of management inspect and inquire.
2. Output is proportional to - understanding and acceptance of instructions.
3. Courtesy and decency - creates high morale and discipline.
4. Loyalty of workers - is recognized in the meetings.
5. Each employee - takes pride in execution of work and his suggestions are considered.
6. Calculated risks - taken in conducting the business.
7. Interruption in production – is controlled effectively.
8. Reminder systems - exists for follow up action.
9. Work delegated - through an organizational chart and up dated when required.
10. Financial condition - reviewed before taking a major decision.
11. Resources reviewed - before taking up a major work.
12. Time availability - considered before giving permission to start a major work.
13. Space - made available for all work.

8.4. Managerial rules

1. Avoid arguments - as it wastes time and generates unnecessary heat.
2. Show respect - to others, for their point of view, but never tell that they are wrong.
3. Admit a mistake - quickly, if a wrong decision has been taken.
4. Begin conversation - with employees in a friendly way.
5. Get consent - from the concerned people first, rather than objections later on.

6. Let others - do the talking first and then summarize the point.
7. Give credit - to others for their good work and practical ideas.
8. Give importance - to others for their independent views.
9. Be sympathetic- to others and listen to them carefully.
10. Issue appreciation letters - for the hard work accomplished.
11. Appeal for cooperation - for implementation of harsh decisions.
12. Dramatize presentation - of ideas to impress upon others to agree to the disputed point.
13. Never abuse or threaten - rather take immediate action, if felt necessary.

8.5. Managerial Techniques

1. Treat employees - with respect and considers them to be honourable.
2. Tell employees - about the change likely to occur and before it happens.
3. Strikes - examines the issues involved; see what went wrong where and in what manner, so as to arrive at a solution through negotiation.
4. Target - if met, pet the employees and re-fix the target at a higher level.
5. Try - to develop team spirit and work with consent, but deal firmly.
6. Appreciate - good work and give credit to the deserving persons.
7. Draw - an outline chart of the organization, define individual functions, fix individual responsibilities, outline individual authority to be exercised and establish lines of communication.
8. Check - individual performances against standard at regular intervals and keep confidential records.
9. Appoint - a committee with terms of references to give recommendations on the burning issues involved and immediately, this will cool the tempers and on receipt of the recommendations, take time to accept them or reject them, if not feasible.

10. Consult - local managers before taking a decision on a controversial local issue, as it may affect them and draw upon their experience, if possible and forge a common front to deal with the problems.
11. Comprehend - the whole nature of an organization.
12. Make a choice - in the available manpower and resources.
13. Choose a right time - to implement a controversial decision.
14. Decide the manner - of execution of an unpleasant decision.
15. Exhibit - sympathy with the employees, but deal with firmness.
16. Maintain - good will with all, but have closeness with few.
17. An advice - is tendered to juniors, but never to seniors (They are informed)
18. Be aware - of the happenings in the organization and in the surrounding areas, through a network of intelligence.
19. Ask questions - from the employees to generate enthusiasm in the organization.

8.6. Managerial Code

1. Set example - rather than issue instructions.
2. Action be based - on principles and rules, rather on adhoc basis.
3. Reading habits - be inculcated in the subordinates.
4. Professionalism - be encouraged, rather than likes or dislikes.
5. Authority - be exercised judiciously, rather than hurting them.
6. Work be done - through cooperation, rather than executed through orders.
7. Toughness - be observed in dealings, but be sympathetic to the grievances.
8. Competence - be developed in the staff, rather than giving instructions.
9. Monetary benefits - be given to the deserving employees.
10. Appreciation letters - be issued to subordinates for extra-ordinary works done.
11. Thanks - is given to subordinates for completing their work in time.

8.7. Managerial Don'ts

1. Don't look - for minor faults in the employees, but have higher objective in mind.
2. Don't be flexible - with the employees, but have firmness to deal with them.
3. Don't be dishonest - with the employees, but have sincerity in the dealings with them.
4. Don't be irresponsible - to the employees, but have the courage to deal with the situation.
5. Don't threaten - the employee, but have the courage to initiated action, if felt necessary.
6. Don't fish - in the troubled waters of the employees, but have calmness to settle the issues involved.
7. Don't loose temper - with the employees, but have confidence to deal with them.
8. Don't argue - with the employees, but have patience to listen to them and win them over.
9. Don't be aggressive - with the employees, but have restraint and speak to them gently.
10. Don't offend - the employees, but have diplomacy and settle the issues.
11. Don't be abusive - with the employee, but have calmness and use polished language.
12. Don't brush aside - the employees, but have patience and listen to them attentively.
13. Don't ignore - over the complaints of the employees, but have sympathy with them.
14. Don't be in a hurry - to take decisions regarding employees, but weigh the pros and cons of the issues involved.

8.8. Japanese management - is considered to be most efficient, successful, has surpassed other philosophies of management, as after Second World War, Japanese economy was in shambles, but its management philosophy turned the economy from ashes to riches and is based upon:

1. Spirit of cooperation and harmony prevails between management and workers.
2. Officers and workers use the same canteen, toilets, etc.

3. No peon is employed and each worker keeps his own area clean.
4. Birthday of every employee is celebrated and a gift is given on behalf of the company.
5. Work begins and ends with physical exercise and prayer.

My personal Experience

In 1984, I was deputed to observe the working of a Japanese team, which was working at Gandhi Sagar Hydel Power Station in Madhya Pradesh. The team used to start their work in the morning with light exercise and prayer, this inculcated the feeling of devotion to their work was excellent, they used to work as planned, they followed their working schedules meticulously, they had the same lunch menu, they worked without gossip, in the evening they all assembled together, which ensured their attendance for the whole day.

8.9. 20 % Efforts - 80 % Returns

1. 20 % of time - produces 80 % of results.
2. 20 % of people - take up 80 % of time.
3. 20 % of counseling - provide 80 % of satisfaction.
4. 20 % of products - bring 80 % of profits.
5. 20 % of study - provides 80 % of knowledge.
6. 20 % of work - provides 80 % of satisfaction.
7. 20 % of efforts - produces 80 % of impact.
8. 20 % of people - donate 80 % of money.
9. 20 % of people - make 80 % of decisions.
10. 20 % of people - in picnic eat 80 % of food.
11. 20 % of priorities - provide 80 % of production.
12. 20 % of people - carry 80 % of responsibility.
13. 20 % of efforts - assure 80 % of success.
14. 20 % of reading - provides 80 % of marks.
15. 20 % of leaders - carry 80 % of responsibility.
16. 20 % of customers - demand 80 % of rights.

8.10. An executive's work

1. A lazy executive - shirks his work.
2. An average executive - completes his work.

3. A good executive - knows what work to do.
4. An able executive - knows when to do the work.
5. An experienced executive - gets the work done in time.
6. A bright executive - creates work for his juniors.
7. A genius executive - completes his work with distinction.

Decision Making

An executive must make a final decision by himself as an individual; he must accept the responsibility for his decision; he must accept the consequences of his decision. If the executive relies on group discussion or majority opinion, then he is acting as a presiding officer. An executive must secure all the available information, seek the best available advice, seek the best assistance and then only, he has to take a final decision in the matter. Once the decision is taken, stick to it, monitor its implementation, if decision is worsening the situation, review the decision, as the decision is as good as the information on which it is based.

8.11. Managing Tension

Tension is a state of mind; soon one gets rid of it; better in life. It has been observed that tension is a major factor in human life, which can lead to other complications, like: depression, anxiety, high blood pressure, insomnia and alcoholism, however meditation is not a cure for these problems, but research has established that meditation does help in reducing tension. Meditation can be learnt at any age and one's education level does not matter in it, however higher education level does help in understanding the processes involved.

During childhood and adulthood, the quantity of Enzyme PP-1 (Protein Phoaphate-1) is less in the brain, but with advancing age, the quantity of Enzyme increases and with this, forgetting the things also increase. Old people remember only the important things; unimportant things they forget soon,;this is part of nature to reduce tension in old age.

8.12. Depression

Depression is caused by inadequate activity of neurons, which release serotonin in the brain. Depression is a combination of inherited, social, environmental factors and is a negative state of mind, which may be due to lack of energy or interest in life or motivation. This state of mind may lead to loss of appetite and weight. Depression can lead to insomnia; can induce anxiety; may produce tearfulness. Depression can be caused by tension, anxiety and phobia, which affect the whole body system and in response to it; heart beat increases; breathing rate increases; liver extracts more sugar; blood pressure increases; blood supply to arms and legs increase to give stability to the body. It has been observed that depression is a symptom of negative thinking, like: a person gets worried that he will never get success in life or in his career. This type of feeling disheartens the person to such an extent that he gets irritated on small things and feels tired all the time.

Managing Depression

1. Calm down, write down the thoughts, which disturb and don't allow the sleep to come, this identifies the negative thoughts.
2. Sit down comfortably, close the eyes and take a deep breath, let it out slowly, use willpower to over come the negative feelings and thoughts.
3. Build the necessary self-confidence, ignore the negative thoughts, try to build positive thoughts and think that you are getting rid off the depression.
4. Stand out, gently stretch the body in an open space, feel that you are getting better and better every day.
5. Shrug shoulders shake hands and arms to develop a feeling of wellbeing.
6. Go for a brisk walk in a garden or by the riverside, feel that you are converting your failures into successes.
7. Punch a cushion or pillow with the feeling that you have over the depression.
8. Laugh loudly, as this is a good exercise that wins the battle against depression.
9. Divert attention to good things in life and engage in constructive work.

8.13. Managing Problem

1. Achieve clear and definite - understanding of the problem.
2. Identify and establish an objective - to be achieved in solving the problem.

3. Evaluate all the possible alternatives - before selecting the best course for action.
4. Keep the other alternative - as a stand by, if the desired result is not forthcoming.
5. Put sincere efforts - in solving the problem and take assistance from others, if desired.
6. Make desired changes- in the action plan, if felt necessary in solving the problem.

8.14. Three Categories of Worries

Worry is a part of modern human life, every one faces it for some time or the other, each worry requires its own strategy to solve, worries fall into three categories:

1. Managing Common Worry

1. Get all the facts, which cause the worry, weigh all the alternatives and decide on the best course of action.
2. Stick to the decision once taken, implement the decision with full force, dismiss all anxieties and wait for the out come.
3. If worry still persists, ponder over the following questions and seek their answers:
    (1) What is the cause of worry, which is causing it?
    (2) Is the course of action selected correct or does it require further modification?
    (3) Is the solution coming in the desired direction?
    (4) If not, then select an alternative course of action, which may to lead to a solution?
4. Divert the mind - to another topic and do not bother about the worry.
5. Mentally get prepared - to face an inevitable, if the odds turn out to be against.
6. Put a full stop - to the worry, as it may be beyond the available means and resources.
7. Ingratitude expected - do not brood upon it.
8. If worry creates health problem - do not pay attention to it.
9. Act to solve the worry - as this is the only way to solve the worry and sooner or later success will definitely come and live with that hope.

2. Managing Financial Worry

1. Write down - the facts on paper.
2. Make budget - that meets the minimum requirement.
3. Spend the money - wisely, as budgeted.
4. Bear in mind - that income just cannot be increased.
5. Borrow from a bank / insurance company - to pay the debts.
6. Insure against - fire, flood and theft.
7. Build a responsible behavior - to spend the money, but do not be a miser.
8. Seek part time employment - for extra earning to meet the unavoidable expenses.
9. Seek cooperation - from family members and housewife in particular.
10. Never indulge in gambling - with the hope to win or invest in lotteries.
11. Postpone the expenses - to a later date, if money cannot be arranged.

3. Managing Complex Worry

1. Learn to relax - in spite of the worry.
2. Take things - easy and wait for improvement.
3. Learn to take rest - before fatigue over takes.
4. Protect health and appearance - as they are most important.
5. Clear desk - of all papers except the concerned documents.
6. Assign priority - to things and tackle them one by one.
7. Make a firm decision - and stick to it.
8. Organize the things - as per priority.
9. Depute the things - to other persons for execution.
10. Put enthusiasm - in the immediate work in hand.
11. Insomnia never kills a man - it is the worry about insomnia, which kills.

8.15. Managing Career

Everyone desires advancement in career, everyone likes to draw more pay or earn higher profits, everyone wish to have job satisfaction, every one wants his work is recognitioned, but all this requires higher level of knowledge and professional skills. For this one requires a life long plan of action and confidence building to share higher responsibilities. One has to keep himself abreast of the latest developments in the professional field, as professional knowledge is growing at a much faster rate these days. One has to put in extra efforts to acquire this ever growing knowledge. This requires study of professional books, magazines and daily newspapers.

Money earned annually through business or salary is a good indicator of progress in one's career. It is still better to think that how much money one will be earning after 5, 10 or 15 years from now. For this, one has to set a target, draw a graph with respect to time in years, see the angle at which the graph rises or remains horizontal or if it has the tendency to go down, then this requires immediate action to set the things right, so that the income again the tendency to rise with time.

8.16. Managing Subordinates

The delegation of power to subordinates is such that they feel responsibility for what they do. They should be told explicitly the lines on which you want them to run the show. Subordinates should be given adequate freedom, but if they make a serious mistake, you have the right to over rule them; otherwise you will not interfere in their affairs. If the subordinates want advice, you are there to help them; however attend the following:

1. Increase the knowledge of subordinates - to increase their efficiency.
2. Improve the skills of subordinates - to tackle difficult situations.
3. Change the habits of subordinates - to improve the work culture.
4. Influence the attitude of subordinates - to become courteous.
5. Know the pulse of subordinates - to know their feelings.
6. Help subordinates - to create a congenial atmosphere.
7. Solve the problems of subordinates - to divert their attention to work.
8. Instruct subordinates - with necessary details, to carry out the work.
9. Stress the importance of time to subordinates - to complete their work as per schedule

10. Pay attention to subordinates - to create the feeling of importance in them.
11. Trust subordinates - to create the feeling of oneness.
12. Motivate subordinates - for higher out put.
13. Teach subordinates - to understand their work.
14. Motivate subordinates - to take interest in their work.
15. Inspire subordinates - to keep their morale high.
16. Identify the sources to subordinates, from where help and information can be obtained in emergency
17. Utilize the services of subordinates - in arranging picnics and cultural activities.
18. Associate subordinates - in decision making.
19. Show appreciation in subordinate's work - to encourage them to do better.
20. Never humiliate subordinates - in front of others.
21. Avoid making a promise- to a subordinate, but if made, keep it.
22. Acknowledge in writing- the good idea of subordinates.
23. Shift a subordinate- to a higher post for short intervals, to build his confidence.
24. Try a subordinate- for higher responsibility on occasions like Boss' leave.
25. Send a subordinate- on special assignment to demonstrate his ability.
26. Assign a subordinate- an opportunity to head an investigation committee.
27. Remember- authority over subordinates merely validate the right to control and direct them.

8.17. Managing Individuals

1. Begin with praise - appreciates their good work and then discusses the issue.
2. Call attention - to a mistake in an indirect way and then discuss the issue.
3. Criticize self - before criticizing others.
4. Do not give - direct order to a very junior individual, but tell him politely, if something is desired to be done.

5. Avoid embracing situations - with the very juniors, but give them chance to save their face.
6. Praise the slightest improvement - if observed in the individual.
7. Uphold an individual's reputation - but let him live up to that.
8. Give an encouragement - to correct the mistake, as discouragement lowers the morale.

8.18. Managing Life Partner

1. Never nag the life partner - in front of others.
2. Never over rule the life partner - reach consensus.
3. Never criticize the life partner - in front of others.
4. Never suspect the life partner - till evidence is available.
5. Never loose faith in the life partner - sympathetically settle the issue.
6. Never loose heart with the life partner - hope for improvement.
7. Never ignore the life partner - encourage for participation.
8. Never be discourteous to the life partner - always use respectful language.
9. Never be dishonest to the life partner - show sincerity in the dealings.

8.19. Managing People

Most important thing in our daily life is people, with whom we interact. Many people make the things happen and society is grateful to them; some people fix targets and achieve them and society is thankful to them; few people have the technique of visualizing the future things and society looks to them for guidance; handful of people have the ability to manage the things and society seeks them to manage their affairs. These handfuls of people study newspapers, magazines, books, learn from others, listen to TV / Radio news bulletins to acquire the latest knowledge in the field of human activity. However, better to know that:

1. People are - imperfect.
2. People are - always defensive.
3. People are - hungry of attention and praise.
4. People are - fond of upholding their dignity.

5. People are - interested in solving their problems.
6. People are - consulting others, when in difficulties.
7. People are - always interested in earning more money.
8. People like - to be addressed politely.
9. People like - to be called by name.
10. People like - to have good friends.
11. People like - to be liked by others.
12. People like - to be treated with courtesy.
13. People like - to be appreciated for their work.
14. People like - to be respected for their opinion.

8.20. Managing Employees

1. Encourage them - to take more responsibility.
2. Associate them - in managerial activities.
3. Take suggestions - from them and give rewards for their suggestions.
4. Give them - incentives for better performance.
5. Provide them - higher standard of living through better canteen services.
6. Maintain clean - sanitary facilities for them.
7. Arrange - picnics and cultural activities for them.
8. Try to make a job - more interesting to them.
9. Develop a sense - of belongingness in them.
10. Routinely send - them on training courses.
11. Train them - to lead their team to a higher level of output.
12. Introduce new employees - to the company's working culture.
13. Pay them - all their dues promptly.
14. Let seniors - exercise control over their juniors.
15. Motivate them - for willingness to work.
16. Respect them - for their skill and work.
17. Create safe working - conditions in the premises.
18. Install first aid boxes - in the working areas.
19. Medical bills - reimburse them promptly.
20. Loan be provided - to purchase essential items.
21. Interest be shown - in the work of employees.
22. Example be set - on sincerity, behaviour and decent talk and on dress code.
23. Cheerfulness - improves working conditions.
24. Sympathy shown - in deserving cases.

25. Encouragement given - to improve efficiency.
26. Diplomacy shown - in dealing with crucial cases.
27. Occasionally inquire - the health of employees and their families.
28. Avoid arguments - with the employees, as it may create misunderstanding.
29. Remember discouragement - retards the work of employees.
30. Group insurance - arranged on a regular basis.
31. Service records maintained- in respect of qualifications, training, leave availed / due, permanent / local address and particulars of families.
32. Parting interview - held, views ascertained on working conditions, reasons ascertained for leaving and a farewell party arranged with a gift.

Five needs of Employees

1. Health needs:

(1) Physical fitness- of employees ascertained annually and medical relief provided, if required.

(2) Maintain good working conditions- this minimizes the employee's distraction.

(3) Avoid emotional behaviour- do not bring it to the place of work from house.

(4) Medical facility- made available in the plant area to meet the emergencies.

2. Primary needs:

(1) Food provided - in the canteen.

(2) Tea break - given after some work.

(3) Family welfare - looked after to create a congenial atmosphere.

(4) Accommodation arranged - to remove distractions.

(5) Recreation provided - during lunch break.

(6) Motivation given - to increase interest in the work.

(7) Discipline maintained - with firmness.

(8) Appreciation given - for good work done.

3. Secondary needs:

(1) Safety provided - at the working places.

(2) Security provided - during odd working hours.

(3) Protection provided - when required or desired.
(4) Respect given - to all employees.
(5) Freedom provided - to follow religious beliefs.
(6) Salary given - in time.
(7) Working hours - regulated and overtime given occasionally.
(8) Punctuality - maintained and monitored.

4. Supplementary needs:

(1) Remunerate employees - commensurate with their performance, responsibility and stand by them to give moral support to their actions, if they are correct.
(2) Maintain good relations - with all the employees.
(3) Provide job satisfaction - to the employees.
(4) Assign specific work - to the employees and encourage them to accept their work as challenge and monitor their performance, till the work is completed.
(5) Reward the employees - for completing the challenging work in record time.
(6) Motivate employees - give them an action plan to complete the work.
(7) Target fixed - for employees with their consultation.
(8) Determine the activities and functions - that employees must perform to accomplish major work in minimum of time.
(9) Admonish employees - for their failure and issue warning letters.

5. Complimentary needs:

(1) Bias never to be shown - to an employee, even if he deserves it as a punishment.
(2) Suggestions invited - from employees, to improve the working efficiency.
(3) Agree to disagree - with the employees.
(4) Patience observed - in dealing with the employees.
(5) Tactfulness observed - in dealing with the employees.
(6) Faith bestowed in the employees - rather than desired.
(7) Temper never is lost - on the employees.
(8) Firmness observed - in dealing with the employees.

Employee's Expectation

1. Expect to be treated- courteously.
2. Expect to be made at ease- with their work.

3. Expect to be welcomed- at work, rather than thrown into it.
4. Expect to be instructed- before start of work.
5. Expect to be made familiar with the work procedure- before start of critical work.
6. Expect to be told before hand- as to what would constitute a good work done.
7. Expect to be provided with proper tools- before start of work.
8. Expect to be awarded with monitory benefits- for accomplishing difficult work.
9. Expect to be thanked- for the good work done in record time.
10. Expect to be compensated- for extra work done.
11. Expect to be seen by their boss- at the work spot, when a major work is going on.
12. Expect to be appreciated- for out of the routine work done.
13. Expect to be provided with incentives- for out of the routine work done.
14. Expect to be patted- for the extra ordinary work done.
15. Expect to be insured- before taking up a high-risk job.
16. Expect to have satisfaction- with respect to salary and service benefits.
17. Expect to be motivated- for doing extra ordinary work and not just ordered into it.
18. Expect to be informed- rather then ordered into a work.

8.21. Managing Self

1. Respect has to be earned, but cannot be demanded.
2. Support has to be obtained, but cannot be bought.
3. Responsibility has to be realized, but cannot be inherited.
4. Proficiency in execution of work has to be demonstrated, but cannot be developed.
5. Potentiality for work is attained by position, but not by boasting.
6. Success in execution of work depends on us, but cannot be assured.
7. Confidence depends on past experience, but cannot be generated.
8. Work execution demands self-efforts, but depends on others cooperation.

9. Help those, who help themselves.
10. We have to crack our own nut, before we can eat it.
11. Sleep well for 8 hours a day.
12. Brain cells get regular work up through puzzle / crossword / brain activity.
13. Brain cells need polyunsaturated fats and amino acids, which are obtained fresh milk, egg yolk, cheese and Soya beans.
14. Yoga is a form of exercise, which helps in blood circulation, while alcohol, drugs, smoking adversely affects the brain cells.
15. Fresh air rich in oxygen gives a boost to our memory.
16. Scents from rose, lily, mint and eucalyptus help in improving concentration.
17. Enjoy the company of friends, family and talk over the worries.
18. Bring joy into life and loud laughter helps in it.

8.22. Managing success:

1. Aspiration - is a contributing factor for success:
   Aspiration depends upon one's ability, capability, personality, character, interest, time available, training, positive thinking, company of good friends, reading habits, endurance, position in society, behaviour, initiative, goal in life, habit of not accumulating homework, availability of resources and taking guardian into confidence, before embarking upon one's aspiration of good career or higher position. In the beginning there are many options and opportunities, but with time, they get narrowed down, as such, right decision at the right time, leads to fulfillment of one's aspiration. In this respect decision making is very important and its execution is still more important, as one has to learn to work with others and has to pay respect to them, then only success in life can be achieved.
2. Family - is a contributing factor for success:
   1. We must not be in a hurry to marry - ideal age is between 26 to 30 years.
   2. We must have fewer children - ideal to have 2 or 3 children.

3. We must save money - ideal is 10 % of earning every month.
4. We must discuss before taking a major decision - with the family members.
5. We must have proper sleep - ideal to have eight hours sleep.

3. Work ethics - is a contributing factor for success:
To overlook work - is dereliction of duty.
To ignore work - is demonstration of incapability.
To forget work - is crime against self.
To be lazy at work - is still a greater crime.
To be negligent at work - is the greatest crime.
As such, action without delay - is the secret to success.

4. Conducting a meeting - is a contributing factor for success:
   1. Circulate agenda - well before the scheduled time for preparation and presentation.
   2. Concerned persons - need to be called.
   3. Restrict number of participants - to the minimum.
   4. Dinner / lunch / tea / snacks - smoothen the proceedings.
   5. Start the meeting - in time.
   6. Stick to the agenda - do not allow drift in discussions.
   7. Control instantly - the hot discussions.
   8. Do not allow interruptions - in the meeting as it wastes time of all.
   9. Do not prolong the discussions - but soon arrive at the conclusion.

5. Behaviour - is a contributing factor for success:
   1. Forget past mistakes - live in the present and work for the future.
   2. Maintain good health - through light exercise in the morning and take a long walk in the evening or go for sports.
   3. Take interest - in the day-to-day news through TV, newspapers and magazines.
   4. Keep acquaintance - with all, friendship with some and intimacy with few.
   5. Give respect to elders - love to youngsters and cooperation to the colleagues.

6. Pay household bills / insurance policy premiums - in time.
7. Think positive side - of the things and avoid negative thoughts.
8. Save regularly - to meet emergency requirements.
9. Stay longer at work / office - than paid for.
10. Do not take home - small items, like: stationery, postage, writing paid etc
11. Do not make personal calls - from office.
12. Do not spend excessive time - on personal matters during office hours.

6. Success formula:

Destiny (D) - is predetermined, but efforts are needed to achieve it. If luck favours, then less efforts are required. If luck does not favour, more efforts are required.

Example – Ones destiny is to become a doctor, but long term efforts are required to learn the bio-subjects. One has to secure high marks for admission in a medical college and to qualify as a good doctor, if luck favours, less efforts are required, if luck does not favour, then more efforts are required,

S = D + E + L + A + W (mnemonic - Delow), where S - Success, D - Destiny, E - Efforts, L - Luck, A - Appropriate time, W - Will-power.

8.23. Organization

Organization is a body of persons working together for a purpose. Organization is a medium through which individuals work in groups on specific jobs. If numbers of individuals involved are large, then some form an organizational chart is required to restore working order in the organization. Organizational chart be based on 'activity analysis', rather than on description of individual positions. Analysis defines responsibility and authority of each individual in the execution of work.

1. Organizing - is arranging the manpower and resources for the execution of work. Organizing has to be done on following governing principles:

1. Do not have too many people reporting directly to one man (Ideal 6 persons).
2. Assign definite responsibilities to each person to carry out specific work.
3. Do not create bottlenecks.
4. Establish priorities for work (top, medium and low)
5. Create proper environment for smooth working.
6. Maintain lists of resources, filing system and records in a retractable manner.
7. Disorganized persons spend hours in trying to find what to do.
8. Each individual has tendency to report to the highest official.
9. Each individual tries to involve the higher official to make a decision or to concur the plan, so that blame cannot be fixed later on for the things going wrong.
10. Use of standard forms and reporting procedures increase efficiency.
11. Do not ask for special reports on minor issues, as this will lead to duplication of work at different places and retrieval of information will become difficult later on.
12. Do not create different forms for different jobs, but consolidate them into few forms, which may suit different job conditions.
13. Do not delegate more powers than essential to the subordinates for smooth functioning of the organization, as later on it will be difficult to withdraw the delegated powers.

2. Organization Development

Organization development is a constant effort towards improving the efficiency of operation in an organization by taking into consideration the changes, which take place in the industrial scenario with respect to: rules, regulations, market forecasts, pollution control, environment up gradation, teamwork, offer of after sale services and job satisfaction to employees.

Development technique suggests that a team of representatives from all sections be constituted for organizational development and issues discussed frankly to arrive at an agreed decision. Decision be implemented expeditiously, as otherwise it looses its value. Long term objectives of the organization are kept in mind always. Objectives can be: performance indicators, market share, cost of production, profitability, fixing of priorities, meeting the targets and this can be implemented in three stages:

Stage 1 - performance improvement planning.

Stage 2 - identification and analysis of impending and impelling forces.

Stage 3 - evolving strategies, action programs for improvement, making arrangements for implementation, but remember that performance improvement is an on-going process, which never comes to an end, as perfection can never be achieved.

My Personal Experience

Organizational structure of an Atomic Power Station is highly complex, as the technology involved is highly advanced, which is beyond the normal comprehension of a technical person, as such, a separate organization was created in 1987 called Nuclear Power Corporation of India. This organization required development at all levels of operation. Public Sector Uundertakings were studied as model for improvement. Observations recorded below neither have any intention of criticism of any undertaking nor offer any suggestions, but are my personal views and are of very general nature:

1. Poor project planning - leads to escalation in cost of projects.
2. Over run in completion of project - leads to increase in cost of production.
3. Poor growth - leads to stagnation.
4. Over staffing and manning - leads to inefficiency.
5. Lack of technological up gradation - leads to out dated production.
6. Inadequate research and development - leads to non-up gradation of products.
7. Poor utilization of resources - leads to idleness of installed capacity.
8. Low rate of return on capital - leads to non-investment of money.
9. Losses get accumulated year after year - leads to closure of unit.

10. Delay in delivery of products - leads to loss in repeat orders.
11. Inability to regenerate funds for development - leads to no growth.
12. Technically non-dynamic - leads to foreign collaboration to improve the products.

Indian Railways have defined a role for themselves that it is in railroad business rather that in transport business, as such, was loosing in transportation business of people and goods, however, it has now turned the corner and now it is a profitable organization. There are well managed public sector units, which are: Delhi Metro Rail Corporation, Nuclear Power Corporation of India Limited and National Highway Authority of India. These organizations are achieving their targets through out sourcing.

8.24. Assessing an individual

Good side	*Bad side*
1. Intellect:	
- Bright	
- Dull	
2. Profession:	
- Good in theory and at interpreting data.	- Poor in theory and unable to deduce.
- Good at practical work.	- Poor at practical work.
- Produces new ideas.	- Seldom original.
- Discerns the essence of the problem.	- Fails to distinguish the problem.
- Selects the best line of action.	- Fails to adopt what is important.
- Expresses well orally and in writing.	- Incoherent in speech and unclear in writing.
- Wide and through knowledge.	- Restricted and superficial knowledge.
3. Administrative:	
- Excellent judgment and foresight.	- Judgment cannot be relied upon.
- Outstanding organizing ability.	- Poor organizer.

- Born leader, gets best out of subordinates.	- Unable to lead and direct subordinates.
4. Personal:	
- Stands out amongst colleagues.	- Apt to be ignored.
- First class at working with others.	- Difficult to work with.
- Prompt, keen and energetic.	- Lazy, apathetic and slipshod.
- Stands by his judgment.	- Never trusts his own judgment.

Career building:

1. Doing something for other - is called helping him.
2. Giving guidance to other - is called training him.
3. Participation in a seminar - is called enhancing one's caliber.
4. Participation in a workshop - is called sharpening one's skills.
5. Participation in a short- term course - is called teaching to do things in a better way.
6. Brain storming in a session - is called igniting an imagination.
7. Professional person - is called an experienced person, as he avoids repetition of earlier mistakes.

We must remember that no one is so perfect that more practice will not help him to do better in life.

8.25. Leaving an Organization

Leaving an organization in a friendly way is an art, which requires special skills to say goodbye. This can be done in the following manner:

1. Resignation / voluntary retirement

Letter has to be simple, direct and clear; should have the date of last day of work, as per the notice period of employment; letter contains new address, telephone number and mobile number. The resignation letter be drafted showing respect to the company bosses and appreciate the service opportunities provided by the company, but never criticize the company, as their help may be needed in future for reference purpose. In an exit interview bad or good feelings may be expressed to the employer, but must spare time to speak to colleagues, associates and appreciate their contribution in the execution of works, as assigned in the organization.

2. Sample Resignation Letter

Subject:

Dear ——— (sir / madam),

This letter is to let you know that I am concluding my employment with ———— (company) with effect from ——————— (date). The time spent with the company has been most rewarding and helpful in my career and I hope that my contributions to the company have been constructive. My relationship with the company has been professional, warm and result oriented.

I have accepted a position, that will enhance my career growth and will expose me to new challenges and will provide opportunities, which I believe are in my best interests.

———————— (Boss' first name), I have the most respect for you and wish best of luck to you, sir and the company. If I can be of any help during my notice period, please feel free to let me know and thanks,

Sincerely,

(Signature)

3. Termination of service

An individual may not fit in the job or the job may not suit him and in both cases, it will be discouraging, shameful and the trauma may haunt one for a long time. In these circumstances, it is better to negotiate a termination and ask for more time to seek another employment or to make alternate arrangements, but never threaten the employer or go for litigation or if one disagrees with the reasons of termination, one has to put them in writing for record in the service / personal file, but never mention the reason of termination in a letter, as it will jeopardize the future employment. If reason is asked in an interview for leaving the job, simply say professional differences with superiors or no potential growth in career with the previous employer.

9

Wisdom

Wisdom is the quality of being wise. It is an ability to use knowledge in the right direction, at the right time, to do right thing. Wisdom pre-judges the coming events and the wise person controls the situation before it goes out of hand. Wisdom can also be defined, as:

1. Learning from another's mistake - is wisdom.
2. Accepting that cannot be changed - is wisdom
3. Changing that ought to be changed - is wisdom.
4. Applying mind in the right direction - is wisdom.
5. Recognizing an error is the beginning - is wisdom.
6. Anticipating the things, before they happen - is wisdom.
7. Friendship of learned is good, but keeping them - is wisdom.
8. Remaining busy in work is good, but working diligently - is wisdom.
9. Setting an example is better than preaching - is the attainment of wisdom.
10. Keep acquaintance with all, friendship with some and intimacy with few - is wisdom in action.
11. Intention is subconscious, dormant, has relationship with career, while goal is conscious, specific, has time frame - wisdom directs the efforts towards the goal.

9.1. Library

Wisdom requires constant use of library. Libraries keep the books according to Dewey Decimal System. System classifies the subjects into 10 main categories of three digits, each category into subcategories, subcategories into sub subcategories, except the books on fiction and biography.

Classification of subjects:

000-099: General works (Reference books, encyclopedias and bound periodicals)
100-199: Philosophy, psychology, conducts.
200-299: Religion, mythology.
300-399: Social sciences, economics, government, law.
400-499: Language (Including some dictionaries and grammars)
500-599: Natural sciences (Mathematics, biology and so on)
600-699: Useful arts (Agriculture, engineering and so on)
700-799: Fine arts (Sculpture, painting, music and so on)
800-899: Literature (Including poetry, plays and essays)
900-999: History (Including geography and travel)

9.2. Knowledge Quotient (KQ)

Wisdom is based on knowledge. KQ is an index, which indicates one's level of knowledge. Modern society is knowledge based. Intelligence is something with which we are born, while knowledge is acquired through use of intelligence. Knowledge is always acquired for a purpose and 98 % of our knowledge has a purpose, while the remaining 2 % knowledge is recreational in nature. TV Quiz: Who will become a millionaire (Kaun Banega Crorepati) presented by Amita Bachhan / Sharukh Khan has increased the level of knowledge of the common people.

KQ score is calculated through a drawn up program and repeated participation in it, increases the score. KQ score is comparative and is relative to other persons, who have attempted KQ questions earlier. Higher KQ score indicates one's higher level of self-confidence and self-esteem to succeed in life. Improvement in KQ score is more important than the first score.

KQ Subjects

1. General knowledge - is study of newspapers and magazines to foresee the future events with certain degree of reliability. This can be confirmed through future events.
2. Public speaking - is participation in programs, where participants are encouraged to speak on current affairs as

per their age group and each exercise is video taped for self-analysis.

3. Creativity - is about giving importance to original intuitive thinking.
4. Team building - is about accomplishing complicated tasks. Management games are adapted for different age group people and they are encouraged to participate in them to demonstrate their skills.
5. Memory training - is to build better capacity for storing useful information and ability to recall the information for use when required.
6. Managing time - is to utilize time in a constructive manner to gain useful knowledge.

9.3. Money

Money is essential in life, but has to be earned through honest means and saved for contingencies. Regarding money it is said, that:

1. Money can buy beds - but not sleep.
2. Money can buy house - but not home.
3. Money can buy books - but not brains.
4. Money can buy meals - but not appetite.
5. Money can buy luxuries - but not culture.
6. Money can buy medicines - but not health.
7. Money can buy amusements - but not happiness.
8. Spend money wisely and invest it for better returns.

9.4. Good

1. Good to forget - an injury.
2. Good to remember - a benefit.
3. Good to be liked - just the way we are.
4. Good to put efforts - for self-improvement.
5. Good is always beautiful - but beautiful may not be good always.
6. Good to admit - that we were wrong, but never tell others that they were wrong.

9.5. Work

1. Regular work - to be done periodically.
2. Priority work - to be done immediately.
3. Routine work - to be done on the same day.
4. Special work - to be done in a planned manner.
5. Creative work - to be done in consultation with others.

9.6. Happiness - is a state of mind and differs from individual to individual, however:

1. Eating fruits and vegetables give selenium and lack of it leads to depression.
2. Needs and wants change with age and accordingly, we must change ourselves.
3. Problems and worries remain in life and we must solve them with our own efforts.
4. Hobbies and recreation are there and we must engage in them to remain busy.
5. Home, we must make it worth living for all the family members.
6. Moderate and light exercise for 30 minutes a day, boosts our mood and morale.

9.7. Talk - is normal conversation, which takes place between people, but success in life depends upon meaningful talk, as through talk only we come in contact with others, participate in meetings and convince others to our point of view.

Nature of Talk

1. Common talk - through it, we convey our thoughts, ideas and emotions.
2. Idle talk - has no useful purpose in life.
3. Popular talk - is for discussing current events.
4. Professional talk - is done by teachers, advocates and speakers.
4. Religious talk - is for delivering sermons.
5. Communicative talk - is an act of conveying news, views, or information.

6. Intimate talk - takes place between close persons.
7. Chat is day-to-day talk - with no meaning.
8. Dialogue is a talk - to understand the point of view of others or express our views.
9. Parley is a talk - between opposing parties or enemies.
10. Rumor is a talk - on current affairs, which is usually vague.
11. Colloquy is a formal talk - between differing parties for exchange of views.

9.8. Time management - is the most precious thing in the world. It is imperative to use it properly. Time utilization makes all the difference in life. We have to save it by avoiding unnecessary talk and unproductive work.

1. Priority fixing - time has to be allotted to each essential work, priority has to be fixed for each job to be taken up as per schedule. Work should not depend upon our mood. We must not think that the work can be taken up tomorrow, as tomorrow never comes. It is said that what one has to do tomorrow, do it day; what one wants to do to day, one must do it now; as an opportunity once lost, it is lost forever and time never comes back.
2. Job listing - helps to allot time to each job, as per the priority fixed. One has to tick mark the accomplished job; at the end of the day, one has to review the job list; what could not be done and reschedule the job, which has to be taken up tomorrow; this applies to studies as well. One must not sleep for more than 8 hours a day; one should go to sleep at fixed hours, say at 22:00 / 22:30 hours (Ideal); one must get up early in the morning at fixed hours, say at 06:00 / 06:30 hours (Ideal).
3. Entertainment, play and sports - are essential in life. Daily some time has to be allotted to these activities. One must not remain idle for a moment, as idleness is devils workshop; idle time amounts to wastage of time, which cannot be afforded. It is essential to keep oneself busy all the time. Successful people have done it earlier and they can be followed.

9.9. Better in life

1. Better to focus on things - we enjoy doing in life.
2. Better to match skills and interests - we would like to do in life.
3. Better be an expert in some thing - try to do the same in life.
4. Better to have different interests - as it creates intereset in life.
5. Better have a job - though it may not suit in life, but affords opportunities to learn.
6. Better have some values in life - though it may change with age and time.

   It has been observed that one starts his career with aim to earn money, but it changes to job security with age and time and later to status consciousness and independence in work.

9.10. Experience scale

Experience scale - experience is dexterity in doing work, which is attained in life during execution of different types of works and the scale is from 0 to 5, as given below;

0 - just beginning of experience.
1 - brief experience.
2 - limited experience with some knowledge
3 - average experience with associated knowledge
4 - extensive experience with good knowledge
5 - extensive repetitive experience with high degree of knowledge.

9.11. Behaviour in Office / Work Place

1. Respect the time of others.
2. Stand up to welcome a superior.
3. Avoid chewing of tobacco products.
4. Maintain confidentiality of information.
5. Maintain loyalty towards boss and company.
5. Remain committed to work and avoid gossip.
6. Give instructions clearly, slowly and politely.
7. Avoid too short, too tight, too revealing clothes.
8. Do not take or borrow things without permission.
9. Maintain punctuality of time in coming and going.
10. Show courtesy and tact in dealing with rude people.

11. Remain cool, exercise self-control and never loose temper.
12. Do not brush hair, change socks, apply cosmetics or use toothpick.
13. Do not discuss family life or take interest in the personal life of others.
14. Acknowledge the presence of other person, as he enters with appropriate greeting.

9.12. Car classification - is based on length and six classes are:

1. Mini car - up to 3,400 mm (Maruti 800)
2. Compact car - from 3,401 to 4,000 mm (Matiz, Santro, Zen, Alto, Wagon R, Uno, Palio, Indica)
3. Mid size car - from 4,001 to 4,500 mm (Maruti Esteem, HM Lancer)
4. Executive car - from 4,501 to 4,700 mm (Skoda Octavia, Mercedes C- Class, HM Contessa)
5. Premium car - from 4,701 to 5,000 mm
6. Luxury car - from 5,001 mm and above

Car driving:

1. Before entry in car - look underneath for any oil, water leakage, flat tyre or any other obstruction for movement.
2. After entry in car - check:
    1. Gear lever - is in neutral.
    2. Hand break - is released.
    3. Doors - are closed properly.
    4. Driver seat - is firmly fixed.
    5. Put on - seat belts.
    6. Back mirrors- adjusted properly.
3. Never in car driving:
    1. Never drive - in gumboots, as they can get stuck under the break pedal or over the accelerator, which may lead to an accident. Do not drive at such a speed that the car can not be stopped in the visible distance, especially during night, rain and snow.

2. Never see - else where, except in the direction of travel, especially while reversing back. Let others enjoy the scenery.
3. Never talk - to passengers, as it diverts the attention.
4. Never approach - a main road / junction at high speed (Ideal speed 15 km / hr in 2nd gear).
5. Never over take - near a pedestrian crossing, red light stop, speed breaker and road narrows.

4. While driving car:
   1. Blow horn - before over taking.
   2. Give signal - to the back car to over take and give signal before taking a right side turn.
   3. Drive always - in the left lane of the road.
   4. Crossing - give way to traffic on the right side to pass first.
   5. Show courtesy and consideration - to pedestrians; they may be suffering from deafness, poor eyesight or may have physical disability
   6. Brake gently and smoothly - but fiercely in emergency, remembering that car travels 10 m before coming to a halt when running at 30 km / hr and 30 m when running at 60 km / hr due to time lag between perception, action, application of brake and momentum of car.
   7. Do not - park on a corner, do not over take on a corner, do not over speed at a corner- as the way ahead is blind and do not drive in a drunken state.
   8. Stop driving - if tired, get down to stretch or walk a while or take a cup of tea.
   9. Children are always impatient - better let them cross and drive from behind.
   10. Elders are always cautious - better cross them from the front.
   11. Animals - always cross them from behind.
   12. While following a vehicle - keep headlights at low beam, this will avoid glare in the rear view mirror of the front car

5. Before going on long journey:
    1. Keep - water, lube oil and a torch light for emergency use.
    2. Check - battery, lights, wipers, brakes, tyre pressures, oil level in sump, brake oil level in the reservoir, stepney, toolbox and exhaust emission (four wheel vehicle using LPG, Petrol and CNG to have carbon-mono-oxide below 3 % by volume and two / three wheeler below 4.5 %)

Four types of drivers:

1. Defensive driver - follow the traffic rules and is a safe driver.
2. Offensive driver - take unnecessary risks and is an unsafe driver.
3. Cautious driver - takes care of other's mistakes and is a good driver.
4. Careless driver - is a dangerous driver and may cause an accident.

Causes of road accidents:

India has the dubious distinction of having the highest number of road accidents in the world and accounts for 6 % of accidents, while number of vehicles is 1 % of the world. Night driving accident deaths are three times higher than daytime figures. Half of road accident deaths are due to drunken driving.

Road accidents in decreasing order of fatalities:

1. Crossing road junction without due care 11,174
2. Turning right without care 8,691
3. Excessive speeds with regard to road condition 5,307
4. Misjudging clearance, distance or speed 4,778
5. Over taking improperly 4,385
6. Inattentive or attention diverted 3,675
7. Opening side door negligently 2,682
8. Stopping suddenly 2,549
9. Failing to comply with traffic signs / signals 2,419
10. Failing to remain in the traffic lane 2,403
11. Loss of control 2,358
12. Swerving suddenly 1,740

13. Following very closely 1,606
14. Turning left without care 1,548
15. Failing to stop at pedestrian crossing 1,223
16. Learning driving 1,183
17. Pulling out from near side without care 902
18. Dazzled by light of the approaching vehicle 891
19. Reversing negligently 877
20. Other person's error of judgment / negligence 863
21. Driving under the influence of drinks / drugs 642
22. Negligently turning round in the road 519
23. Cutting in hurry 449
24. Inexperience in driving a new type of vehicle 372
25. Fatigue and sleep 278
26. Moving off suddenly without care 263
27. Illness 230
28. Changing traffic lane without care 180
29. Hampered by a passenger / animal / luggage 49

Total number of accidents surveyed 65,210

9.13. Learning from Mistakes

1. Mistake - if happens by mistake, it is an experience.
2. Mistake - if done intentionally, it is easy to correct.
3. Mistake - if done for trial, it can be correctly.
4. Mistake - if repeated, it forms a habit.
5. Mistake - if repeated for a longer period, it becomes a trend and very difficult to correct.
6. Mistake - if adopted by the family, it is impossible to rectify.

9.14. Category of Habits

Habit is an acquired behaviour pattern, which if followed against one's own will, will soon become a part of life. Scientific research has proved that an action, if repeated for 21 days, becomes a habit, which determines 95 % of thoughts, feelings and actions.

Good habits - are positive actions, which lead to happiness, growth, success in life and are:

(1) Eating habit - determine weight and health.
(2) Social habit - determine relationship with others.

(3) Work habits - determine success in career.
(4) Sleeping habit - determine how fresh one gets up in the morning.
(5) Spending habit - determine the bank balance.
(6) Buying habit - determine how one stuffs his house.
(7) Setting goal habit - determine the level of achievement in life, but 97 % of population do not have any goal in life; it is 3 % of population, which have and they achieve success in life.

Bad habits - are negative actions, which lead to unhappiness, retard growth, lead to bad health, loss of money, loss of memory and are:

1. Alcohol - is made by fermenting sugary or starchy foods, such as grains or fruit juices. Small amount of alcohol relaxes, increases appetite, relieves anxiety and this feeling slowly leads to addiction. Once the habit is formed, the body slowly gets used to small amounts of alcohol and body desires to have more quantity of alcohol to derive the same amount of old feeling of pleasure. More quantity of alcohol is harmful to body. Withdrawal symptoms from the habit are: trembling, headache, anxiety, nausea, confusion, fever and hallucination.

Four Stages of Alcoholism

1st Stage: Occasional drinker - takes on certain occasions, like: picnics, parties, festivals, some times friends force him to company them and slowly the reluctant drinker starts taking interest in drinks.He desires to have more and more drinks on different occasions.

2nd Stage: Habitual drinker - takes regularly in controlled quantities, seeks the company of others to justify his behaviour, as the drinker gets used to drinks, his body demands for larger quantities of drinks to derive the same amount of pleasure and slowly the quantity reaches a dangerous level.

3rd Stage: Addicted drinker - cannot live without drinks. He will go to any extent to get drinks in large quantities to satisfy his need. Drinker may sell his household items or can steal items for sale to get the required money to buy drinks. He requires hospitalization to get rid off the habit.

4th Stage: 24 Hour drinker - remains drunk through out day and night. He becomes a nuisance to family and to society. Ones a person develops an extra ordinary taste and craving for drinks, he takes the drinks shamelessly in spite of opposition from near and dear ones. From this stage onwards, downfall of a person starts in an irretrievable manner and consumption of drinks in large quantities leads to damage of liver, indigestion and loss of appetite. Person cannot think properly, ultimately he embraces an untimely death.

Different types of alcoholic drinks:

1. Beer - is alcohol made by fermentation from malted barley.
2. Brandy - is strong spirit distilled from wine.
3. Gin - is spirit distilled from grain.
4. Rum - is spirit made from sugar cane.
5. Whisky - is alcohol made from grain.
6. Wine - is made from fermented juice of grapes or other fruits and is intoxicating in nature.

2. Caffeine - is found in coffee, chocolate and less in tea, which makes the brain and body active for some time. After some time, when the effect goes down, one feels to take coffee again, however caffeine in moderate doses improves mental ability, reaction time, memory, reasoning skills, but coffee at bedtime removes sleep. Caffeine is addictive and symptoms of caffeine withdrawal are: headache, drowsiness and loss of concentration.

3. Tobacco- is a plant, whose dried leaves are not even eaten by animals, as they have an extra ordinary sense to smell it out as a poisonous substance. Insects too avoid contact with tobacco and run away from it. Man is worst in this respect and use tobacco in different ways:

(1) Tooth powder - use of tobacco in tooth powder is habit forming. It is very much prevalent in India and in course of time leads to mouth cancer.

(2) Snuff - is made out of tobacco, is sniffed in through the nose and is habit forming. It is also prevalent in India and in course of time leads to lung and mouth cancer.

(3) Smoking - smokers smoke cigarettes, cigars, biddies and pipes. They subject others also to passive smoking, who inadvertently inhales smoke from air, which surrounds them. Smoking increases heart beat, blood pressure and rate of breathing. These effects remain for 20 minutes, after elapse of this time, an urge is again felt to smoke and the process keeps on repeating. Smoking is highly addictive in nature and smoke contains:

1. Tar - inflames the tissues of lungs, which causes heart, lung and cancer diseases and 90 % smokers admit that they would like to stop smoking, but cannot do so due to lack of will-power. Samuel Johnson said that cigarette is a white cylindrical object filled with tobacco, with fire at one end and fool at the other end.
2. Carbon-mono-oxide - is picked up by hemoglobin in the blood stream, which reduces oxygen supply to the body parts. This is the cause that smokers get tired soon. Acitel-di-hydride also enters into the blood stream, which induces sleep, reduces tension, suppress the normal thought process. This is interpreted by smokers as relief and leads to more and more smoking.
3. Nicotine - acts as a tranquilizer, which produces a feeling of: well-being, relaxation on a temporary basis, reduces ability to concentrate, but give rise to high blood pressure. Nicotine is absorbed through the lungs and reaches the brain within few seconds. This mimics an action of a naturally occurring brain chemical called Acetylcholine, by docking with receptor molecules, which activate the pleasure centre in the brain.

   Nicotine withdrawal symptoms are: irritability, anxiety, sleeplessness and loss of concentration.

Nicotine is addictive and slowly brain starts to rely on nicotine to work in a normal way. Brain slowly becomes less sensitive to its own natural chemical called Acetylcholine. One cigarette has 2 milligram of nicotine. Nicotine is so poisonous that the quantity contained in a cigar, if injected directly into the human blood stream of a normal healthy person, he will die within few minutes.

Nicotine in small quantities may invigorate the nervous system of a person in the early stage, but as the human body system gets used to it, the system demands more and more of nicotine, till a habit is formed. Habit once formed, it becomes difficult to leave. A normal smoker inhales about 100 milligrams of nicotine every day. This quantity constricts arteries of hands and feet, which make the heart to beat more rapidly to increase blood pressure. One cigarette contains 2.2 parts per million of en-nitro-so compound, which causes lung cancer.

4. Carcinogenic substances - increase the risk of mouth cancer, teeth decay, bad breadth, ulcers, lung cancer, blood clotting, increase in cholesterol level, lead to heart attack, coughing, insensitivity in fingers, urinary cancer, impotency and produce heart burning.
5. Stop smoking - smokers try to stop smoking with patches, N.R.T. or with will- power, but they still want to smoke, because their subconscious mind wants them to smoke, which controls their habits, addictions and phobias. Hypnosis is a sleep like state brought on by another person, who then influences the sleeper to do many things, which normally the sleeper will not agree to do in consciousness state. Hypno-therapy is used effectively to transform the subconscious mind to stop smoking. If tension, worry, anxiety build-up; do not smoke; do not take drinks / drugs, but go for a walk, this diverts the mind or engage in constructive work.

It is estimated that a smoker looses 5 minutes of his life by smoking a single cigarette. Smooker meet their unnatural death early, annually 8, 00,000 people in India and 70, 00,000 people in the world meet their early death due to smoke related diseases. United Kingdom has banned smoking in public places.

4. Gutka - tobacco is an ingredient part of Gutka. Gutka is highly addictive in nature. Gutka is the worst form of use of tobacco, as it remains in direct contact with mouth tissues for a longer period of time and is three times more dangerous than smoking. Gutka has two carcinogenic substances: Nicotine and Methyl Nitroso. Both these substances mix with mouth saliva and the mixture slowly changes the DNA structure of the mouth tissues, which causes cancer. Cancer progresses in two stages: Early Stage and Advance Stage; each stage has two steps:

Early stage cancer - 1st Step: Mouth opening reduces to half, 2 cm blisters form in the mouth, which do not heal with normal treatment, but cancer can be treated through an operation.

Early stage cancer - 2nd Step: Blister increases to 5 cm, no pain is felt, but patient can be treated through an operation and laser treatment can work.

Advance stage cancer - 1st Step: Blister increases more than 5 cm, pain is felt. This is the stage where cancer is detected in India. This stage requires major operation; face gets deformed, which requires further operation. Plastic surgery and radiotherapy treatment may improve the situation..

Advance stage cancer - 2nd Step: Inner tissues of mouth deteriorate; bone becomes visible; cancer becomes incurable; patient takes liquid diet, as he can not chew any thing solid; patient can not speak properly; patient dies with great suffering. It was disgusting to see a patient in this stage of suffering in a Delhi hospital.

9.15. Indian Armed Forces

Knowledge on the working of armed forces is very essential, as country's security and well-being depend upon them. India is a vast country stretching 3,214 km North to South and 2,933 km East to West. India is a peace loving country, has never invaded any other country in the long history of last 1,000 years, but has a past history of foreign domination. Indian Armed Forces have taken part in 1st and 2nd World Wars along with British Forces.

Indian Army

Army has strength of 12 corps, 30 divisions and 3,454 tanks; army tanks and infantry combat vehicles are mostly of Russian origin, which have advanced nuclear, biological and chemical warfare capabilities. Army has a strength of 11, 00,000 personnel (9, 80,000 in Uniform + 1, 20,000 Civilians) and employs Gorkha soldiers of Nepali origin. Army has an annual budget of Rs.31, 000 crore. In olden days, army units under Indian Rulers, used to be disbanded immediately after their defeat.

Comparison with other armies:

1. British Army - has a strength of 1, 90,000 personnel. It is currently deployed in 80 countries around the world.
2. Chinese Army - is called Peoples Liberation Army (PLA). It is the largest Army in the world and employs 22, 00,000 personnel (2002). Chinese Civil War lasted from 1945 to 1949 and 12, 00,000 people were killed. Korean War backed by China lasted from 1950 to 1953 and 12, 00,000 people were killed.
3. Pakistan Army - has 5,50,000 personnel (5,20,000 in Uniform + 30,000 Civilians) and has 2,285 tanks

Indian Army structure - Army Headquarters is in New Delhi. Army functions through seven commands. It is the commands, which are responsible for planning, execution, monitoring and control of army operations. Commands are:

1. Central Command - headquarters at Lucknow.
2. Eastern Command - headquarters in Kolkatta.
3. Northern Command - headquarters at Udhampur.
4. Southern Command - headquarters at Pune.
5. SouthWestern Command - headquarters at Jaipur.

6. Western Command - headquarters at Chandigarh.
7. Training Command - headquarters at Shimla.

Each command has 3 Corps, each Corps has 3 Divisions, each Division has 3 Brigades, each Brigade has 3 Battalions and each Battalion has 800 Soldiers. Division is an independent fighting arm, which has Artillery, Armed Brigade, Engineering Regiment and Signal Regiment. Regiment is a body of soldiers commanded by a Colonel.

Defence Intelligence Agency (DIA) - was established in 2002. Intelligence process has seven steps: 1 Collection, 2 Analysis, 3 Assessment, 4 Dissemination, 5 Co-ordination, 6 Action and 7 Evaluation. Intelligence system assigns responsibility to independent groups and this minimizes overlap of operations.

Indian Army history

1765: British East India Company - raised the Indian Army on modern lines. Army had command and control structure at par with British Army structure. British Officers held senior ranks in the army.

1897: Saragarhi Battle - took place on 12. 09.1897. One non-commissioned Indian officer with 20 other soldiers fought the battle at Saragarhi post in North West Frontier Province (Now in Pakistan) against 12,000 armed tribals. Indian soldiers fought up to their last man. This established bravery of Indian soldiers in the battle field.

1914: 1st World War (1914 - 1918, 4 years) - 85, 00,000 people were killed. War started, when Austrian Archduke Franz Perdinand was gunned down in Serbia. Austrians wanted to teach a lesson to Serbia, but soon other nations joined the war. On the first day of battle of Somme 60,000 British soldiers were killed. Australia, Austria, Belgium, Britain, France, Germany, Hungary, India (Under British Rule), Japan, New Zealand, Russia, Turkey, United Kingdom were involved and 10,00,000 British soldiers were killed.

1939: 2nd World War (1939 - 1945, 6 years) - War started on 01.09.1939 and ended on 10.08.1945. War was the deadliest, longest in human history; 8, 65, 00,000 people (3 % of world population) were killed, 60 % of war casualties were civilians as a result of aerial bombing. USA for the first time in human history dropped Atomic Bomb on Hiroshima in Japan and second Atom Bomb on Nagasaki in Japan.

Allied Forces - lead by United Kingdom suffered 5, 00, 00,000 casualties (Military 1, 70, 00,000 + 3, 30, 00,000 Civilians); Axis Forces - lead by Germany and Japan suffered 1, 20, 00,000 casualties (Military 80, 00,000 + 40, 00,000 Civilians). People reported missing 2, 45, 00,000 people (Believed to have been killed)

Poland suffered the worst; 60, 00,000 people (17.2 % of population) were killed. Soviet Union suffered the highest number of casualties; 2, 66, 00,000 people were killed and the highest number of casualties occurred at Volgograd (Stalingrad) in Soviet Union (USSR), where 11, 09,000 Russian soldiers were killed; 6, 50,800 were seriously wounded. All casualties occurred, because Russian dictator ordered his troops not to retreat; Hitler of Germany not allowed his Nazi Army to retreat, when it was encircled by the advancing Russian Army. Battle ended on 31.01.1943 with the surrender of Germany

Countries of the European Union (EU) have shown the way, as to how to live in peace and harmony with neighbours. EU has set an example for the rest of the world to follow, sooner it happens, better for humanity.

1947: 1st Kashmir Operation (1947 - 1949, 2 years) - took place in October 1947, when Pakistani Kabailees backed by Pakistan Army invaded Jammu and Kashmir (J&K). India responded by sending Army to defend the state against invasion. In 1948 on 15th January, General K. M. Cariappa became the first Commander-in-chief of the Indian Army. In J&K, cease-fire was arranged in January 1949 under UN auspices. This enabled Pakistan to hold on to portion of J&K, which is now called Pak Occupied Kashmir (POK). J&K cease-fire agreement was signed in July 1949; 1,100 Indian soldiers were killed in the operation.

1962: Chinese attack - China invaded Eastern part of India and Ladakh Region in Jammu and Kashmir. China occupied large parts of Indian Territory. India suffered a humiliating defeat on the Himalayan borders, which compelled the Indian political leadership to pay more attention to armed forces; 3,250 Indian soldiers were killed.

1965: 2nd Kashmir Operation - started, when Pakistan invaded Rann of Kutch in Rajasthan. The conflict spread to Punjab, Jammu and Kashmir and cease-fire was arranged on the initiative of Russia; 3,264 Indian soldiers were killed.

1971: Indo-Pak War - started, when more than 1, 00, 00,000 Hindu refugees were forced to leave the then East Pakistan; on liberation the country was renamed as Bangladesh. Shimla agreement was signed in July 1972; 3,843 Indian soldiers were killed.

1987: Siachen Operation - started on 26.06.1987, when Pakistan Army occupied Siachenglacier area in Jammu and Kashmir. This is the world's highest battle field (6,400 m above sea level). Ultimately, the invading Pakistan Forces were driven out.

1987: Sri Lanka Operation (1987 - 1990, 3 years) - Indian Peace Keeping Force under took operation along with Sri Lankan Forces against Tamil Rebels; 1,157 Indian soldiers were killed.

1999: Kargil Operation - started when Pakistan Army occupied Kargil sector in Jammu and Kashmir and the invading forces were driven out after a long drawn out battle; 522 Indian soldiers were killed.

Anti-terrorist operation - Indian Army is constantly engaged against terrorist activities and every year about 300 soldiers are getting killed.

Indian Navy History

1612: East India Company Marine (EICM) - in 1608, East India Company from Britain came to India. In 1612, Britain built a small port at village Swally, near Surat in Gujarat and established a small Navy called East India Company Marine (EICM). The force was formed on arrival of warships from United Kingdom under the command of Captain Thomas Best. EICM had command and control structure at par with British Navy, but operated under the control of East India Company. EICM defeated Portuguese

Navy on 05.09.1612 in Indian waters. Britain established supremacy in the Indian Ocean.

1686: Bombay Marines (BM) - EICM under took operations against Maratha Empire warships and defeated them. British trade was concentrated in and around Mumbai; West Coast of India and to protect trade EICM was renamed Bombay Marines (BM).

1824: Burma War - BM participated in war of 1824; under took operations against Portuguese, Dutch and French warships. BM eliminated pirates from Indian waters.

1830: Her Majesty's Indian Navy (HMIN) - Bombay Marines (BM) was renamed as Her Majesty's Indian Navy (HMIN) and with British capture of Aden, HMIN's commitment increased to whole of Arabian Sea and Indian Ocean.

1840: China War - of 1840, HMIN took active part in the war.

1863: Bombay Marine (BM) - Her Majesty's Indian Navy (HMIN) was renamed again as Bombay Marine (BM).

1887: Her Majesty's Indian Marine (HMIM) - Her Majesty's Indian Navy was renamed as Her Majesty's Indian Marine (HMIM) and two divisions: were formed: East Division with Headquarters at Kolkata and Western Division with Headquarters at Mumbai.

1892: Royal Indian Marine (RIM) - Her Majesty's Indian Marine (HMIM) was renamed as Royal Indian Marine (RIM) and operated 50 warships of different types.

1934: Royal Indian Navy (RIN) - Royal Indian Marine (RIM) was renamed as Royal Indian Navy (RIN), as Navy's commitments and jurisdiction had increased vastly.

1941: 2nd World War (1939 - 1945, 6 years) - most devastating naval attack in naval history took place on 07.12.1941, when Japan attacked American Navy Fleet in Pearl harbor; destroyed 9 warships (3 cruisers, 3 destroyers and 3 frigates); 88 warplanes; attack lasted from 07:02 hrs to 09:45 hrs (Local time). Japan lost 5 midget submarines; 27 warplanes. RIN was not involved in this devastation.

1947: His Majesty's Indian Ship (HMIS) - Royal Indian Navy (RIN) was split between India and Pakistan; Indian warships were assigned the prefix HMIS (His Majesty's Indian Ship); Pakistan warships were assigned the prefix HMPS (His Majesty's Pakistan Ship)

1950: Indian Navy (IN) - India becoming a republic on 26.01.1950, Royal Indian Navy was renamed as Indian Navy (IN); warships carry the prefix INS (Indian Naval Ship).

Indian Navy is the oldest continuing armed force of India. Navy has strength of 55,000 personnel (48,000 Sailors + 5,000 Aviation personnel + 2,000 Marines). Indian Navy in terms of personnel is the world's fifth largest Navy and operates 161 warships of different types including conventional submarines 19 and aircraft carrier one. Indian warships and submarines are mostly of Russian origin; have nuclear radiation detection, protection, decontamination capabilities. Navy has an annual budget of Rs 4,600 crore. In 2004, January Indian Navy has purchased a Russian aircraft carrier Admiral Gorshkov for Rs. 6,900 crore and renamed her as INS Vikramaditya.

Comparison with other Navies

1. American Navy - is called US Navy. It is world's largest Navy, operates 318 warships including submarines; has 7, 38,000 personnel (3, 83,000 Uniformed + 1, 85,000 Civilians + 1, 70,000 Marine Corps). Marine Corps is a separate armed force of America, but forms part of US Navy. US Navy operates world's largest nuclear powered aircraft carrier, called US Nimitz (Length 332.9 m, propellers - four developing 2, 60,000 bhp, speed 56 km / hr, aircraft 85, crew 8,880 (Ship personnel 3,200 + Aircraft personnel 5,680).
2. British Navy - is known as Royal Navy (RN); has 36,000 personnel; operates submarines having nuclear capabilities built on Trident II ballistic missile system. British Marines form part of Royal Navy (RN) and carry out amphibious operations. Royal Navy is the second largest Navy in the Western world in terms of tonnage. In 1982, has under taken full-scale combat operations against Argentina and the operation lasted for three months to recapture Falkland Islands from Argentina
3. Chinese Navy – operates 65 submarines and 27 submarines are nuclear powered.

4. Pakistan Navy - has 22,000 personnel; operates 10 warships and submarines.

Indian Navy Operations

1961: Operation Vijay - was launched to liberate Goa from Portuguese Rule. INS Delhi fired on two Portuguese warships on 18.12.1961; sank one warship; scuttled the other warship; supported Indian Army's advance by firing on citadel and on airport. Portuguese Navy's warship Alfanso De Albukark was damaged; the warship was captured along with the crew.

1965: Pakistan conflict - Pakistan Navy attacked Dwarka port in Gujarat, but the damage was minor. INS Delhi at Mumbai fired on Pakistan Air Force warplanes on 04.09.1965. During this operation, I was serving on board INS Delhi as engineer and War Service Medal was awarded to me.

1971: Operation Trident (Western Front) - Indian Navy launched operation on 04.12.1971; attacked Karachi Naval Base and port (Pakistan); this major naval operation was so successful that 4th December every year is celebrated as Navy Day.

Naval Engagement (Near Karachi)

Indian Navy Warships INS Nirghat and INS Nipat attacked Pakistan Navy Destroyer PNS Khaibar and sank it; PNS Shahjahan was damaged.

Indian Navy Warship INS Veer attacked Pakistan Navy Minesweeper PNS Muhafizb and sank it.

Naval Engagement (Near Saurashtra Coast)

Pakistan Navy submarine PNS Hangor (Shark) attacked Indian Navy Frigate INS Khukri and sank it; 18 officers and 176 sailors were killed. INS Kirpan was damaged.

Sequence of operation:

PNS Hangor, a Daphne class submarine built by France. PNS Hangor launched on 28.06.1968; 1971 inducted into Pakistan Navy; sailed in the early hours on 22.11.1971;

patrolling Kathiawar Coast of India; on 09.12.1971 extended patrol Northward to investigate radio-transmissions intercepted on her sensors. PNS Hangor picked up two contacts on her passive sonar set; first attempt to attack INS Kirpan and INS Khukri failed due to speed disadvantage.

PNS Hangor managed to foresee the movements of Indian warships; took up an advantageous position on the path of the patrolling Indian warships at 19:00 hrs; waited for the Indian warships to return; at 19:57 hrs fired a homing torpedo at the Northerly warship INS Kirpan from a depth of 40 m (120 ft); torpedo missed the target; instantly PNS Hangor fired a second torpedo on the Southerly warship INS Khukri; torpedo hit INS Khukri with a loud explosion; INS Kirpan instantly turned round to attack HNS Hangor; in a hurry, PNS Hangor fired the third torpedo on INS Kirpan; INS Kirpan was hit and a distant explosion was herd. Immediately after these attacks, PNS Hangor turned Westward into deeper waters to avoid detection.

Operation Python (Eastern Front): was launched to liberate Bangladesh.

Aircraft carrier INS Vikrant - was equipped with Sea Hawk and Alize aircraft. Aircrafts attacked Pakistan Navy 3 Patrol Boats, 7 Gun Boats, 10 Merhant Navy Ships and one ammunition ship and sank them all. One Indian Navy Alize aircraft was destroyed.

Indian Navy Destroyer INS Rajput - attacked Pakistan Navy Submarine PNS Ghazi and sank it, as it was causing threat in the Bay of Bengal.

1988: Operation Cactus - was launched in Maldives, when Tamil Mercenaries attacked the island country.

History of Indian Navy warship INS Delhi

1933: HMS Achilles - Leander class light cruiser of the Royal Navy (British Navy); commissioned on 06.10.1933; crew 550 peace time crew; 680 war time crew; built by Cammell Laird at Birkenhead, Liverpool, England, UK; length 169.1 m (554.9 ft), beam 17.1 m (56 ft), draught 5.8 m (19.1 ft); Admiralty steam boilers 6, geared steam turbines

(Parsons); 4 propeller shafts (72,000 horse power); 4 Gun turrets of 152 mm (6 inches) bore, double barrel mounting (Originally); 3 Gun turrets, when handed over to India in 1948.

1937: New Zealand Division - of British Navy was formed on 31.03.1937; HMS Achilles started serving this division.

1939: 2nd World War - HMS Achilles was assigned to patrol South American Coast; warship arrived at Falkland Islands (Under British rule) on 22.10.1939; assigned to South American Division and allotted to Force 'C'.

On 13.12.1939 - a force consisting of HMS Achilles, HMS Ajax and HMS Exeter detected smoke on the horizon; 06:16 hrs confirmed to be German Navy warship Admiral Graf Spee (Heavy cruiser, fitted with 280 mm (11 inch) guns, gun range 36.4 km, commissioned in 1936, two propeller propulsion with eight 9 cylinder double acting two stroke diesel engines developing 52,050 horse power, speed 53 km / hr and crew 1,150).

HMS Achilles engaged German Navy warship Admiral Graf Spee at range of 20 km in a fierce battle. HMS Achilles got hit; got damaged; her four crew members got killed and Captain W.E. Parry was injured. German warship Admiral Graf Spee too got hit; got damaged; her 36 crew members got killed; both side warships were closing in for an even more intensive fighting; range got reduced to 7 km at 07:15 hrs.

German warship Admiral Graf Spee suddenly broke off engagement at 07:45 hrs; headed towards the neutral harbour of Montevideo in Uruguay in South America; entered harbour at 22:00 hrs for urgent repairs; buried her dead crew members.

1941: Royal New Zealand Navy - was created in September; HMS Achilles joined Royal New Zealand Navy as HMNZS Achilles.

1943: HMS Achilles was operating off the coast of North Australia with US Forces near New Georgia Islands (Solomon Islands); warship got hit on 05.01.1943 by a bomb on 'X' Gun turret; warship was damaged; warship went for repairs at Portsmouth in UK from April 1943 to May 1944.

1948: HMIS Delhi - HMS Achilles was recommissioned, as HMIS Delhi on 05.07.1948 under the Command of Royal Navy (British Navy) Captain H.N.S. Brown; crews 17 Royal Navy Officers, rest were Indians. HMIS Delhi under the Command of Captain Brown under Indian flag went on goodwill cruise to East Africa, Seychelles and Mauritius.

1950: INS Delhi - on 26.01.1950, India became a republic; HMIS Delhi was prefixed as INS Delhi (INS - Indian Naval Ship); In June 1950 Commander A.K. Chatterji became the first Indian Commanding Officer of the warship; Prime Minister Jawahar Lal Nehru boarded the warship for an official visit to Indonesia.

1956: Cinema Film Battle of River Plate - was shot along with other British warship and at this juncture I joined the warship as an engineer.

1978: INS Delhi was decommissioned - on 30.06.1978 for scrap in Mumbai; 6" Gun turrets were removed; one gifted to New Zealand, now on display at the entrance of Devonport, RNZN Base in Auckland; second gifted to Indian Military Academy at Dehradun, Uttarakhand.

Indian Air Force

Is the youngest armed force of India; raised in 1932; manpower of 1, 40,000; has 32 attack Helicopters; has 730 warplanes (650 aircrafts are of Russian origin, rest are from Britain, France); has an annual budget of Rs 8,200 crore.

Comparison with other Air Forces:

1. Chinese Air Force - manpower 4, 70,000; largest air force in the world in terms of manpower; has capability to build fighter planes.
2. Pakistan Air Force - manpower 40,000; has 353 fighter aircrafts.
3. US Air Force - is the largest Air Force in the world in terms of aircraft; has 179 bombers, 1,666 fighters, 1,279 trainers and 1,289 other aircraft (Total 4,413 aircrafts - 2002 figure).

Indian Air Force (IAF) history:

1932: Royal Indian Air Force (RIAF) was established on 08.10.1932; No. 1 Squadron was formed in Karachi (Pakistan) on 01.04.1933

1942: RIAF No. 1 Squadron flew into combat operations during 2nd World War on the Burma Front from 01.02.1942 to 12.03.1942

1947: RIAF under took air operations in Jammu and Kashmir to support Indian Army and 32 officers and airmen lost their life in one and a half years of operation.

1961: IAF took part in liberation of Goa from 18.12.1961 to 19.12.1961. (Goa was Portuguese colony since 1535)

1962: IAF took part in Indo-China conflict

1965: IAF Operations during lasted for 22 days, when on 08.09.1965 Pakistan Naval Ship Babar shelled Dwarka in Gujarat.

1971: IAF under took a massive air operation during liberation of Bangladesh.

1987: IAF went into air operations in Sri Lanka from 29.07.1987 to 24.03.1990 for the longest operation in its history, which lasted for 32 months.

1988: IAF under took part during Operation Cactus and airlifted massive loads to Maldives in the Indian Ocean.

1999: IAF launched Operation Safedsagar to regain control over Kargil in Jammu and Kashmir.

IAF Garud – comprise of 1,080 soldiers (Commando force); acts as an emergency response team; is the recent most force raised in India.

Indian Paramilitary Forces:

1. Indian Coast Guard - has 58 ships; 37 aircrafts.
2. Indo-Tibetan Border Police
3. Border Security Force
4. Central Industrial Security Force - functions under Ministry of Home Affairs in peacetime; under Ministry of Defense in emergency.
5. Central Reserve Police Force - is deployed through out the country to maintain law and order during disturbances.

9.16 Atom Bomb:

1945: 1st Atomic Bomb Test:

1st Atomic Bomb Test - was conducted by United States of America on 17.07.1945. Explosive device was based on fission of Plutonium, which on explosion produces large amounts of heat energy, flash, radiation (Gamma rays), high energy X - Rays. These X - Ray's heat up air in the form of fireball of temperature 3, 00,000° C. Atomic (Nuclear) explosion is measured in kilo / mega / giga tonnes of TNT.

1st Atom Bomb attack on Hiroshima in Japan:

US President Truman during 2nd World War ordered dropping of Atom Bomb on Japan. The attack was carried out on 06.08.1945 at 08:15 hrs (Japanese time) by US Air Force B-29 Bomber, named Enola Gay. Atomic Bomb was code named Little Boy, which contained 60 kg of plutonium; bomb exploded with a force of 15,000 tonnes of TNT; 67 % of Hiroshima city was destroyed; 10 sq. km of area was devastated.

Aftermath of atomic explosion:

1. Instantly - 1,55,200 people were burnt to death within a radius of one km.
2. Black-rain - rained for one hour.
3. Radius of 3.5 km - people were severely burnt.
4. Radius of 2.3 km - wooden houses collapsed.
5. People suffered - serious nuclear radiation effects in the form of cataracts, leukemia, cancer; worst part was that doctors did not know how to treat the radiation victims, as it was for the first time in human history that mankind was subjected to a nuclear attack.

2nd Atom Bomb attack on Nagasaki in Japan:

2nd Atom Bomb was code named Fatman. It was dropped on 09.08.1945 at 11:02 hrs (Japanese time). The attack was carried out by US Air Force, which instantly burnt 70,000 people to ashes.

1950: Accidental release of heaviest Atom Bomb:

Atom Bomb weight 19,050 kg, length 7.47 m, when was being carried by US Air Force MK 17 B-36 Bomber, accidentally fell near Albuquerque in New Mexico. Bomb's high explosive device detonated upon impact with ground, but due to some technical problem the atom bomb did not explode. Thank God that mankind was saved from holocaust.

1952: Hydrogen Bomb:

Is the most devastating atom bomb ever devised by mankind to destroy humanity?

1. Bomb as developed by USA uses hydrogen isotope deuterium / tritium; bomb is a thermonuclear device; Uranium U-238 casing encloses the triggering device of TNT; bomb core has Uranium U-235; inside the core is Lithium-6 Deuteride fusion fuel.
2. Fission - TNT explosion compress U 235; this causes fission nuclear reaction, fission causes fusion in the core of the bomb, which releases Neutrons.
3. Fusion - in the configuration some neutrons strike Uranium U-238 casing.
4. Fission - Uranium U-238 casing produces fission nuclear reaction; whole bomb on a test explosion produced force of 5, 00, 00,000 tonnes of TNT. This is the reaction, which is going on in the Sun and sustains it to shine.

1961: Test of the most powerful Atom Bomb:

Atom Bomb was named Tsar Bomba; bomb tested on 30.10.1961 at 08:33 hrs GMT; explosive force 5, 70, 00,000 tonnes of TNT; device tested by Soviet Union; test carried out on a remote Arctic island of Novaya Zemlya; explosion shock waves encircled the Earth three times.

1961: Neutron Bomb:

USA developed the nuclear device; bomb is a thermonuclear reaction type; produces a limited explosion; gives out large amounts of lethal neutron and gamma radiation; these kill all living beings in its range without loss to property; radiation waves are short lived.

1974: 1st Atomic device test of India:

Atomic device was tested on 18.05.1974 at 08:05 hrs (IST); yield of 10,000 tonnes of TNT; yield was based on seismic 'P' wave signals, as recorded at 11 stations in 7 countries

(1 USA, 2 India (Gauribidanur), 3 Sweden (Hagfors), 4 Norway (Norsor), 5 UK (Eskadhlemuir), 6 Canada (Yellowknife) and 7 Australia (Warramunga); tremors averaged 5.0 on Richter Scale.

1. Test preparations - was done at Pokhran in Rajasthan; device was placed 107 m deep in a 'L' shaped hole in the Earth; melting point of soil was 1250 – 1300° C; water content of soil 4 %; 'L' shaped shaft was sealed; television cameras were placed to monitor the explosion. Several months before the experiment, meteorology stations were set up near the surface ground zero; experiment was carried out in the atmospheric stability category 'D'.
2. Facilities installed - for on the spot checking of fission product contamination of water, soil and vegetation were installed; several hundred deposition trays and thermoluminescent dosimeters were installed in a radial grid at various distances and at different angules.
3. Monitoring - high speed movie cameras were located at 1.5 to 4 km away from the point zero; formation of mound was photographed; mound rose with a velocity of 30 m / second; mound formed a dome 170 m in diameter, 34 m high; dome was not ruptured by the cavity gases during its growth and fal; crater has an average radius of 47 m and 10 m depth; vaporization phase was completed in 125 microseconds; shock melted in 575 microseconds.
4. After explosion - no increase of radiation levels above the earlier existed level of 0.02 mr / hour was observed; after 30 minutes, health-physics team went in jeep up to 135 m of the crater lip; cleared the area from radiation point of view at 09:20 hours; surveillance teams using helicopters moved in the down wind direction; declared the area to be clear of any radiation; roadblocks were cleared at 10:00 hrs.

   Helicopter went down to 30 m above surface ground zero; declared the area to be safe; monitoring team went up to the tip of the crater monitoring for crevices and fissures; air, milk and deposition samples of dust were collected from different locations for analysis; samples were found to be normal.

1991: Graphite Bomb (G-bomb):

G-bomb was developed by USA; it works by exploding a cloud of ultra-fine-carbon-fiber-wires over electrical installations; this leads to short-circuit; bomb was first used in Iraq, when USA disabled 85 % of Iraq's electric power supplies during Gulf War.

1998: 2nd Series of atomic tests carried out by India:

Series of under ground tests were carried out on 11.05.1998; three tests were carried out; later two tests were carried out.

Heaviest conventional bomb - is called MOAB (Massive Ordnance Air Blast); weighs 9,752 kg; bomb developed by USA; it is a guided weapon.

Stockpile of nuclear warheads - as reported by foreign intelligence agencies:

1. Britain - 300 warheads.
2. China - 400 to 410 warheads
3. France - 400 to 482 warheads.
4 India - 100 to 150 warheads (15,000 tonnes of TNT explosive power)
5. Pakistan - 25 to 50 warheads.
6. Russia - 13,000 to 20,000 warheads.
7. USA - 10,500 to 12,000 warheads.

Iran and North Korea - are suspected to have nuclear warhead building capability.

9.17. Indian Missile System - is an integrated guided missile development program,; started in 1983 for development of five different types of missiles for the three armed services:

1. Prithvi - is a tactical surface to surface, short-range battlefield ballistic missile, size 1m x 8.5 m length; liquid fueled missile; first test fired on 22.02.1988; three versions:

   Prithvi I (Army) - warhead 1,000 kg; range 50 – 150 km
   Prithvi II (Air Force) - warhead 500 kg; range 250 km

Prithvi III (Navy) - named Sagrika; fired from ships and submarines
Equivalent Pakistan missile Hatf I - range 60 – 100 km

2. Agni - is a strategic intermediate range ballistic missile:
Agni I - is solid fueled; single stage; road mobile; surface to surface medium range missile; first test fired on 22.05.1989; warhead 1000 kg; range 1500 km
Equivalent Pakistan missile Hatf II - range 280 km and Shaheen I range 750 km
Agni II - solid fueled; two stage; rail mobile; surface to surface guided missile; first test fired on 11.04.1999; warhead 1,000 kg (nuclear capable); range 2500 km
Equivalent Pakistan missile Shaheen II - range 2000 km
Agni III - solid fueled; rail mobile; range 3,500 – 4,000 km (Under development)

3. Akash - is a swift medium range surface to air missile:
Akash is anti-missile missile; surface to air; first test fired on 14.08.1990; range 25 – 30 km; missile similar to Patriot missile of America.

4. Nag - is anti-tank guided missiles; operates on fire and forget principle:
Nag can be fired from helicopter; road mobile; first test fired on 29.11.1990; range- 4 km; suitable for all the three services.

5. Trishul - is a quick reaction; surface to air short-range missile:
Trishul (Army and Air Force) - is an anti-missile missile; surface to air missile; was first test fired in Nov. 1991; range 9 km
Trishul (Navy) - reaction time 2.5 seconds; speed 2 mach (twice the speed of sound); was first test fired in June 1998 from INS Dronacharya

6. Astra - is an air to air missile:
Size 4 m length; solid fueled; air to air guided missile; range 60 – 100 km; speed 4 mach fitted with electronic jamming devices not to be detected on RADAR; pay load 15 kg.

7. Dhanush - fired from ships; land targets can be attacked.

8. BrahMos - is a short-range cruise missile; size 8 m length; named after River Brahmputra in India and River Moskova in Russia; speed 3 mach (3,500 km / hr); fired from land,

sea, sub-sea and air based platforms; range 290 km; warhead 300 kg; weight 3 tonnes; has stealth low radar signature with fire and forget computer controlled guidance system.

9. Surya - range 5,000 km (Under development)
India imports 80 % of its weaponry from outside; budget of Rs 21,500 crore

10. Satellite Launch Vehicle (SLV) – is developed by Indian Space Research Organization (ISRO), Legend: A - Advance, P - Polar, G - Geo-synchronous

Vehicle	*Weight*	*Length*	*Pay load*
SLV	17 t	22 m	40 kg
ASLV	39 t	23.5 m	150 kg
PSLV	294 t	44 m	1200 kg (Orbit 820 km, Sun synchronous)
GSLV	401 t	49 m	1540 kg (Orbit 36,000 km, Geo-synchronous)

Pluto planet probe - was launched on 20.01.2006 by NASA in USA; after traveling for 9 years will reach the planet in 2015; traveling speed 21 km / sec (75,600 km / hr); speed is 14 times faster than a bullet fired from a rifle; bullet speed 1.5 km / sec (5,400 km / hr).

9.18. Basic Units of Measurement

1. Meter (m) = 16, 50, 763.73 wavelengths of Krypton 86 atom.
2. Kilogram (kg) = International prototype.
3. Second = 1 / 86,400 part of a mean solar day, since 1967, the second has been redefined as Second (s) = 9,19,26,31,770 periods of radiation of ground state of Cesium 133 and the element is used in atomic clocks to measure time in millionth of a second accuracy.
4. Ampere (A) = produces a force of 2×10^{-7} Newton / m length of 2 conductors.

5. Kelvin (k) = 1 / 273.16 thermodynamic temperature of triple point of water.
6. Candela (cd) = luminous intensity surface of 1 / 6,00,000 square m of black body.
7. Mole (mol) = unit of substance equal to the amount of substance of a system which contains as many elementary entities as there are atoms in 0.012 kg of carbon12.

Supplementary units of measurement:

1. Radian (rad) = measure of plane angle with the vertex at the center of a circle and subtended by an arc equal in length to the radius.
2. Steradian (sr) = measure of a solid angle with the vertex at the center of a sphere, enclosing an area of the spherical surface equal to that of a square with sides equal in length to the radius.
3. Pascal (Pa) = one Newton per square metre, unit of pressure, 1 kg / cm = 98,066.50 Pa and one bar = 10^5 Pa, 1 Torr = 1 mm / Hg pressure.

Derived units of measurement:

1. Density denoted in kg / m^3.
2. Energy denoted in Joules (J).
3. Newton (N), one kg achieves an acceleration of one metre / second / second.
4. Stress denoted in Newton / m^2.
5. Dynamic Viscosity in Newton second / m^2 (Centipoise American unit).
6. Kinetic Viscosity in m 2 / second (Centistoke American unit).
7. Work in Joule.

Radiation units of measurement:

1. Grays (Gy) - is the amount of energy absorbed and 1 Gy = 1 Joule / kilogram
2. Sievert (Sv) - is the product of Dose x Quality factor
3. One milli Sievert (msv) = 100 millirem

Indian numbering system:

1 lakh = 1,00,000 = 100 thousand
10 lakh = 10,00,000 = 1 million
1 crore = 1,00,00,000 = 10 million
10 crore = 10,00,00,000

100 crore = 100,00,00,000 = 1 billion
Frequency - is measured in cycles per second (Hertz); M (Mega) = 10^6, G (Giga) = 10^9,
T (Tera) = 10^{12}, P (Peta) = 10^{15}, E (Exa) = 10^{18}

Hertz	*Name*
3,000 MHz	Radio waves
3,000 MHz - 300 GHz	Micro waves
300 GHz - 400 THz	Infra red rays
400 THz - 750 THz	Visible light- velocity 3, 00,000 km / sec
750 THz - 300 PHz	Ultra violet rays- cause suntan, sunburn and cancer in humans and is detected by insect eyes. Ultra violet rays from Sun are absorbed in the Ozone layer in the Earth's atmosphere
300 PHz - 30 EHz	'X'-Ray equipments
30 EHz & above	Gamma rays- cause genetic mutation, cell damage and radiation sickness

Aircraft Flying Terms

Mach - is the speed of sound and 1 Mach = 1,238 km / hr at sea level.

Altitude - is the distance between aircraft and sea level.

Height - is the distance between aircraft and ground.

Elevation - is the distance ground and sea level.

Datum - is any reference level.

Aircraft propeller - displaces large quantities of air at low velocities e.g. aircraft speed = 725 km / hr, the velocity of air stream going back will be around 16 km / hr

Jet propulsion - small quantity of air is accelerated to high velocity e.g. aircraft speed = 965 km / hr, the velocity of jet in relation to surrounding air will be also around 965 km / hr

9.19. Temperatures

1. Supernova explosion = 10,000 crore degree centigrade C
2. Highest temperature obtained in laboratory = 510 crore C
3. Nuclear explosion = 100 crore degree C
4. Center of Sun = 1.4 crore degree C
5. Surface of Sun = 6 thousand degree C
6. Blue dwarf star = 50 thousand degree C
7. Melting point of tungsten = 3,380° C (Highest for any metal)
8. Bulb filament = 2,550° C
9. Molten lava = 600° C
10. Highest recorded on Earth = 57.8° C (Libya in 1922)
11. Lowest recorded on Earth = - 89.2° C (Vostok in 1983)
12. Human body = 37° C (Normal)
13. Seawater freezes = - 18° C
14. Air turns into liquid = - 200° C
15. Outer space = - 270° C
16. Absolute zero = - 173.15° C (Thermal energy of an object disappears and is the coldest possible temperature in the universe)

9.20. Categories of Industries

Industries have been categorized with respect to pollution into four categories:

1. Green industry - is less polluting and a standard application form constitutes to establish it. Permission is given to operate for a period of 5 years, subject to payment of consent fee for the said period.
2. Orange industry - carry out activities as classified under F of MPD-2001. These industries are not permitted to operate under Green category, as such; these industries are categorized under Orange category.
3. Red industry - carry out hazardous and noxious activity. They fall under the category of heavy or large industries, as specified in MPD-2001. These industries come under Central Pollution Control Board and follow Supreme Court of India directives for the purpose of categorization and identification of various industries under H (a) and H (b) category. These industries are categorized as Red industry and are not permitted to operate in the National Capital Territory of Delhi.

4. G-1 industry - fall under Group G-1 in MPD-2001 and operate in light and extensive industrial areas.

9.21. Categories of explosives - explosives have been categorized with respect to explosion risk into four categories:

1. Category X - those explosives, which have a fire or slight risk of or both, but the effect is localized.
2. Category Y - those explosives, which have a fire risk or a moderate explosion risk, but not the risk of mass explosion.
3. Category Z - those explosives, which have a mass explosion risk and major missile effect.
4. Category ZZ - those explosives, which have a mass explosion risk and minor missile effect.

Classes of explosives - explosive compounds have been classified depending upon the nature of the constituents of the compounds and the eight classes are:

Class 1 - gunpowder
Class 2 - nitrate mixture
Class 3 - nitro compound
Class 4 - chlorate mixture
Class 5 - fulminate
Class 6 - ammunition
Class 7 - fire works
Class 8 - liquid oxygen explosive

9.22. Pollution

1. PM 10 pollution - is caused by polycyclic-aeromatic-hydrocarbon particles, which get produced from rubbing of vehicle tyres on roads. Size of particle is less than 10 micron. These floating particles in the air, find their way into human body through breathing. They cause cancer, respiratory diseases and heart problems.

2. Sound pollution; loudness of sound - is measured in decibels (dB); dB scale:

0 dB	-	Threshold of human hearing (Speed of sound in air = 1,220 km / hr)
20 dB	-	Soft whisper
40 - 50 dB	-	Normal conversation

80 dB - Vacuum cleaner, factory
120 dB - Jet aircraft taking off
130 dB - Threshold of ear pain
140 dB - Space rocket lift off
160 dB - Eardrum rupture

Recommended Sound Levels

When loudness of sound increases beyond a limit, it leads to irritation, tension and in course of time to deafness. Legend: Day (0600 – 2200 hrs), Night (2200 – 0600 hrs)

Code	*Area*	*Day*	*Night*
A	Industrial	75 dB	70 dB
B	Commercial	65 dB	55 dB
C	Residential	55 dB	45 dB
D	Silence	50 dB	40 dB

Silence area - is 100 m around hospitals, educational institutes and courts.

3. **Respirable Suspended Particulate Matter (RSPM)**
RSPM are the deadly pollutant particles present in the exhaust of diesel vehicles. When inhaled; they travel to the blood stream through lungs; aggravate heart condition of patients; cause asthmatic reactions in persons. Permissible limit for these particles is 100 microgram per cubic meter. Benzene is a big carcinogenic factor; its maximum permissible limit is 1 % in petrol.

4. **Water Pollution**
Insecticides, pesticides, chemical fertilizers, untreated sewage, when enter into rivers; they cause water pollution; water from most of the Indian rivers is highly polluted; water is not even fit for drinking; at places water is not even fit for bathing. Under ground water sources are also getting polluted and the effects of pollutants are:
Arsenic - produces serious skin diseases.

Cadmium - mental tension and body growth gets hampered.
Cobalt - produces burning sensation in the chest, weakness in bones and low blood pressure.
Detergent - upsets stomach.
Mercury - produces pain in the chest and headache.

5. Green House Effects

In the last 100 years, carbon-di-oxide gas in the atmosphere has increased by 25 % and it is still increasing at an alarming rate, if not checked in time; this will lead to inundation of low lying areas on Earth, like: Bangladesh and Mauritius.

9.23. Time Scale of Technical Progress

50: Hero - of Alexandria in Egypt built a steam reaction turbine.

1452 - 1519 AD: Leonardo Da Vinci - designed:

1. Vehicle propelled by 8 men.
2. Tank like vehicle with sloping sides to shield against artillery fire.
3. Cannon with rapid firing mechanism.
4. Flying machine with 4 flopping wings, but it could not fly.
5. Parachute.
6. Vertical take-off aircraft using an aerial screw (Propeller).
7. Diving bell and suit for under water exploration.
8. Bicycle-chain.
9. Giant crossbow operated by pulleys and used for shooting.

1629: Giovanni Branca - designed steam impulse turbine.

1770: Nicholas Cugnot of France - made the first car run by steam engine with boiler installed in the front, but it was very inconvenient to drive.

1831: Michel Faraday - proved principle of electro-magnetic induction that when a wire cuts a varying magnetic field, electrical potential is induced in it and current flows.

1853: On 16th April 1853 - first train ran from Mumbai to Thane in India. Currently, India has 6, 24,000 km route railway track; out of which 1,56,000 km route is electrified (25,000 V - DC).

1876: Thomas Alva Edison (1847 – 1931) - established an 'Inventions Factory'; registered 1093 US patents; he was called father of inventions.

1878: Gramme - built the first direct current generator.

1881: World's first experimental hydro-electric power plant was built in Germany.

1882: Thomas Alva Edison (1847 - 1931) - began inventing things from the young age of 12 years; he established chemistry laboratory in the home; built worlds first thermal electric power generating station in New York (USA); plant produced direct current (DC) electricity; plant supplied power to 80 homes. He invented the first record player, first cinema projector and in all invented 1,000 things, like: electric bulb in 1879 AD.

George Westinghouse used Nikola Tesla's invention; established world's first thermal electric power generating station; plant produced alternating current (AC) electricity and to day, all power stations in the world use this method.

1883: Gustat De Laval - of Sweden built the first single stage reaction turbine.

1884: Charles Parsons - built the first stem turbine of 400-watt capacity.

1886: Bainz and Daimler of Germany made the first car run by an internal combustion engine.

1888: Steam nozzle patented in Sweden.

1888: Nikola Tesla - introduced for the first time poly phase alternating current system.

1890: Single-phase 75 kilowatt turbo-generator was installed in England for public service.

1891: Parsons - built the first steam-condensing turbine.

1893: Rudolf Diesel - of Germany patented internal combustion heat engine.

1897: Working diesel engine was demonstrated.

1898: America built its first diesel engine.

1899: First thermal power station of I KW was established in Kolkata in India.

900: America built its first turbine of 1.5 Megawatt, which weighed 52.7 kg / kW.

1901: Parsons- built the first 3 phase, 1.5 MW turbo-alternator.

1903: America designed 5 MW set.

1904: World's first geothermal power station was built at Lardarello in Italy.

1909: America designed 12 MW set.

1919: India launched its first cargo ship on 5th April.

1941: World's first wind power in Vermont in USA was established.

1954: World's first Atomic Power Station was built at Obninsk in Russia; plant used 550 kg 50 % enriched uranium.

1957: World's first satellite Sputnik was launched by Soviet Union on 4th October.

1957: World's first animal Laika (Dog) was launched into space by the satellite Sputnik by Soviet Union on 3rd November.

1960: World's first solar power station was built in Turkmenistan.

1961: World's first cosmonaut Yuri Gagarin of Soviet Union went into space; he circled the Earth aboard Vostok satellite on 12th April.

1967: World's first tidal power station was built in Rance Estuary in France.

1968: World's first orbit around the Moon was made by Apollo satellite of USA on 21st December 1968

1969: World's first astronauts Neil Armstrong and Edwin in Apollo - 11 mission landed on the surface of Moon on 21st July 1969. Moon's surface temperature on Sunshine side remains 130° C; in shadow - 90° C.

9.24. Devastating Accidents

1921: Ammonium nitrate (3,000 tonnes) - exploded on 21.09.1921 at Oppau in Germany; killed 561 people up to 7 km away; 100 people were disabled; 1,500 people were injured; 7,000 people became homeless; environmental damage extended up to 10 km away.

1942: Coalmine explosion - took place on 26.04.1942 at Honkaiko Benxihu in China; 1,549 miners were killed.

1945: Attack on passenger liner – occurred on 30.03.1945 at Sea during 2nd World War, when German liner Wilhelm Gust Loff (25,484 tonnes) was torpedoed off Gdansk, Poland by Soviet S-13 submarine; 7,700 people were killed, who were fleeing from the advancing Soviet forces; 300 people survived.

1960: Spacecraft accident - took place on 24.10.1960, when at Baikonur Space Center in Russia (Kazakhstan); Rocket - 16 valve leaked resulting in fire; 91 people were killed.

1979: Chlorine gas release - a train accident took place on 11.11.1979 at Mississauga, near Toronto in Canada; 60 tonnes of Chlorine gas escaped; 2, 40,000 people were evacuated for a week from 125 Sq km area; there were no casualties.

1981: Train accident - took place on 06.06.1981 at Samastipur in Bihar in India; train hit a buffalo; train plunged into River Bagmati; 900 passengers killed.

1984: Fire accident - took place on 19.11.1984 in Mexico City in Mexico; 6,000 tonnes of liquid petroleum gas caught fire; fire lasted for 18 hours; 500 people were killed; 100 people were disabled; 7,079 people were injured; houses up to 300 m were destroyed; 39,000 people were evacuated.

1984: Gas leakage - occurred on 03.12.1984 at Bhopal in India; run-away reaction occurred in Union Carbide Company's storage tank; 30 tonnes of Methyl Isocyanate Gas got released into the atmosphere; 2,000 people were killed immediately; 1,000 people died after few days; 10,000 people received disabling injuries; 2,00,000 people got injuries over an area of 10 sq km.

1985: Japanese airliner - Boeing 747, flight # 123 crashed on 12.08.1985; 535 passengers were killed near Ueno in Japan; 4 passengers survived; aircraft was flying at 8 km height, when aft-pressure bulkhead failed resulting in failure of rudder and elevator.

1986: Nuclear reactor accident - occurred on 26.04.1986 at 01:23 (Local time), when Chernobyl No. 4 nuclear power plant reactor blew its dome in USSR (Ukraine); 31 people died; 17, 00,000 people were exposed to dangerous levels of radiation.

1986: Hazardous chemical warehouse - caught fire on 01.11.1986 at Basle in Switzerland; 30 tonnes of hazardous chemical including 150 kg of mercury compounds washed into the River Rhine; 250 km of river course got polluted leading to severe damage to flora and fauna.

1995: Train accident - took place on 28.10.1995; train in a tunnel caught fire in Baku Azerbaijan; 300 passengers were killed due to carbon-mono-oxide poisoning, when toxic material caught fire.

1996: Airliner collision - occurred on 12.11.1996, when a Saudi Arabian Boeing 747 aircraft on a scheduled flight from Delhi collided with Kazakh Ilushin 76 aircraft on a charter flight 80 km Southwest of Delhi; 351 passengers and crew were killed.

1996: Boiler explosion - paddle steamer Sultana was sailing on River Mississippi in USA; ship's boiler exploded; ship sank; 1,650 passengers killed; 741 people survived.

2000: Ammunition depot fire accident took place on 20.04.2000 at 16:30 hrs at Bharatpur in Rajasthan in India; fire originated outside the boundary in tall dry grass; fire spread into the depot, where 30,000 tonnes of ammunition was stored; fire tenders were rushed from Alwar, Agra and Mathura; fire brought under control on 29.04.2000 at 22.00 hrs; 12,111 tonnes of ammunition costing Rs 376 crore was destroyed; 2 persons died; 10 persons were injured.

Accidents Due to Human Failure

1. Production personnel failure - America was stunned when Challenger exploded; quality control of NASA had warned that the space shuttle was not fully prepared for flight; production personnel said that the show must go on; challenger met the disaster.
2. Airline crew failure - Eastern Airline jumbo jet bound from New York to Miami on a regular flight No. 401; plane reached Miami airport for landing; light that indicates proper deployment of landing gear failed to light; plane started flying in circles over the swamps of Everglades of Florida; cockpit crew busy in checking wether gear actually deployed or indicator light is defective; other crew members tried to help the flight engineer to determine the cause; no one noticed that the aircraft was loosing height; plane flew straight into the swamp; killing dozens of people.

9.25. Commercial Things

1. GDP (Gross Domestic Product) - of a country is domestic production of agriculture, non-agriculture and industrial production in a year and is an index of a country's progress. GDP = Consumption + Investment + Export – Import. GDP of India is Rs 27, 55,034 crore and stands 12th in ranking after USA (First), Japan, China and South Korea.

2. **Gold**

Yellow gold - is an alloy of: silver, zinc and copper and 18 / 22 carat yellow gold is popular for making jewelry in India. White gold - is an alloy of: silver, zinc and platinum and 18 / 22 carat white gold is popular for making jewelry in Western countries.

Purity of gold - is expressed in carat, in marking, in purity % and in parts, as shown below in the table:

Carat	*Marking*	*Purity (%)*	*Parts* *Gold*	*Alloy*
24	Pure gold	100 %	24	00
23	958	95.8 %	23	01
22	925	92.5 %	22	02
21	875	87.5 %	21	03
18	750	75 %	18	06
14	585	58.5 %	14	10
10	417	41.7 %	10	14
09	375	37.5 %	09	15

3. Gems - carat is a unit of measuring the weight of gems and 1 carat = 0.2 gm.

4. Trade credit - is a form of working capital funding; reputed firms can count upon it to run a company. Need for working capital arises, as there is an operating cycle of a company, which requires time to materialize, like: converting cash into raw materials; raw materials into finished products; finished products into recoverable bills; finally bills into recovered cash, which acts as working capital.

5. Fixed deposits - are raised from public for investment in current assets; interests are around 14 %.

6. Hundi - is a bill of exchange on the buyer of the goods and lorry receipt as evidence of dispatch of goods. The borrower is allowed to draw funds, when he submits the documents to his bank, which scrutinizes them and sends the documents at the buyer's location. The collecting banker collects the payment from the debt owed by the company to the shareholders / partners in a partnership firm. This includes paid up share capital, retained earnings and reserves. There is no legal obligation to pay interest on equity capital.
7. Short term finance - is required to buy raw materials and consumables; to meet expenses of running a business or company.

9.26. Millionaires in the world as per American Forbes magazine, their numbers has increased to 793; 78 are ladies; 40 are Indians; some of them are:

1. Bill Gates – an American citizen; cofounder and chairman of Micro Soft Corporation (Software company); he is the richest person in the world; he is maintaining this position from the last 12 years; his personal wealth is estimated at Rs 2, 25,000 crore; he does not have a college degree; he dropped out of Harvard college in USA to establish Micro-soft Company.
2. Lady Hind Hariri - she is the youngest amongst all the rich persons; age 22 years; she is from Lebanon.
3. Lakshmi Mittal - age 51 years; heads steel empire, which spread to 10 countries; his headquarters are in London in UK. He has turned the loss making steel plants into profit churning plants through innovative ideas (Steel Authority of India is a loss making concern). Mittal is an Indian; retains his dark blue Indian passport; owns TV Channel B4U with his friend Kishore; net worth $ 1.4 billion; ranks 327 in the world.

Millionaires (Crorepati) in India - number of millionaires in: Mumbai - 17; Delhi - 10; Bangalore - 7; Pune – 3; Hyderabad – 1; Ahmadabad – 1; some of them are:

1. Dhiraj Lal Hira Chand (Dhirubhai) Ambani (1932 – 2002) - was the most successful industrialist in India and every Indian

is proud of his achievement. He was born at Chorvad in Junagadh district in Gujarat on 28.12.1932; father was schoolteacher; Ambani failed in 10th class; went to Aden (British colony); started his business as distributor of consumer products in 1949. Ambani's work influenced company's management to such an extant, that he was made Chief Manager (Marketing).

Ambani returned to India in 1958; came to Mumbai in 1959; with Rs.500/- in his pocket established Reliance Commercial Corporation; started export of consumer products to Europe. Ambani started his textile business in 1960 with working capital of Rs.15, 000; manufacturing activities started in 1966 at Naroda, near Ahmadabad; employed 70 workers; gave the mantra, 'Work is worship'.

Ambani started his business career in Mumbai in a rented office with a table and a chair; cost Rs.150/- with no telephone; within 25 years, built Reliance; assets Rs.80, 000 crore; shareholders 60, 00,000; employees 85,000; turn over Rs.60, 000 crore; profit Rs.4, 600 crore; contribution to the total revenue of Government of India 5 %.

Ambani established world's largest earthquake resistant (Richter scale 9) oil refinery at Jamnagar in Gujarat; invested Rs.25,000 crore; Reliance is the first Indian Company to have issued 100 year bonds in America; surpassed Henry Ford's Ford Motor Company and Bill Gate's Microsoft Company. Reliance is engaged in: oil-exploration, refining, distribution, research, petrochemicals, power, finance, insurance, polyester staple fiber, filament yarn and telephone and Internet services.

Ambani's wealth Rs 23,588 crores; ranked 138 in the list of richest persons in the world; received following awards:

1994 - Businessman of the year and membership of Textile Institute of UK.

1998 - Star of Asia and business hall of fame.

1999 - Industrialist of the century and most popular Chief Executive.

2000 - One amongst the three richest Indians.

2001 - Lifetime achievement award.

Ambani suffered a heart attack in 1986; suffered brain hemorrhage on 24.06.2002; passed away on 06.07. 2002; property passed on to his two sons: 1 Mukesh Ambani - Managing Director and Chairman of Reliance Industries and 2 Anil Ambani - Managing Director and Vice Chairman.

2. Azim Premji - at the age of 21 years; left engineering course at Stanford in USA; father expired in 1966; took over father's small vegetable oil processing uni; founded giant Wipro Company; diversified into producing soap and medicines. He believes in professional management; personal wealth Rs 18,964 crores; ranks 41 in the list of richest persons in the world.

3. Malvinder Singh and Shivainder Singh - Ranbaxy Industries; property worth Rs 5,086 crores.

4. Sunil Mittal - Bharti Telecom; property worth Rs 5,000 crores.

5. Shiv Nadar - age 56 years; miracle man of India; self-made man; multiplied his crores through technology; heads Hindustan Computers Ltd; survived Silicon Valley recession. He ranks 378th position in Forbes' list of richest persons in the world; his mantra - success is a journey and not a destination; 25 years ago started his business from one-room apartment in Delhi; today, he is the largest PC maker in India.

He is a non-resident Indian based in USA. He is an electrical engineer from Coimbatore in India. He has worked with Cooper Engineering as a systems analyst and practices Yoga. His industrial assets are worth Rs 4,299 crore; ranks 378 in the world among rich persons.

6. Kumar Mangalam Birla - age 34 years, is at the helm of India's second largest business empire, which produces: cement, viscose staple fiber, aluminum, apparels, software, provides services in the insurance field. He is a chartered accountant; has done MBA from London Business School. He is credited to have introduced performance management and professional appraisal system. He brought down the

average age of top executives from 64 to 45 years. Good news under his stewardship is that the growth of Birla Group has doubled to Rs 2,737 crores and the group is at the 200th position in the world.

9.27. Highly Paid Chief Executives in India

Chief Executive	*Company*	*Yearly salary in lakhs of Rupees*		
		1998-99	*1999-00*	*2000-01*
Late Dhirubhai Ambani	Reliance Industries	114.00	509.00	885.00
Mukesh Ambani	Reliance Industries	93.00	406.00	713.00
Anil Ambani	Reliance Industries	93.00	406.00	713.00
Azim Premji	Wipro	-	186.43	428.94
Brijmohan Lal Munjal	Hero Honda	125.47	191.28	418.42
Pawan Lal Munjal	Hero Honda	113.22	84.04	412.68
Matsuo Yamasaki	Hero Honda	7.88	8.50	405.30
Kejuni Yenagida	Hero Honda	-	2.91	402.78
Vivek Pal	Wipro	-	158.20	402.20
H. R. Khusrokhan	Glaxo India	-	70.60	228.60
N. S. Shekhria	Gujarat Ambuja Chem	-	-	201.53

9.28. Will

Will is a written document that shows that after one's death, how his property is to be distributed amongst his inheritors. It is better that a Will be written soon a person crosses 75 years of age or earlier, if the health warrants it. It is better to consult the inheritors, before writing the Will, as this will avoid unnecessary controversies, which may arise after one's death. A trusted person can also be appointed, who can execute the Will in accordance with the instructions, one places in the Will.

A simple Will on a stamp paper is written, which makes the intention clear; two independent witnesses attest the Will and it is registered with a Notary, though registration is not necessary, but it reduces the burden of proof on the claimants. In the case of bank locker, it is better to go for a joint holding to avoid future complications. Will can be written in the following manner:

I .... (Name) ...., son of .... (Father's name) .... normally residing at .... (Address) .... being of sound mind and memory, hereby revoke any Will that I may have made hitherto and declare that this Will made at .... (Address) .... on ...... (Date) ......to be my last Will.

In order to prevent any litigation amongst my heirs, it is my wish that all my properties and assets should be distributed amongst my heirs in the manner, as described below:

I hereby appoint the following two persons:

Name and address of the 1st executor- ....

Name and address of the 2nd executor- .... to be executors of this Will.

The 1st executor ... (Name) ... shall administer the disbursement of my properties and if he is unable to take up this responsibility, the 2nd executor .... (Name) ...... shall administer the disbursement. The executor so appointed shall act as guardian of my minor person who may benefit from my Will.

I have been enjoying full ownership and control over the following properties:

Immovable property: .... (Full details, address, names and percentage of share of other co-holders, if any) ....

Movable property: (A) ... (Cash) ..., (B) ... Bank a/c (Saving, Current, Fixed) ...., (C) ... Insurance ..... (D) .... Jewellery .... (E) .... Shares .... (F) ... Others ...

I declare that all my belongings shall be distributed amongst the persons mentioned by me as follows:

Serial No.	*Property*	*Name, Address, Relationship to me*
1.		
2.		
3.		
4.		

Following are my special instructions before commencing disposal of my properties:

I have allocated Rs .... /- to my daughter ... (Name) ... aged ... (Years), who is residing .... (Address) .... On the demise of my daughter, the returns from this money is to be transferred to her daughter, if she is a minor at the time of demise of my daughter, then it will be under custody of executor.

I have kept aside cash value of Rs ..... /- for expenses that may be incurred on my illness, if any or to meet the expenses for my funeral and related ceremonies. Any legal expenses, unpaid taxes etc. shall be met out of this money. The balance from this money after all payments and any other residue of my property, I bequeath to my wife.

This Will has been prepared in the presence of the following two persons as witness:

(Name and address of the 1st witness) ....

(Name and address of the 2nd witness ....

Signature and name of person making the Will

9.29. Achieving Excellence in Life

1. Define goals early in life; write them down; put efforts to achieve them.
2. Determine the time frame into which the goal is to be achieved.
3. Identify the obstacles that stand in the way of achieving the goals; plan to overcome the obstacles.

4 Make a list of peoples and organizations, which can render help in achieving the goa; tap their resources as and when required.

5 But never loose heart, as goals require sincere efforts and put more efforts with hope that the goals will be achieved in course of time.

THE END

FOUR BASIC ASPECTS OF HUMAN LIFE

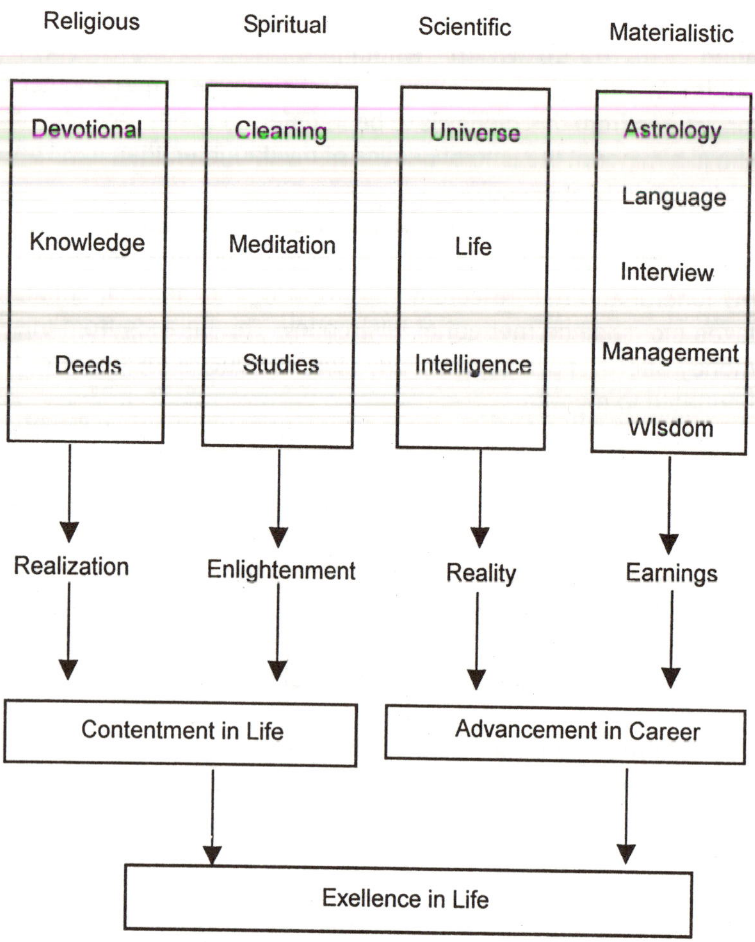

Index

B

C

F

G

N

R

S